Books by Ann Rule

Too Late to Say Goodbye
Green River, Running Red
Heart Full of Lies
Every Breath You Take
. . . And Never Let Her Go
Bitter Harvest
Dead by Sunset
Everything She Ever Wanted
If You Really Loved Me
The Stranger Beside Me
Possession
Small Sacrifices

ANN RULE'S CRIME FILES

Vol. 14: But I Trusted You and Other True Cases
Vol. 13: Mortal Danger and Other True Cases
Vol. 12: Smoke, Mirrors, and Murder and Other True Cases
Vol. 11: No Regrets and Other True Cases
Vol. 10: Worth More Dead and Other True Cases
Vol. 9: Kiss Me, Kill Me and Other True Cases
Vol. 8: Last Dance, Last Chance and Other True Cases
Vol. 7: Empty Promises and Other True Cases
Vol. 6: A Rage to Kill and Other True Cases
Vol. 5: The End of the Dream and Other True Cases
Vol. 4: In the Name of Love and Other True Cases
Vol. 3: A Fever in the Heart and Other True Cases
Vol. 2: You Belong to Me and Other True Cases
Vol. 1: A Rose for Her Grave and Other True Cases

Without Pity: Ann Rule's Most Dangerous Killers

The I-5 Killer
The Want-Ad Killer
Lust Killer

IN THE STILL
OF THE NIGHT

The Strange Death of Ronda Reynolds
and Her Mother's Unceasing Quest for the Truth

Ann Rule

Free Press

New York   London   Toronto   Sydney

Free Press
A Division of Simon & Schuster, Inc.
1230 Avenue of the Americas
New York, NY 10020

Copyright © 2010 by Ann Rule

All rights reserved, including the right to reproduce this book
or portions thereof in any form whatsoever.
For information address Free Press Subsidary Rights Department,
1230 Avenue of the Americas, New York, NY 10020

First Free Press hardcover edition October 2010

FREE PRESS and colophon are trademarks of Simon & Schuster, Inc.

For information about special discounts for bulk purchases,
please contact Simon & Schuster Special Sales
at 1-866-506-1949 or business@simonandschuster.com

The Simon & Schuster Speakers Bureau can bring authors to your live event.
For more information or to book an event contact
the Simon & Schuster Speakers Bureau at 1-866-248-3049
or visit our website at www.simonspeakers.com.

Manufactured in the United States of America

1   3   5   7   9   10   8   6   4   2

Library of Congress Cataloging-in-Publication Data

ISBN 978-1-4165-4460-9
ISBN 978-1-4391-7185-1 (ebook)

For Barb Thompson and All Parents Who Grieve
For Their Lost Children

and

For Families and Friends
of Violent Crime Victims (fnfvcv.org) in Everett,
Washington—Who Are There to Help

I know that my Father in Heaven knows me
    and loves me.
He has blessed me with the only mother I
    would ever have chosen.
My mother has flaws and faults as anyone
    does.
One thing she never failed to do is to love me.

—Freeman Thompson, Ronda's brother,
    speaking for himself—and for Ronda, too

FOREWORD

LEWIS COUNTY, WASHINGTON, lies just about halfway between Seattle and Portland, Oregon. The only towns of any size are Centralia and Chehalis, the county seat. With a population of about 15,000, Centralia is home to twice as many people as Chehalis. There is an outlet shopping mall in Centralia, and a number of motels and restaurants close by Interstate 5 to serve bargain shoppers and salesmen. For all the drivers of cars and trucks whizzing by at seventy miles an hour, there are the locals who live and work in Lewis County—on farms or homes in hamlets with quaint names: Onalaska, Salkum, Mossyrock, Napavine, Fords Prairie, Winlock, and Toledo. Mount Rainier looms to the east, as do numerous forests and lakes.

Rivers twist and interlace all over Lewis County, and they often flood areas of the county, wreaking havoc on homes in their path. In the past few years, unfortunate residents have often just recovered from the devastation of floodwater damage when another watery catastrophe strikes.

But life goes on for the longtime residents of Lewis County, and most rebuild, with foundations that are high enough to resist the next flood.

Among my own family's archives is the journal that my grandfather-in-law, the Reverend William J. Rule, a Methodist minister, kept as he went on horseback through the heavy woods that once covered Lewis County. Reverend Rule had come to America from Cornwall, England, and he was both a preacher and an expert on draining water from mines. He wasn't thirty yet, and he stood barely over five feet tall. He had worked in the coal mines of Cornwall before he came to America, and he had never been on a horse when he became a circuit rider in the far Northwest as it existed in 1881. With only a Bible and a wobbly saddle, he struck off into the dark fir trees and waterways around Mossyrock and Salkum. He preached, ate, and slept in welcoming farmhouses deep in those woods, and occasionally hardworking farmers' and loggers' wives would wash his clothing. Just as often, they tried to arrange meetings with local spinsters, since they worried that he needed a wife to take care of him. As he rode precariously through the dank forest of Lewis County, there was a constant threat of cougars and bears. But somehow he survived and moved up to proper churches around Washington state.

Seeing Lewis County in 2009, it was impossible for me to recognize any of the landmarks in Grandpa Rule's journal. Since his time, trees have been cut, replanted, and cut again. And again. Several generations of a new society have been born. Many residents have moved away to the big cities: Seattle, Spokane, and Portland, Oregon. But the cores of pioneer families have remained, with the same surnames popping up in every census tabulation. Everyone who lives there seems to have some connection to everyone else.

Elected officials, their names familiar on ballots, tend to stay in office in Lewis County for decades. Although those elected have their cheerleaders and their critics, voters are reluctant to change horses. Locals say that most of these officials retire, or die in the middle of a term, and when that happens the powers that be have someone already picked to step into the vacant position. It is a well-oiled machine. Some say with a wink, "The good old boys make sure they get the 'right' people in office."

If that is true, voters don't seem upset—they reliably rubber-stamp familiar names on the ballot. There are few instances of new blood or a breath of fresh air coming in.

Go south eighty-five miles or so from Centralia and Chehalis and you reach Portland, Oregon. Go north about the same distance and you arrive in Seattle.

For many, Lewis County is only a place that flashes by the window as their cars race along I-5, but many stop there to eat or to stay overnight. When my children were young, we always took a break at Fort Borst Park, hard by the freeway and crowded with so many tall fir trees that they often shut the sun out. The park boasted a real—historic—fort where settlers fought off Indian raiders, some slides and swings, and a small zoo filled with dispirited-looking animals.

The Washington state reformatory for boys is in Lewis County; the delinquent girls' facility used to be there, but it's been moved. The first road signs with directions to what is left of Mount St. Helens, whose top blew in a gigantic eruption a quarter century ago, appear in Lewis County.

One newer and bizarre roadside attraction in the county consists of four or five towering "art" pieces built on tall poles—a weathervane said to be the "world's largest," a statue of Christ, a miniature Statue of Liberty, and a couple whose messages are more obscure. Seattle monument builder Dominic Gospodor has placed them there on land he owns along the northbound lanes of I-5.

Lewis County's longest-standing oddity is probably the "World's Largest Egg." It was an apt tourist magnet until the 1950s, Winlock was the second-largest egg producing town in America. The first mammoth egg was fashioned of canvas, debuting in 1923 as part of the hoopla surrounding the opening of the Pacific Highway. It has been upgraded three or four times since then using plastic and fiberglass. Local business boosters have been happy to donate funds for "the egg" since its "hatching" in 1923, and the newest giant egg is made of concrete, painted like an American flag. Twelve feet long and weighing 1,200 pounds. It sits atop a pedestal on a ten-foot pole on the grassy median that runs through Winlock's center. Even though Winlock's egg production has dropped drastically, the hamlet of a thousand citizens still hold its "Egg Day Festival" on the fourth weekend of June.

(Two thousand miles away, the town of Mentone, Indiana, makes an identical claim about *their* concrete egg.)

Those who live in Lewis County and tourists, too, eat at The Country Cousin, Mary McCrank's, or Kit Carson's.

On one hand, Lewis County is a little countrified and corny, wholesome as pumpkin pie; on the other, cynics say almost everyone in public office or government employ has "a dark secret."

That is probably an exaggeration, but not everything that happens there is visible to the naked eye.

In the main, people in Lewis County are friendly and welcoming to visitors. But for those who make their homes there, the ease of communication through the small towns makes hiding secrets almost impossible. Few who engage in extramarital affairs can hope to keep their wanderings private, for gossip ripples through Lewis County like the first flickering of a forest fire. Some have said that Lewis County is like "a little Peyton Place," but that can be said of any small town—going back to Sherwood Anderson's fictional *Winesburg, Ohio*. Everyone experiences things that we hope to keep private; they are simply easier to detect in smaller communities. Some secrets aren't all that interesting to other people; some are devastating and change lives forever . . .

*   *   *

LEWIS COUNTY HAS HAD its share of homicides, suicides, and accidental deaths, and many of them are connected in some way either to the I-5 freeway, which long since replaced the Pacific Highway—"Old 99"—as the fastest north-south roadway, or to the trains that rumble through at almost every hour of the day and night.

Coroner Terry Wilson has ruled on the "manner of death" for most of them for seven four-year terms in office. Bald, with a florid complexion and an inscrutable expression on his face most of the time, Wilson is neither a medical doctor nor a forensic pathologist. He is a "PA," a physician's assistant. He earns $35,000 a year as coroner, and works in a local clinic as a PA, too. That isn't particularly unusual, because many of the outlying and/or smaller counties in Washington employ the coroners' system, while Pierce, King, Snohomish, Spokane, and larger counties have medical examiners who *are* medical doctors and even forensic pathologists. The latter, of course, are the best educated, the most skilled, and the most experienced in detecting time, cause, and manner of death.

Either medical examiners or coroners can make or break the successful solution to a sudden and violent death.

Ronda Reynolds was thirty-three and healthy and beautiful when she died on December 16, 1998. She was still what would be considered a bride—though on the verge of divorce—when her brain was destroyed by a single bullet just beside her right temple.

But *why* and *how*? Almost a dozen years later, both those who had known and loved her and those who had only read about her were still asking those same questions.

*   *   *

ON THE SECOND DAY of November 2009, on the fourth floor of the Lewis County Law and Justice Center, a precedent-setting hearing began. It was a civil hearing, one long sought by Barbara Thompson, Ronda Reynold's mother. Although Ronda, a former Washington State Patrol trooper, had been dead for nearly eleven years, there were questions about what really happened to her and what might have led up to the tragedy just before that long-ago Christmas. There had been few solid answers, only massive speculation that seemed to grow every year.

The hearing in the Chehalis courtroom was not for a judge and jury to decide on who—if anyone—had killed

Ronda; it was to evaluate Coroner Terry Wilson and his staff's handling of Ronda's case. Had Wilson been irresponsible and derelict in his duty on December 16, 1998, and thereafter? Under his orders, his staff had done a perfunctory investigation of her death. Had it been enough? Or had her dying been swept under the rug and dismissed?

Barb Thompson believed fervently that it had.

*   *   *

IT WAS STILL DARK at 6:20 on that cold morning in 1998 when Ronda's husband of less than a year—Ron Reynolds—called 911. He told the sheriff's dispatcher that his wife had committed suicide. It appeared to be what mystery writers like to call "an open-and-shut case."

But was it?

Coroner Wilson did not go to the scene of Ronda's death himself, nor did he attend her autopsy. He rarely, if ever, went to crime scenes, and since he wasn't a medical doctor, he couldn't perform a postmortem exam, but he hadn't even bothered to attend Ronda's. Instead, the same deputy coroner, Carmen Brunton, who had responded to the Reynolds's home and observed the deceased, was present at Ronda's autopsy. Before she was hired by the coroner's office, Carmen, a middle-aged blonde, had had a career as a beautician and hair dresser.

Dr. Daniel Selove, a mobile forensic pathologist who was often called upon by counties with a coroner's system, carried out the actual postmortem procedure.

Over more than a decade since Ronda's death, Coroner Wilson had changed his mind several times. His office first concluded that Ronda's death was "undetermined." And then her manner of death was deemed "suicide." Wilson's third decision was, once again, "undetermined." Remarkably, the Lewis County coroner changed his mind for the third time and officially decided that she had perished by her own hand—that she was after all a "suicide."

This hearing was to determine why it had taken so long and why there were so many missteps along the way. Why would a coroner with twenty-seven years on the job vacillate for eleven years? The sheriff who was in office in 1998 had retired and been replaced, and in the interim many of the investigating detectives had resigned, retired, or been transferred out of the detective division.

Except for those who loved Ronda, a handful of trained investigators and one lawyer—who all either volunteered their time or greatly reduced their usual rates—Ronda Thompson Liburdi Reynolds would have been forgotten long ago, her ashes scattered to the winds near Spokane where she had grown up, her lovely face captured on photographs in an album and on her mother's website.

And that would have been a travesty of justice.

Ronda wasn't a perfect person, no more than any of us is. Still, the one word I've heard continually when I ask people who knew her to describe her is *courageous*. And not only in her career as a female state trooper, but in her personal life.

As someone who had friends on both sides of the quandary, this case was a hard call for me. I spent a lot of time playing devil's advocate with myself—trying to look at the mystery of Ronda's death from all points of view. In only two of my books have I had an instant intuition that something was wrong. One was when I heard the first news broadcast about an Oregon mother and her three children who had been attacked by a "bushy-haired stranger." One child was dead, the other two critical.

Oh, that poor woman, I thought, only to have suspicion replace my sympathy in less than a minute. As cops say, "Something was hinky."

That poor mother, of course, was Diane Downs.

PART ONE

Realized Dreams,

Lost Dreams

CHAPTER ONE

AS WE FILED INTO the courtroom on the fourth floor of the Law and Justice Center in Chehalis on that rain-swept morning in November, there were more media present than spectators. Odd—because everyone I'd talked to in Lewis County knew about Ronda Reynolds's puzzling death eleven years earlier, and each had ventured an opinion. Still, Lewis County residents who were lucky enough to still have jobs didn't dare risk taking extra days off. They would catch up on what happened in *The Chronicle*, the local newspaper, or from Paul Walker at KITI Radio, who would attend the hearing every day.

ABC, NBC, and CBS affiliates in Seattle sent cameras and reporters from KOMO, KING, and KIRO so that the hearing could be featured as a lead-in on their evening and late night news. Some reporters—particularly Tracy Vedder of KOMO and Sharyn Decker of *The Chronicle*—had followed Ronda's case for years. Others hadn't even been living in Washington state when she died and were playing catch-up on a case that had vanished from the headlines a long time ago.

The waiting area on the fourth floor was full of people—some appearing for their own trials, and some whose presence there I could not pinpoint. There were an inordinate number of overweight young women who were either pregnant or carrying babies in fussy clothes. There were young-ish men with earrings, wearing motorcycle-themed and obscure band T-shirts under leather jackets. And there were staid people in their sixties or seventies.

Were they there to support Coroner Terry Wilson, or to show their concern for Barb Thompson? As it turned out, most were prospective jurors who would be selected or rejected not only for this hearing, but for other cases about to be tried. Among them was Dennis Waller, an editor at *The Chronicle*. Some were defendants out on bail, and others seemed only to be passing through on other legal business.

Judge Richard Hicks, who was a superior court judge in Thurston County (just north of Lewis County), had been summoned to preside over this hearing. He was the epitome of what laymen expect a judge to look like—a husky man with a shock of white hair and a beard to match, his eyes missing nothing as he peered through black-rimmed glasses. Although he could be jovial, there was no doubt that he was in complete control of this courtroom. He was also bending over backward to follow all the rules of trials held in Lewis County, right down to the usual court hours.

Initially, Judge Hicks had been appointed as the sole authority who would decide whether Coroner Wilson had been derelict in his duty and/or mismanaged the investigation into Ronda Reynold's sudden death. But Hicks chose to add a twelve-person jury. The opposing attorneys—Royce

Ferguson, representing Barb Thompson, and John Justice, who had been retained by the Lewis County prosecutor's office to represent Terry Wilson—chose eight women, four men, and two alternates to listen to the witnesses, hear the circumstantial evidence surrounding Ronda's death, and view the physical evidence. They would render a verdict, but it might be moot; if he didn't agree with them, Judge Hicks still held the option to overrule their decision.

Attorneys, police officers, and even coroners from other counties observed the action in this starkly modern, windowless courtroom with its original rock-hard oak benches. If they scrunched together, as many as 180 spectators could fit onto those benches. Whatever the verdict would be about Coroner Wilson's responsibility in this still-unsolved death, this was a landmark case. Newspapers and television reporters disseminated the testimony from Seattle to Portland each day.

I had followed the violent and mystifying death of Ronda Reynolds since it occurred, and was as curious as everyone else. Naturally, I was anxious to hear the witnesses' testimony, consider the circumstantial evidence—which was rumored to be weighted heavily against suicide—and see what physical evidence might be accepted by the Court. Several copies of a shiny white binder about six inches thick that appeared to be a collection of police reports, statements, and photos spurred curiosity in the gallery and the media. One copy sat on the plaintiff's table, and another on the defense's.

What was in it? I wondered. If Judge Hicks should accept the material in that binder into evidence, I would find out. I wanted to read each page.

Yet whatever results would emanate from this hearing, they wouldn't change my mind about writing a book about

Ronda's death. There were almost as many sides to this story as colored glass splinters in a kaleidoscope. I didn't know if I would be writing about a brutal crime, a pitiful suicide, or something else. I knew only that sometimes everything has to be told, no matter how embarrassing or distasteful the truth may be. There is never real closure for those who lose someone they love to violence, or for those who have had the white light of suspicion focused on them for decades.

So attention must be paid.

I know my readers, and I know that most of them are well-read and often sharp amateur sleuths. In the death of Ronda Reynolds, they may make the final decision on guilt or innocence. For almost twelve years, I have tried to work my way through the tangled mass of statements and leads.

In the end, I hope to present all sides of this haunting case, even though I suspected early on that there would be some principal players who might not talk to me at all.

As it happened, I was right.

*   *   *

EVEN THOSE WHO VIEW a glass as half full have moments when they wonder if their lives are too perfect to last. For some, the warm, wafting breezes of spring, redolent with the fragrance of flowers, are difficult; there is too much nostalgia to deal with. For others, a new love can bring with it a fear of losing something more precious than they ever could have imagined. Similarly, holidays are times fraught with tension for many people.

Everyone hopes for a warm and loving gathering of family and friends, doors locked against the outside world once everyone arrives. And yet there is an almost subliminal fear that someone we love could be in an accident on the way to Grandmother's house or wherever the celebration is to be held.

At Thanksgiving and Christmas, weather conditions can be icy and stormy, making roads dangerous to traverse and weighing down the wings of planes.

We worry, usually silently, and watch the clock until our roll call is complete. To lose someone on a holiday means that every anniversary that comes after will be marked by sorrowful remembrance.

I suspect that mothers agonize the most. Even when our children are grown, we would much prefer them to be safe beneath our wings, and sometimes we long for the days when we could tuck them into cribs and know that we were there to protect them from any harm.

Barb Thompson was like that, even though she seldom betrayed her concern. She wanted her two children to grow up, realize their dreams, and fly free. By the 1990s, she had let go of her babies, as all good mothers have to. She was confident that they were independent and fully capable adults, able to take care of themselves.

And they hadn't let her down; her daughter, Ronda, in her thirties, had been a Washington State Patrol trooper for almost a decade, for heaven's sake, responsible for the safety of others as well as herself. If she couldn't take care of herself, what woman could?

Barb's son, Freeman, was ten years younger than Ronda. Barb was very young when Ronda was born, only nineteen, and it probably was just as well that she had only her daughter to raise then. It wasn't easy for Barb. Bringing up her children on her own much of the time was a challenge. Nevertheless, Barbara always put them first, and she usually worked two—or even three—jobs to support them.

Although she and her mother, Virginia Ramsey, had

tangled often when she was a child and a teenager, it was
Virginia who became Barb's strongest support. Virginia had
been married for more than twenty years to the only man
she had ever loved, bringing up three children on "less than
a shoestring," when Barb's father deserted her for another
woman. She was totally devastated.

"Somehow," Barb recalled, "Ronda's birth gave her a
reason to go on, and I sure did need her. She took care of
Ronda—and, later, Freeman—while I worked as many jobs
as I could, helped me raise my little girl. She never complained. My mom was always there—and Ronda cherished
her grandmother."

Although Ronda was born two months premature—
with no fingernails, eyebrows, or lashes yet—she was a
pretty, serene baby and she was easy to care for from the
moment Barb took her home from the hospital in Southern
California in September 1965.

Barb married twice, and had romantic relationships
from time to time, but the core of her family was her
children—Ronda and Freeman—and her mother, Virginia.
They saw each other through many hard times and always
emerged together.

Ronda loved horses as much as Barb did, but she had
another dream for her life. Ever since she was about five,
she had watched *Dragnet, Adam-12,* and *Mayberry R.F.D.*
avidly. She decided then that she would be a law enforcement officer—a sheriff, maybe, or a detective. In fact, she
wanted to grow up to be a Washington State Patrol trooper.
At the time, that seemed unlikely; there were no female
officers when Ronda was a little girl. There weren't even
any short troopers. The image of the Washington State Patrol was one of tall men wearing blue-gray uniforms and
wide-brimmed hats. (In many ways, it still is, and motor-

ists are surprised to be stopped by small women with soft voices.)

Barb figured she would grow out of that, but Ronda never wavered. Although she was a very feminine little girl, she loved riding wildly on her horse, and was fascinated with police officers.

Nothing daunted Ronda. She took on challenges all of her life, and as she grew up, she knew that women were beginning to take their place beside men in law enforcement. She never gave up on her plans to be a trooper, although she could not have imagined some of the problems her femininity would bring in a male world.

The lovely girl from Eastern Washington wanted it all— as people tend to say about women who work and hope to have a family home life, too.

Ronda wanted to marry one day and, especially, to have children.

And she almost achieved it all. She shared many characteristics with her mother, but perhaps the strongest was that they were both stubborn and single-minded. Each of them had had to face more than most women could imagine, but they didn't give up on improbable or impossible goals, despite all the naysayers who warned them they couldn't win.

Like all other mothers and daughters, they had some arguments when Ronda went through her teen years, but they loved each other devotedly. Ronda respected her mother and appreciated the sacrifices she had made, and the long hours she'd worked over the years.

*   *   *

IT WAS WEDNESDAY, December 16, 1998, nine days before Christmas. Ronda lived over on what Washingtonians call "the coast," and the rest of her family lived three hundred miles away in Spokane. Barbara was looking forward to a five-day visit from Ronda, as were her grandmother and brother. It wouldn't exactly be a Norman Rockwell Christmas, although Spokane could count on snow. It was far colder in Eastern Washington than it was in Seattle.

Ronda's visit wasn't really to celebrate the holiday; she was going home to those who loved her for comfort and advice. Her second marriage was ending, and although she had no trouble finding a job, none of them was what she had wanted for most of her life. A few years earlier, after eight years as a Washington state trooper, she had resigned from the force. In her mind, she had had no choice, but she grieved for the career she loved more than any other.

Twenty-some years ago, there were only about thirty-five female Washington state troopers; today there are 1,200 sworn officers in the state patrol and 5 percent of them are women, about sixty of them. That didn't matter to Ronda; she always assumed that she would be one of the small percentage of women who made it.

And she was right. With her grades in high school and community college close to a 4.0 GPA, she was a shoo-in. Well, not quite. The state patrol winnowed out applicants scrupulously. Candidates had to be nineteen and a half years old, with 20/25 vision and their weight proportionate to their height. Ronda met all those requirements, too.

They could not have felony convictions or misdemeanor convictions involving theft, crimes of violence, assault on a family member, larceny, moral turpitude, controlled substances, or hit-and-run accidents.

Any prior conviction for driving under the influence of alcohol or drugs had to be at least seven years in the past. When they met all those standards, the few applicants who emerged were required to pass a fitness and agility test. Perhaps more important, they would be subjected to a background investigation, and then had to successfully pass a polygraph examination.

Ronda sailed through; her record was pristine. Having chosen her career when she was in grade school, she'd been careful to live the kind of life that the state patrol wanted to find when they did background checks on prospective new hires.

Ronda was welcomed as the youngest female cadet ever hired. She was twenty, and her life was turning out just as she hoped it would.

Cadets must go through eight months of grueling training before they can hope to become road-worthy troopers. Their "boot camp" in Shelton, Washington, is similar to Army and Marine Corps training. They are often wakened in the wee hours of the morning, grabbed out of their cots by the ankles, and held upside down. They are ordered to do push-ups in the mud and cold rain long before the sun comes up, and to jog in the dark.

The WSP cadets are always at the bottom of the totem pole. As they toughen up, they derisively call the Criminal Justice Training Center law enforcement students from other departments "Club Med members." Part of Washington state's training for young police officers involves traveling from the Burien training academy and spending time at the state patrol's Shelton academy to focus on driving skills.

"They weren't nearly as military as we were," a ten-year female veteran of the state patrol recalls. "And they were nowhere near as disciplined as our group of cadets. We kind of resented them because whenever there were visiting students, we had to 'step back' and let them eat first. Lots of times, we were the last to eat."

About a third of Washington State Patrol cadets failed to finish the eight-month training program. They washed out for a variety of reasons: some for ethical standards that didn't meet the Patrol's level, some because they couldn't grasp the defense tactics that they had to learn before they could go out on dark roads in one-man cars and face who knows what. Some couldn't take the lack of sleep, the physical demands, and the harassment.

But Ronda could.

I myself have worked a one-man car—back in the day—and it can get lonely and scary out there. Being a patrol trooper is, in many ways, more dangerous than being a detective in the Women's Bureau of the Seattle Police Department, as I was when I was her age. Washington state permits windows that are tinted so darkly that an officer cannot see who is inside. It takes a sixth sense, faith, and caution for troopers to stop a car where the driver and passengers are virtually invisible. Some of the most benign-appearing drivers, pulled over for a burned-out taillight or for driving only a few miles over the speed limit, can turn out to be killers on the run.

Ronda entered the Washington State Patrol academy on September 8, 1987, and with credit for her earlier years as a trooper cadet in her teens, she became a commissioned trooper on January 8, 1988. She stood proudly in her new uniform in the rotunda of the state Capitol in Olympia as then Governor Booth Gardner shook her hand and camera flashes highlighted her new badge: #954.

Her first assignment was to patrol I-5, the busiest highway in Washington State, near the Seattle Detachment. Next she went to the Grays Harbor WSP detachment in Aberdeen. These were early days in the history of females on the Washington State Patrol, and Ronda deliberately armed herself with a protective emotional shield, appearing far tougher than she really was. Her close women friends knew that she was loving, vulnerable, and often "grossed out" by some of the jokes and remarks the men went out of their way to tell.

But Ronda didn't show it.

Connie Riker worked as a dispatcher for the Patrol in Bremerton, and her territory—#8—consisted of many counties, including Clallam, Jefferson, Wahkiakum, and Grays Harbor. She met Ronda when she and another trooper had a delivery to make in Aberdeen. It wasn't long before Connie and Ronda became fast friends. On occasion, Connie rode along with Ronda in what was usually her "one-man car."

Connie was appalled at the lewd comments and forbidden jokes that Ronda had to put up with. "There was a huge sexual harassment problem in the Patrol then, but Ronda felt she had to get along with the guys—and she could put on a different persona when she was around them. The guys were used to 'taking care' of women—which was kind of the opposite of their naughty stories—but Ronda didn't want to be taken care of. She was so strong.

"If Ronda was a man, you would call her 'cocky,'" Connie explained. "She believed she could do anything then. And she was so empowering to me. She told me the Aberdeen Police was hiring, and that she could introduce me to the chief. I remember how she said, 'Connie, you can *do* this. You will be great!'"

She mentored me, and she once said, 'Yeah, you have to put up with a lot of crap working with a bunch of men,' and then she said, 'But won't it be cool to break the "no females" barrier in Aberdeen?'"

Inspired, Connie applied to the Aberdeen Police Department, passed all the tests and interviews, and was offered a job as a police officer. She and Ronda were both thrilled.

"But I injured my knee," Connie said, "and I couldn't take the job. And then I got cancer. I lost touch with Ronda after I was transferred to Tacoma for six months. Later, I went to the Department of Licensing."

Connie Riker and Ronda Thompson both loved horses and that gave them an additional bond during the time they both lived in Grays Harbor County.

Connie still remembered how happy Ronda was the early summer she married another Washington state trooper, Mark Liburdi, and they moved to a wonderful horse farm in McCleary. Ronda loved Mark's three kids, and the newly married couple seemed to get along well. She asked the Patrol to officially change her name to Ronda Liburdi.

"Their house was so very neat," Connie recalled. "I finally said, 'How do you do it? You're both too busy to keep it this clean!' "

The ranch house was sparely and purposely furnished. Connie saw that Ronda liked nice things, and she chose quality rather than quantity.

On their ride-alongs, Ronda and Connie talked through the nights, especially when there were few calls from dispatch.

"She had a wonderful personality, so giving," Connie said. "One thing about Ronda—as tough as she could seem to be, she needed a man in her life. She was very pretty and she seemed always to have a boyfriend, but once she met Mark, she expected to be with him forever."

Would Ronda commit suicide? It was a question that always came up when I was talking to her old friends and working partners.

"No!" Connie shouted. "In order for Ronda to have killed herself, she would have had to have a complete personality replacement. She was very strong. She ran the domestic violence program in Lewis County, and she wanted to believe in the people she loved. I've seen suicides in my own family, and Ronda just wasn't like that. Whatever happened, she would have gone on to the next phase of her life. She wouldn't give up."

Ronda had a number of close women friends, possibly because she didn't feel any need to compete with them; she wanted them to be successful, too. Another was Claudia Self, who worked in the Grays Harbor County Prosecutor's Office.

Claudia offered to help Ronda fill out follow-up and field investigation reports. Ronda was a rookie then, and the reports had to be perfect because they were often used in trials or other legal hearings. Claudia empathized easily with Ronda when it came to working as the lone woman in a domain mostly populated by males. She had hired on as an officer in Idaho, and she too had lived through the not-so-subtle repartee and sexual innuendo—and sometimes outright inappropriate touching—that Ronda faced.

"Ronda put on this veneer that she was rough and gruff, when, inside, she was soft and tender," Claudia recalled. "She never swore, but she gave as good as she got. She would change tires and take on other challenges that weren't that easy for her—because she felt she had to keep proving herself. She was sometimes rebellious because she had to be, but she was really a very vulnerable woman who just wanted to be loved."

"She was religious, too," Claudia said, although she admitted that Ronda was sometimes a "drama queen" when she let her emotions get away from her. "One of the male troopers teased her once when she got her hair cut very short. He said, 'If somebody didn't know you, Ronda, they'd think you were a dyke.' She got so mad at him!"

Her husband, Mark, let Ronda fight her own battles to prove she was as capable as any male on the Patrol. He knew she could handle herself.

Like most of her friends, Claudia found Ronda's sense of humor hilarious, and her fearlessness rather daunting. On a moonless winter night Claudia rode along with Ronda on back roads surrounding Ocean Shores, a community once touted as a resort town. Old-time big-band stars bandleader Kay Kyser and singer Ginny Simms had invested heavily in Ocean Shores some sixty-five or so years ago, but it had never lived up to their entrepreneurial expectations.

Off season, in the darkest part of the night, Claudia found it scary. As they drove slowly through pockets of fog that clung like smoke to the road, something or someone suddenly jumped from the thicket of trees and scotch broom directly into the path of their patrol car. Ronda just missed hitting the figure, and Claudia's heart thumped in her chest.

It was a person, a youngish-looking man who came up to the driver's window. He evidently hadn't noticed that it was a police unit; Ronda was driving the sergeant's patrol car that night, and it had no cage separating the front seat from the back. The stranger had been drinking; the odor of alcohol permeated their car.

"He looked like a kid," Claudia said. "Sixteen—seventeen, maybe. That might have been the reason Ronda didn't frisk him for a weapon. She gave him a ticket for 'Minor in Possession of Alcohol' and drove him to where he wanted to go."

There was something about him that gave Claudia Self

a creepy feeling, and she didn't relax until he was out of the squad car. She asked Ronda why she hadn't searched him, and Ronda shrugged and said, 'Oh, he's just a kid.' "

Several weeks later, Claudia heard a bulletin about a twenty-year-old man named Raymond Baca who had just been arrested for murdering a woman on the beach. He had stabbed her many times with a screwdriver.

Claudia called Ronda and asked her if she recognized the name Baca. Ronda couldn't place him.

"That's that guy that jumped in front of our car that night in Ocean Shores," Claudia said. "I guess we were lucky. What he did to that poor woman was awful."

And they *were* lucky. Maybe they'd survived because there were two of them. Maybe it was because he realized he'd jumped in front of a police unit.

Baca had a record in California for violent attacks, too. Ronda was chagrined at herself because she hadn't searched him at the time—or handcuffed him—but she took the valuable lesson to heart. She *wasn't* superwoman. Still, she stuck with her motto, "No fear."

Asked if Ronda might be likely to take her own life, Claudia scoffed, just as the rest of Ronda's family and friends had. "I would say she was kind of dramatic, but she would *never* kill herself—especially shoot herself in the head.

"For one thing, she was very, very, vain about her appearance," Claudia Self said. "That's not meant as a criticism—it didn't bother me. She always dressed perfectly, her uniform was spotless, her nails were just so, and she was careful about her makeup. I can't even imagine Ronda shooting herself in the head. She wouldn't have wanted anyone to find her like that."

More than that, it simply wasn't in Ronda's psychological profile to take that way out. If she suffered disappointment in love or anything else, Claudia felt, Ronda would simply change her life and move on.

"I remember Ronda the last time I saw her. She was working security at Macy's in Olympia on the weekend of—or maybe after—Thanksgiving. I asked her how things were going with her new husband, Ron Reynolds, and she said she 'had her issues with him,' but it didn't seem serious.

"The last time I saw her she had a smile on her face."

After her disappointing resignation from the Patrol, with eight years as a trooper, Ronda had started working in store security for Walmart and then for Macy's. In the past few years, Ronda's life seemed to crash down around her like boulders breaking free of unstable cliffs in the mountain passes. Her first marriage—to fellow trooper Mark Liburdi—had ended in divorce, and her second marriage of less than a year's duration was almost over. She was far from giving up; she was too strong for that, but she needed to go home to be with her family while she decided what to do next.

Ronda never spent much time weeping about her misfortunes in life. Rather, she got mad, and she had always managed to come back wiser—but not more bitter. In that, she was like her mother. The two of them would talk, and weigh different options.

Everyone who knew her was convinced that Ronda would rise like a phoenix from the ashes of her marriage to Ron Reynolds.

*　*　*

ALTHOUGH BARB THOMPSON kept her mouth shut, she never understood Ronda's attraction to Ronald Reynolds. He was forty-six, fourteen years older than Ronda was, a grade school teacher, and a presiding overseer in the Jehovah's Witnesses religion. He was tall, with graying light brown hair, wore glasses, and had a thick brush of a mustache. Reynolds wasn't nearly as handsome as Mark Liburdi, the trooper who was her first husband.

But he listened to Ronda when she turned to the Jehovah's Witnesses for counseling, and he always seemed to know just what to say to make her feel happy and serene.

Mark and Ronda had met Reynolds when they went to Kingdom Hall services and learned that Ron and his wife of more than twenty years, Catherine "Katie" Huttula, lived several houses down the street from the Liburdis' home in McCleary. The Reynoldses had five sons, three of them still living at home.

They were quite open with Mark and Ronda, and Mark recalled that Ron had confided that he and Katie had had a problem with drugs when they were much younger. Katie was still struggling with her own addictive personality and often stumbled.

At that point, the Liburdis' union was in trouble, and it looked as if Ron and Katie weren't holding together very strongly, either. Ronda had never expected to get divorced, but it appeared that she was headed for that and she felt like a failure.

When Ronda was grieving for the loss of her first marriage, the career she had loved, and her failure to carry any of her pregnancies to term, Ron Reynolds had offered himself as her spiritual counselor, and her concerned advisor. Ron was in the process of divorcing Katie.

At first, Ron might have seemed only a safe place to jump to, but Ronda soon found it easy to fall in love with him. She was very vulnerable in 1997, and Ron made her believe in herself, and he seemed solid. She didn't really know what his financial situation was, but his job as an elementary school teacher paid well. Before his father's death, Ron had moved Leslie Reynolds into a trailer in McCleary behind his own house and cared for him. It wasn't much of a move; prior to the older man's illness, he had lived right next door. Ron had inherited that house.

The thought of taking on care of the elderly man and three pubescent boys who resented her because they sided with their mother in the divorce was a bit challenging, but Ronda thought they could grow to be a family—in time. Mark had brought three children into their marriage.

Ronda was confident she could come to love the Reynolds boys. She already found Ron's dad endearing.

*   *   *

BARB THOMPSON HAD NEVER MET Ron Reynolds, and she had no chance to form an opinion on his suitability to marry Ronda. She was a little concerned that he was so much older than Ronda, and that he already had five sons and an ex-wife he'd been married to for over twenty years. She would have hoped that Ronda would wait longer to marry him, and give herself enough time to truly know him— but Ronda was adamant. She loved him, and she believed in him.

Reynolds had used a "reverse seduction" ploy with Ronda, and that troubled her mother. The two women had always talked about problems in their lives—even intimate ones. But this was a strange courting technique to Barb.

Ron had confessed to Ronda that he was impotent, and felt it wouldn't be fair to her for them to fall in love. He had, in fact, attempted to make love to her, with negative results, proving what he'd told her was true. She hurt for him and his male pride, but it didn't make her love him less. When they tried intercourse again, Ron was miraculously able to achieve an erection and he thanked Ronda profusely for making him feel alive again.

Barb never believed that for a second, but Ronda was so happy to hear that she was capable of bringing Ron's sexual potency back to life. Ronda had always been a one-man woman, and as strong as she was, she seemed to feel incomplete without a significant male in her life. Ron seemed like the answer.

They quickly became engaged, setting their wedding date for January 2, 1998.

Barb was taking care of close to twenty prize horses—along with a few cows—on her ranch, making it almost impossible for her to leave Spokane to attend Ronda's wedding—especially since her mother, Virginia, and Ronda's brother, Freeman, really wanted to go. Someone had to stay home and take care of all the animals. Sometimes it seemed as though she always had a pregnant mare, and she needed to be there as "midwife."

Barbara's brother, Bill Ramsey, a graduate of the U.S. Naval Academy and a decorated helicopter rescue pilot during the Vietnam War, flew up from Colorado to take Barb's place. He considered it a great honor, since he adored both Ronda and Freeman; they were like his own children. Bill and Barb were very close; she could think of no one more suited to stand in for her. They had been there for each other all their lives—through both happy times and very difficult periods.

Barb wasn't avoiding Ronda's second wedding ceremony, and if marrying Ron made Ronda as happy as she sounded, her mother gave the union her blessing. Barb and

Ronda agreed they would all get together for Mother's Day in May—if not sooner.

Ron and Ronda were married on the second day of the new year Friday. The ceremony was held in the Abel House Bed & Breakfast, in the hamlet of Montesano, in Grays Harbor County.

Ronda wore a white satin dress that gramma Virginia made with a bolero to match, and a string of pearls, and carried a bouquet of tiny roses and lilies of the valley. Ron wore a business suit, a colored shirt, and tie, but he made the street wear more festive with a rose and lily of the valley boutonnière. Both of them smiled widely for their wedding photo.

Ron didn't care for one of Ronda's friends—Cheryl Gilbert*—and had urged Ronda to avoid her if possible. Mark Liburdi had felt the same way about Cheryl, who was a security guard at the Lucky Eagle Casino and a reserve officer in Elma, Washington.

Claudia Self described Cheryl as "coarse and crude." "I never understood why Ronda befriended her—unless, typical of Ronda, she felt sorry for Cheryl."

Ron complained that Cheryl clung to Ronda and had no respect, he felt, for their private time. Possibly he didn't know that Cheryl was working off some bad-check charges she had made on Ronda's account when she was married to Mark Liburdi. Ronda didn't want to turn her in.

Ron agreed that Cheryl could continue cleaning their house, but he didn't want her at their wedding. Since it was a small affair, Ronda didn't invite Cheryl. But she showed up anyway, and Ronda didn't have the heart to ask her to leave. She even posed for one awkward snapshot with Cheryl.

---

*The names of some individuals have been changed. Such names are indicated by an asterisk (*) the first time each appears in the narrative.

Ronda had such high hopes for her second marriage, but she may have wed too soon. There were any number of things the couple didn't know about each other. Ron had seemed so kind, so thoughtful when she was struggling to find her equilibrium, but he changed after they wed. Not a lot at first. Ronda figured that it was just the adjustment that all new couples have to make until they get into the rhythm of living together. She had known him as her spiritual advisor, as another woman's husband, and, briefly, as her lover.

She had had no idea what he might be like as a husband.

At first they lived in Ron's house in McCleary, in Grays Harbor County. It is a town of 1,500 people, nestled beside State Highway 12 as it heads southwest toward Aberdeen and the Pacific Ocean. Salmon and bottom fish fisherman pass through McCleary in droves during the season. Like several other small towns in the area, McCleary has its traditions. It draws a modicum of fame for its summer festival—the Bear Festival—where the gourmet treat is, of course, bear stew.

Shortly thereafter, Ron was hired by the Toledo School District in Lewis County to be an elementary school principal. He'd always been popular with his students, and he had earned his master's degree and was considering going for a doctorate in education.

The couple bought a house together on Twin Peaks Drive in Toledo. Ronda contributed $15,000 of the down payment. They weren't at all deterred by the violence of the wildly popular television mystery series also called *Twin Peaks*.

Because she was in negotiation with the state patrol over just how much her retirement package would be, she borrowed that sum from her mother, promising to pay her back when she got the retirement money owed her. Ronda knew she wouldn't receive her full retirement sum of $12,000 to $15,000 because she owed the Washington State Patrol money for a time period where she had mistakenly taken sick pay as well as state compensation for an on-the-job injury. She also had money coming from the sale of a home and acreage she and Mark Liburdi owned together.

Even though she had put up $15,000 toward their new house, Ron explained to his bride that his ex-wife, Katie, had taken everything away from him in their divorce, and he just wasn't comfortable putting half interest in their new house in Ronda's name. It wasn't that he didn't trust her, of course, but he'd just gone through losing everything so he could be with her. He promised to add her name to the house deed later.

Ronda said she understood. She trusted him completely and knew how devastated he was when many of the possessions and money he'd worked for for years were taken away and given to Katie.

They moved in in August, seven months after their wedding. Ron didn't have any furniture of his own any longer, so Ronda brought all of her furniture to their new house. Some of it was quite new, and other pieces—like her grandmother's china cabinet and paintings—had great sentimental value for her.

Ron moved his three youngest sons in with them. Still mourning the recent death of her beloved Rottweiler, Duchess, Ronda brought her new rottie pup, Jewels, an aged stray Rottweiler she'd rescued and named Daisy, and her feisty Jack Russell terrier, Tuffy. If there had only been room, she would have brought Clabber Toe, her beloved horse, too.

It was 1998. Ronda still hoped for a truly happy marriage, two or three babies, and to be a continued success in her new career in store security and loss prevention.

Barb Thompson was in no hurry for Ronda to repay the loan she'd extended, but her daughter assured her that that would happen as soon as she received the money that was due to her.

The last thing anyone expected were dark clouds ahead for Ronda; she had paid her dues and suffered so many painful emotional setbacks in the first three decades of her life. Those days were over, and Ronda didn't envision anything but happiness in her future.

Ronda would never see 1999.

PART TWO

911:

Sudden Death in Toledo

CHAPTER TWO

IT WAS 1:40 A.M. IN SPOKANE, Washington, on Wednesday, December 16, 1998. Barb Thompson was jarred from sleep by the sound of her phone ringing. Groggy, she reached across her bed for it, knowing that after it rang five times her answering machine would pick up. She didn't want to wake the man who shared her home—"Skeeter"—as he was ill and often in pain that made it hard for him to sleep.

Barb grabbed the phone on the third ring, and muttered, "Hello."

She heard only the buzz of the dial tone.

She lay awake, wondering if she had been dreaming—but she was sure the phone really had rung. Expecting it to ring again, she waited.

There was nothing more.

*   *   *

BARB HAD TALKED TO RONDA only a few hours earlier. Her daughter had been calling from her home in Toledo, a tiny town with a population of under 700. Barb had never been there, although the Reynoldses had lived there for several months. She suspected she would never see Ronda's house; Ronda had called her three days before to tell her that Ron had asked for a divorce.

Ronda said then that she would be flying to Spokane on that Wednesday, scheduled to arrive at 12:59 P.M. She had considered flying out of Portland but had decided to take an Alaska Airlines flight from SeaTac Airport in Seattle. David Bell, a longtime friend and a police sergeant in Des Moines, Washington, had offered to drive the seventy-five miles to Toledo to pick her up and drive her back north to SeaTac Airport. Dave and Ronda had once been sweethearts and, after a decade, they still remained solid friends who depended on each other.

Barb and Ronda, mother and daughter, had talked for a long time around eleven on Tuesday night. Her mother was relieved to hear that Ronda was quite upbeat in her attitude when she said she didn't mind walking away from her eleven-month marriage. Still, she was determined to recoup the thousands of dollars she had put into the house, along with all her efforts in painting, decorating, and making it a home.

"I'm actually looking forward to getting on with my life, Mom," Ronda said. "I just need a few days with you guys to decide a definite course of action."

"You're sure?" Barb asked. "You don't have to put on a happy face for me. You know that."

"I'm sure. I'm fine. I can't wait to see you all tomorrow."

Freeman, Ronda's "little" brother, who was seven inches taller than she was, would take Barb to the airport in Spokane to pick up Ronda. Then they would swing by Gramma Virginia's house—which was right next door to Barb's.

They were all beside themselves with anticipation; they hadn't had a chance to really visit with Ronda since Mother's Day, when they'd had brunch with Ron and Ronda. That had been perfectly pleasant, and there were no warnings at all that the Reynoldes' marriage might not be as sound as it looked.

Probably Ronda herself had no concerns about that. Her first husband, Mark Liburdi, had married again and Ronda was friendly with both Mark and Krista. In a phone conversation with Krista Liburdi in the spring of 1998, Ronda had bubbled with enthusiasm, saying, "I only hope that you and Mark are as happy as Ron and I are."

Mother's Day was when Ronda had put an adorable tumble of black puppy fluff in her mother's arms. This was Young Daisy, or just plain Daisy. She was a good-size dog now, and Barb wanted to show her daughter what good care she had taken of her. Ronda also had a new filly she hadn't seen since Mother's Day when the colt was only a few days old. And, of course, there was Clabber Toe. He would recognize Ronda at once, and it wouldn't be long before the two of them would go galloping off across the Spokane acreage.

Freeman pulled up in front of the Spokane airport, and Barbara asked him if he wanted to go to the gate to meet his sister.

"No, Mom. You go. I think I can wait. I'll watch the door and get her baggage when you guys get back here."

He hadn't quite brought his car to a complete stop when Barb leaped onto the curb and whirled around to close the door.

"Slow down, Mom," he laughed. "She's not going anywhere. You have plenty of time."

Barb Thompson walked into the main terminal, realizing at once that she'd forgotten the airport was in the midst of a massive remodel. She had to walk all the way to the far north end of terminal to reach the Alaska and Horizon airlines arrival gate.

It suddenly became intensely important that she glimpse Ronda and give her a big hug. But when she got to the gate, she found out that Ronda's flight had been canceled, and the next flight from Seattle wasn't scheduled to arrive until just before 3 P.M.

Freeman's face dropped when he heard that. "She's on flight 2198 now," his mother told him. "It's due in at 2:55 P.M. It's not that much longer."

It was just a little over two more hours, but it seemed an eternity to Barb and Freeman. They drove home, not stopping at Gramma Virginia's house. The phone was ringing as they walked in the door. Barb expected it to be Ronda, calling as she always did if she had a change in plans so they wouldn't worry. But it was her own mother, demanding to know why they hadn't dropped in with Ronda.

"Her flight was delayed, Mom," Barb said. "We have to go back to the airport at three. Freeman's on his way to your house now to grab a bowl of cereal. He'll pick me up at two-fifteen."

"Darn," Ronda's grandmother said. "I don't know if I can wait that long."

Barb tried to make her mother feel better by telling her that Ronda would surely have called if she had changed her mind and wasn't coming. Ronda *always* called.

"You're right, Mom," Barb said, soothing Virginia Ramsey. "I just want her here now, too. Maybe she'll decide to transfer after her probationary six months at Macy's, and take a store security job with them in Spokane. Then we'll have her here all the time. Wouldn't that be great? Don't get your hopes up, though. You know how she feels about the weather over here."

Barb busied herself loading the dishwasher, and just as she'd put the last plate in its slot, she glanced out the window over the kitchen sink. She saw a green and white squad car parked at her mother's house. It looked like a Spokane County sheriff's unit.

She wasn't alarmed. Whenever there was a loose or injured horse, the deputies usually came to her to ask her who owned it. She was the "go-to" expert on horses in her end of the county.

Daisy sat by the door expectantly, her whole body wiggling with delight as she was about to meet someone new. Daisy knew no strangers. She was always looking for someone to play with.

Barb was usually glad to help round up wayward horses, but it never took less than two hours. Right now she didn't want to be delayed when she was just about to go back to the airport to pick up Ronda.

But she realized that she couldn't refuse to help; she lived so close to a four-lane, much-traveled highway. Ronda, of all people, would understand and she could call Gramma Virginia when she landed if Barb wasn't home.

She opened her front door, and an older man stood there, gazing with some doubt into Daisy's brown eyes. Barb grinned at the stranger, and said, "She's okay—she doesn't know she's a Rottweiler. She's hoping you've come to play with her."

At that point, Barb Thompson saw that her visitor had a bar with writing etched on it pinned to his shirt. She leaned forward and read "Chaplain."

But what was he doing at her front door? Her world

tilted only a centimeter off its axis, and she felt a knot in her stomach. A chaplain usually meant something bad had happened to someone.

She would not allow herself to believe that had any connection to her.

"Are you Barbara Thompson?" the gray-haired man asked.

"Yes, I am," she said, opening the door wider. "But I only have a couple of minutes. We have to get to the airport to pick up my daughter."

He hesitated for a moment, and then said, "I have a message here. I'm so sorry to tell you that your mother has passed away and you need to call your father."

Relief washed over Barb's body. Whatever had happened, it couldn't involve her or her family. "That can't be right," she said. "My father passed away years ago, and my mother lives right next door. You were just at her house."

The chaplain pressed on. "I have a message that you are to call your father at the coroner's office in Lewis County."

She felt dizzy. Lewis County? She didn't know anyone in any Lewis County. Lewis County, where? What state?

"Do you have a telephone number? Do you have a *name*?"

He shook his head, apologizing. "I'm sorry—but that's all I have."

"Was there anything about a Ramsey, or a Thompson, Liburdi, or Reynolds?"

Again, he shook his head. If he hadn't arrived in a sheriff's car, she would have thought the man was demented—someone who went around knocking on strange doors and scaring the hell out of people. Why *didn't* he have more information? This could all be resolved so quickly if he only had a name to give her.

"*Your* name is Barbara Thompson, right?" he pressed.

"Yes, that's me. But my mother is right next door and she is very much alive. There must be a mistake here."

"This *is* 7711 West Highway Two,* isn't it?"

"Yes."

"This is definitely the address and name I was given, and I was told to tell you that you need to call your father."

Barbara wished Freeman would show up. The "chaplain" was giving her the creeps.

She suddenly recalled that there was another Barbara Thompson living in Spokane, a woman who worked at the racetrack. In the past, she had received some of the other Barbara's mail and phone calls. She didn't have any idea where the other woman lived, but she was sure the sheriff's office could find out. Barb looked at her watch and told the chaplain that she really had to leave for the airport. He nodded and went to his car. Barbara called Freeman, reminding him it was time to go.

Once more, Barb jumped from her son's car and headed for the Alaska/Horizon arrival gate. Luckily, Ronda's plane wouldn't land for another fifteen minutes. Barb knew she had plenty of time, but she found herself running down the corridor, darting between people, baggage, children, and strollers. All the chairs were taken when she got to the gate, but she didn't care. She stood with her eyes glued to the double doors that would soon spring open and release scores of passengers. And Ronda would be one of them.

"It was Christmastime," Barb Thompson remembered a decade later. "Joy and laughter were in the air. We would be having Christmas together for the first time in nearly eight years. Ronda had to leave on the twenty-first to get back to her job, so we planned Christmas dinner and our gift exchange early. It was enough that we could just be together."

It was 2:50 P.M. and Barb watched the incoming planes circle in the cold sky and then taxi in to their gates. Finally, she saw the Alaska Airlines jet and knew it must be Ronda's plane. She watched the ground crew wave their big orange wands and lead it into a covered ramp, and heard its engines winding down.

In her mind, she could see Ronda's face. She knew her daughter would be one of the last to deplane; she liked to let all those with babies, as well as the elderly and disabled passengers, exit safely, and Ronda always grinned widely when she saw her mother's face change from impatience to delight.

Barb stretched and strained her neck to see beyond the departing passengers as far as she could. At three, the last of them straggled in—a mother holding a baby in one arm, and a little girl about five crying and pulling on her other arm.

No one else. But that could not be. Two flight attendants walked past Barb, pulling their luggage, talking and joking, and the plane's door slammed shut behind them. She wanted to confront them and demand to know where Ronda was. But she didn't.

"I was suddenly nauseated," Barb Thompson recalled. "My mind whirled and I felt dizzy. *Where was Ronda?* I could see the chaplain's face in my mind now. His words were screaming in my ears. 'Your father wants you to call him at the Lewis County Coroner's Office.' It hit me like a ton of bricks. Oh, my God! My *baby*! No, no, it can't be! He hadn't been talking about my little girl. She must have just fallen asleep and didn't get off the plane. Any moment now the doors will swing open and there she'll be there."

But Ronda wasn't there. She hadn't been on the plane, or even on the manifest of passengers.

Barb made up every possible reason why her daughter hadn't arrived as she had promised—every reason *but* the one that tortured her the most. She simply could not face that possibility.

Finally, she dialed Information and asked for the number of the Lewis County Coroner's Office. When the operator asked her the state, Barb still didn't know. At length the operator came back on the line and gave her a number beginning with a 360 prefix. Barb's knees buckled. That was Ronda's prefix. But Lewis County hadn't meant anything to her; she thought Ronda lived in Thurston County.

Knowing what she didn't want to know, Barb Thompson called the number for the coroner's office. She identified herself to the female voice that answered.

"Are you Ronda Reynolds's mother?"

"Yes . . . I am."

"I'm sorry to inform you that your daughter died this morning."

"How?" Barbara didn't recognize her own voice. It was hollow.

"Your daughter committed suicide."

Barb didn't believe it.

She never did. For more than eleven years, Barb Thompson worked to discover the truth about her daughter's death, to remove that word *suicide* from Ronda's death certificate.

But nothing ever fit. Nothing ever matched. There are a number of suspects in Ronda's death, and as many motives. The main players each have their own theories—their particular script of what went on on that frigid night in December 1998.

And some of them know more than they have told.

CHAPTER THREE

THE LEWIS COUNTY SHERIFF'S COMMUNICATIONS dispatcher had received a call on the 911 line at 6:20 on the cold morning of December 16, 1998. The man calling in identified himself as Ron Reynolds and asked that an emergency vehicle respond as soon as possible to his home on Twin Peaks Drive. When asked what the situation was, Reynolds said that his wife had committed suicide with a pistol.

He spoke in a flat, oddly calm voice as he explained that he wasn't sure just what had happened because he himself had been asleep for the past "few hours." "I didn't hear the shot," he said. "She must have muffled it with a pillow or something."

"Does your wife have a pulse?" the dispatcher asked.

"I don't know—I can go check."

The dispatcher heard him set the phone down and return a few minutes later.

"I can't find any pulse," Reynolds said.

Lewis County deputy sheriff Gary Holt was dispatched to the Reynolds home just a minute after the school administrator called 911.

The Lewis County road deputies were spread thin in the county at that time of day, patrolling many miles from one another. It took Holt twenty-one minutes to arrive at the ranch-style home in Toledo. He wasn't quite sure what to expect, although, from the dispatcher's instructions, it sounded like a cut-and-dried suicide. At any rate, something was terribly wrong at Ronda and Ron Reynolds's house. When Holt walked up to the residence, he was directed to the master bedroom at the end of a hall to the left of the front entrance. Emergency medical technicians were working over a woman who lay on her left side on the floor of a closet that was just off the bedroom. There was a bathroom adjacent to the closet.

Holt noted a pistol lying across her forehead. She appeared to have suffered a head wound, and had bled profusely.

Ron Reynolds was quite well-known in Lewis County because of both his teaching career and his leadership in the Jehovah's Witnesses. But he was no longer connected with the church; when he left his wife, Katie, and moved in with Ronda, he left the Witnesses.

He spent a lot of money on Christmas gifts for his sons in December 1998—it was to be his sons' first Christmas with presents since they were very young. Josh hadn't even been born until his parents spent fifteen years in the Jehovah's Witnesses.

As the first deputy on the death scene, Gary Holt, surveyed Ronda's body, he noted that Ron seemed unnaturally calm, perhaps in shock. Ron told Holt that he had fallen asleep about 5 A.M. He was exhausted, he said, from trying to keep Ronda awake all night because she had been "thinking about suicide."

When his alarm clock jolted him awake at 6 A.M., she wasn't in bed beside him, and Ron said he'd searched their home and couldn't find her. He told one officer that he'd checked the living room couch, and another officer who arrived shortly after that he had gone to the kitchen, thinking Ronda might be in there feeding her dogs.

Only when he returned to their bedroom had he thought to push open the door of the walk-in closet off the master bathroom and look inside. He recalled moving a pillow from over his wife's head to check for a pulse. When he detected none, he called 911. (This was his second version of events; earlier he'd told the emergency dispatcher that he had *not* tried to find a pulse in his wife's wrist or neck arteries.)

The EMTs who were now kneeling beside the shooting victim in the closet found her body was still warm—but that could be accounted for by the electric blanket that covered her. It was turned on, powered by an extension cord stretching across the bathroom.

Ronda Reynolds wore white flannel pajamas with a pink rosebud pattern. The paramedics checked for lividity—the livor mortis that occurs when the heart stops beating and blood sinks to the lowest part of the body, eventually leaving fixed purplish-red stains or striated marks there. Where the weight of the deceased rests on a hard surface, the skin blanches white. If a body is moved before lividity is complete, there will be secondary (or dual) lividity, a lighter shade of pink than the first. Ronda's blood had settled to the left-front portion of her body first. (Later at the morgue, there was a shifting of bloodstains to her back, indicating that while lividity was almost complete, some of her blood had seeped through to the lower portion of her back when she was placed on a gurney to be transported to the funeral home.)

The EMTs also checked for signs of rigor mortis, a stiffening of the joints that begins soon after death. The jaw itself is usually the first area to begin to harden. They were surprised to hear that her husband said he had seen her alive at 5 A.M. Rigor seemed far more progressed than it normally would be within an hour and a half of death. Both the degree of lividity and rigor mortis would tend to place Ronda Reynolds's death at about 2 A.M.—four hours earlier than the time that her husband discovered her.

There might be more injuries on Ronda's body, but the wound that was instantly apparent when the medics pulled down the electric blanket had surely resulted from a fatal shot; it was just in front and slightly above Ronda's right ear, but they wouldn't be able to tell if it was an entrance or an exit wound until the massive amount of blood was washed from her face, throat, and hair.

Ron Reynolds's younger three sons who were living with him and Ronda had apparently been wakened from their sleep by strange voices and lights going on. Jonathan was seventeen, David fifteen, and Joshua ten. Apparently concerned that the boys would be distressed by the police activity, Ron had told them all to get up and to dress quickly. Then he had instructed Jonathan to drive himself and his two younger brothers to their mother's home. Katie Huttala lived some twenty miles away.

Deputy Holt, who had only a glimpse of the boys in the front hallway who were fully dressed and carrying extra clothes, agreed, thinking—erroneously—that the detectives could just as well talk to them later at Katie's house. Perhaps they could, but the probe was damaged when three of the main witnesses to Ronda's death left. Their initial emotions, impressions, memories would never be quite as fresh again. Other people might talk to them, and tend to confuse them. Detectives had no opportunity to take any statements from them or even to ask any questions. Indeed, the boys were hustled out of the house before most of the sheriff's team realized they were gone.

At the very least, the investigators would have asked Jonathan why there was such a heavy cloud of incense coming from his room.

Ron Reynolds called Tom Lahmann, the superintendent of the Toledo School District, and Bill Waag, the principal of the Toledo Middle School, and they hurried over to offer him emotional support.

The crowd in the Reynoldses' house grew larger. David Bell, who was a sergeant with the Des Moines, Washington, Police Department and Ronda's longtime friend, arrived. He said he was keeping his promise to drive her to SeaTac Airport to catch her flight to Spokane.

Oddly, Cheryl Gilbert showed up minutes later, saying that she was Ronda's very best friend and had come to pick her up and drive her to Portland to catch a Spokane flight from there. The distance to the Portland airport and the SeaTac Airport just south of Seattle was approximately the same, as was the flight time to Spokane from each.

A phone book, opened to the yellow airline pages, still sat in the master bathroom near the phone there. Ronda had surely made reservations to fly *somewhere* from one airport or another, but the investigators would have to check with Alaska Airlines before they knew for sure what her travel plans had been.

Cheryl Gilbert was baffled and said she had no idea that Ronda had decided to fly out from Seattle; she was positive Ronda was leaving from Portland. She appeared harried at finding the situation in the Reynolds home, but not terribly upset.

Ron Reynolds was stoic, apparently determined to keep from giving in to emotion. It seemed that he hadn't yet accepted that Ronda was gone.

Even rookie police officers soon learn that human beings react in many different ways to tragedies and sudden death; some go all to pieces, sobbing and shaking, while others may seem calm when they are really in deep shock.

Although it hadn't even begun to get light on this morning only five days from the shortest day of the year in Washington state, the death scene was crowded and becoming more so. Ideally, the fewer people allowed at the site of an unexplained death, the better. Two investigators are enough to take photographs, hold opposite ends of a measuring tape, and gather, preserve, and label evidence. Usually the first to arrive are patrol deputies or police patrolmen who keep the scene secure until detectives can respond. The presence of family, friends, neighbors—and even police supervisors—raises the risk of contamination of physical evidence.

Jerry Berry, the detective who would soon take over the investigation of Ronda Reynolds's death, calls them "Looky-Loos," and he includes members of the sheriff's department and "the brass" who invade a crime scene.

To begin with, there were just two deputies—Bob Bishop and Gary Holt—along with the paramedics. Deputy Bishop had arrived only three minutes after Holt did. When Bishop observed Ronda's body, he saw that she lay on her left side, was covered with an electric blanket—which was turned on—and had her head on a pillow.

"I didn't see any weapon," Bishop wrote in his report.

*   *   *

As THE AID CREW gathered up their gear, ready to clear the premises, Gary Holt asked Ron Reynolds to step into the kitchen. He wanted to tape an interview of Reynolds's recall of events while they were still fresh in his mind. The three boys were gone, but at least Ron was still there.

Ron told him that he had come home the night before at about 8:30. He and Ronda had had a prolonged argument; they were in the process of separating. He said he was worried when she began talking about suicide. He had told her to stop talking about killing herself, to stay with him and not leave him.

"I'd found the empty holster for my gun," he continued, "and I asked her where the gun was. She told me she'd given it to Dave Bell—a friend of hers—for safekeeping, so I wasn't as concerned then because I knew it wasn't in the house."

(When Jerry Berry read Bishop's follow-up report, he shook his head slightly. He'd learned that Reynolds was a black powder expert and a hunter, and it was rare for men interested in guns and ballistics to allow their weapons to be given away. Especially to his wife's old boyfriend. His intuition told him that Ron would have been angry if he thought Ronda had given his father's handgun to anyone.)

When Reynolds spoke to Deputy Gary Holt that first morning at 7:13, he said he'd done his best to stay awake all night so he could watch over Ronda in her depressed state, but by about five in the morning he became so exhausted, he figured he must have fallen asleep. The last thing he remembered was that he sensed his wife was in bed next to him. When he was awakened by his alarm clock at six, she wasn't there. He hadn't heard any unusual noises during the hour since he dropped off to sleep.

"I began to look for her, and I found her in the bathroom closet on the floor," Reynolds said.

"I took her pulse," he told Holt once more.

He had seen the terrible injury just below her right temple, and called 911.

This was only the second statement the school principal had made. There would be many more as some investigators dug deeper and others were ready to mark Ronda's case "Closed. Death by suicide."

Something bothered Deputy Bob Bishop. Ron Reynolds said that he hadn't heard a gunshot because both the bathroom and closet doors were closed. And yet Ronda died only about twelve to fifteen feet from the bed where he slept. Bishop walked to the closet door, did a double take, and looked in again. Ronda's feet were exposed and extended over the door's sill. Ron had said the door was closed and he had opened it to find his wife. But Bishop realized that it would have been impossible to shut the closet door because Ronda's lower legs extending over the sill would have blocked it.

Strange.

It was a grim puzzle with different detectives apparently observing different aspects that jolted them in this sad and sudden death.

Deputy Gary Holt wrote in his report that he had seen the .32-caliber Rossi revolver (Ron's gun) in Ronda's left hand. David Bell hadn't taken it out of the house after all. But Bishop's memory was that the blanket covered her left hand and "the gun was in the blanket."

In fact the blanket was clutched so tightly in her left hand that it took some effort to loosen it.

Ronda was right-handed. Ron was left-handed.

Deputy Holt's first statement said that Ronda was lying on her left side and the pistol was resting "next to her forehead."

But a police photograph of Ronda showed her in the classic fetal position. She lay on her left arm and her right arm was tucked under her right breast—not a position consistent with a self-inflicted gunshot wound to the right side of her head. Could she have somehow shot herself in the head—and then clutched the blanket with her left hand and moved her right arm until it was tightly caught beneath her right breast before she died?

It seemed unlikely.

It would take a neurologist or forensic pathologist to say what deliberate actions a person suffering a gunshot wound into the brain could execute.

Nevertheless, Holt tended to believe Ron Reynolds, who assured him Ronda had killed herself. Her manner of death appeared to have been set in stone from that first 911 call. Nothing, perhaps, is more devastating to an efficient and thorough death investigation than deciding too soon what has happened. Once minds are closed, it becomes extremely difficult to consider other possibilities.

Ronda Reynolds appeared to have taken her own life. Her husband had said so in his first call for help. Thus far, every lawman—save, perhaps, Deputy Bob Bishop—accepted that out of whole cloth. Still, it was difficult to understand why she had made so many plans for the immediate and distant future if she intended to commit suicide in the darkest hours before dawn.

It was apparent that Ronda had planned a trip; her

three suitcases were nearby and neatly packed, and her makeup and personal items were in her red Suzuki Tracker parked in the driveway. The rear plastic window was partially unzipped.

Holt walked down the hall to a bedroom near the front of the house. He could smell the strong odor of incense coming from what they learned later was Jonathan's room. It was heavy enough that it had to have been snuffed out very recently.

Why was Jonathan burning incense at six in the morning?

Homicide Detective David Neiser arrived at the house on Twin Peaks Drive at eight minutes to eight. Chief Criminal Deputy Joe Doench was already there. Although Doench would not write a report about his reason for being there, he observed the scene and put out a call for Detective Jerry Berry to respond and give his take on what had been found so far in the Reynoldses' house.

Neiser said later that he had removed the handgun after observing that it "was between her two hands," although when he peeled back the pillow that had been over her head, he noted the horizontal imprint of the gun barrel etched deeply into her skin from her right temple across her forehead. He agreed that the wound was just above and to the right of Ronda's right ear, and the blanket was grasped in her left hand.

Neiser tried later to explain to his sergeant—Glade Austin—why he had moved the gun even before photos were taken of its original position. He said he didn't know why—it had been an automatic reaction, his wanting to get a loaded gun into a safer place.

Jerry Berry, whose name suggests more of a cartoon character than a dedicated homicide detective, was initially the other half of the investigating duo. Berry, of the Lewis County Sheriff's Office at that time, is a shrewd and dogged detective, and he was assigned to work the crime scene, looking for evidence, while Dave Neiser would interview any witnesses who might show up.

Berry took photographs of the home's interior, and found a number of perplexing aspects of the so-called suicide. Ronda's hair was swept up and back, as if someone had run their fingers through it, possibly to check her bullet wound. Or she could have been dragged—but there wasn't room for that in the closet, and, more telling, there was no blood trail there or in the bedroom. Or in the entire house, for that matter.

Someone had used lipstick to write on the bathroom mirror:

I Love You!
Please call me
(509-555-0202)

It was Ronda's grandmother's number in Spokane. Was it Ronda's hand that had written the lipstick message? Berry noted that Ronda would have had to get on a stool or really stretch to reach that high a spot on the vanity mirror. And a handwriting expert would have to be called in to see if Ronda had written it, or if someone else had.

Berry caught his own image in the mirror as he photographed the bright red message. The words could not possibly be construed to be a permanent goodbye note.

Even when he examined the puzzling note on the mirror, the handwriting expert could not determine who had written it. However, he doubted it had been Ronda Reynolds.

"Most people write on a blackboard or a mirror at their

own eye level," he commented. "This is far above where Ronda's eye level would have been."

Again, if she had been suicidal, why would she have left such a message? It sure wasn't a suicide note; was she so organized that she had tried to make her suicide look like murder? And *when* was it written there?

The bathroom and the bathroom closet were immaculate, just like the rest of the house. Ronda's shoes were wrapped in tissue paper, stacked in their original boxes and lined up neatly, clothes hung on hangers that all faced the same way, and other items were stored in plastic bins with covers. Ron's dress shirts were carefully starched and ironed.

The only out-of-place object was a gift box of cheeses, smoked meats, jellies, and crackers just to the right of Ronda's body. Berry figured it might have been used to prop up the dead woman's arm.

Jerry Berry found a prescription container for Ronda for Zoloft, an anti-anxiety medication, but the date on the bottle was May 1998, and there were still a number of pills in it. If she had been taking too many Zoloft pills, or even if she had taken them as prescribed, they would have been gone months earlier.

The queen-size waterbed with its blue sheets and blue-and-white quilt in a "wedding ring" pattern appeared to have been slept in on only one side. If an observer stood at the foot of the bed facing straight ahead, the rumpled area was on the left.

That turned out to be Ron's side.

Ronda's usual spot was on the right, and it was barely rumpled. The pillows still on the bed matched the one placed over Ronda's head.

There was an empty half-gallon bottle of Black Velvet

whiskey on the bed stand on Ronda's side of the bed. When dusted for fingerprints, the bottle had none at all! The detectives would learn that Ronda didn't drink hard liquor—preferring wine coolers, or Zima, or a beer on a hot day, and those only on occasion. Ron said that the last time he looked at the bottle, it was approximately a quarter full.

He hadn't drunk any of it, he said.

*   *   *

A DEATH INVESTIGATION is such a delicate procedure. The best detectives must always view it first as a homicide, second as suicide, third as accidental, and finally as a natural death. They begin with a jumbled scene, items that may or may not be essential physical evidence, witness statements, forensic science aspects such as blood spatter, DNA, hair and fiber comparisons, forensic odontology, autopsy findings, ballistics, and all manner of possible evidence that will help to either convict or clear suspects. This is particularly important when the victim dies in his or her home, and if the suspect(s) also had reason to be there. For instance, unknown fingerprints are far more telling than those of people whose usual place of residence has become a death scene.

The only absolute way to connect a fingerprint with a killer is to find it pressed into a victim's wet blood, dried there as a silent, irrefutable statement.

There were dozens of possibilities for significant finds in the small house on Twin Peaks Drive. In the icy predawn hours ten days before Christmas, the Lewis County sheriff's staff had just begun to open puzzle after puzzle, peeling off layers like the brightly colored Russian dolls that fit one inside the other until the last, tiniest doll is revealed.

But most of those Lewis County deputies and detectives

at the death scene believed Ron Reynolds's declaration that his wife had died a suicide, and their minds were virtually made up that that was the true manner of death.

Jerry Berry wasn't nearly ready to declare a category into which Ronda's death fit. He was a man who approached any death scene with a jaundiced eye, and he had any number of questions in his mind, even as the case was only a few hours old. He noted things that disturbed him, and expected that the investigation would continue for days—even weeks.

It's not at all unusual for detectives to spend twenty-four hours or even more at a death scene, working alongside bodies of victims until the time is right to remove them. That wasn't true of Ronda's death. Lewis County didn't have a medical examiner, but instead operated with a coroner, as do many small counties in Washington and other states. Some coroners aren't even medical doctors, much less forensic specialists.

Coroner Terry Wilson had been in his elected post for twenty-seven years, and some of his calls on manner of death had troubled Jerry Berry in the past. Wilson did not come to the house on Twin Peaks Drive, but instead dispatched his deputy Carmen Brunton.

Carmen had worked in Wilson's office for a long time. She was a middle-aged, stylish woman with thick blond hair that she wore short and swept up. Her usual mien was stern and her face gave few hints about what she was feeling.

The time Carmen had arrived was never established accurately. Her report says she was notified of Ronda's death at 6 A.M. That could not have been; Ron Reynolds didn't call the sheriff's line until 6:20. Since it had taken most of the deputies twenty minutes to half an hour to reach the Reynolds's home, it was likely Brunton didn't get there until around 7 A.M.—at the earliest. When she did, she wrote that rigor mortis had set into Ronda's lower legs, and later she noted on her report that the reddish-purple stains of lividity had begun on Ronda's back when she was at the funeral home.

There was no indication that *anyone* had taken the dead woman's liver temperature with a thermometer probe. That could have further pinpointed her time of death.

After finding Ronda Reynolds on her left side, the investigators had rolled her onto her back for photos. It was apparent that the blood that flowed from her head wound had soaked her pajama top, hair, and the carpet beneath her. If she had been shot somewhere else, and her body then moved into the closet, there would have been blood in some other area of the house or in one of the couple's vehicles.

And there was none.

Carmen Brunton also said that the wound near Ronda's ear looked like an *exit* wound and that there appeared to be an entrance wound inside her mouth. Both of her opinions—which would suggest suicide—were erroneous.

Ronda's body was removed to Brown's Funeral Home in Centralia, and Deputy Coroner Brunton signed the first of several death certificates on Christmas Eve. The manner of death was listed as "Undetermined," while the cause of death indicated "a contact gunshot wound to the head." Brunton estimated Ronda had died "within minutes" after being shot.

That was technically possible. Ronda might have been unconscious and/or paralyzed, but she would have had to live for quite some time for her heart to pump out that much blood. The heart of a healthy person may well keep beating, even though all brain activity is gone. As it beats, blood will flow or leak from arteries and veins—even though the victim is already "brain dead."

There was no question at all that Ronda was deceased, and that she had passed from this life many hours earlier. The question that loomed from the very beginning was, of course, what was the manner of her death?

CHAPTER FOUR

As THE LEWIS COUNTY INVESTIGATORS worked at the scene of Ronda Reynolds's death, her mother Barb was three hundred miles away, happily planning for her daughter's Christmas visit and counting the hours until she and Freeman would pick Ronda up at the airport. Nothing seemed to be amiss; the only odd thing in Barb's Spokane home that morning was her memory of her phone ringing in the wee hours—and the dead silence she heard when she answered it. She had practically forgotten about that.

She knew that Ronda was sad that her second marriage was failing—just as the first had, but her daughter hadn't seemed truly distressed when they'd talked the night before, sometime between ten and eleven-thirty. Ronda had called her grandmother on Sunday or Monday to tell her that Ron was going back to his first wife, but there had been rumblings of trouble for months—so it wasn't really startling news, and Ronda seemed to be coping with the breakup as well as could be expected.

Ronda hadn't mentioned suicide. Of course she hadn't. It was unthinkable. "She was upset—she was distraught," Barb Thompson recalled. "She had just been hit with an outright, unmistakable request for a divorce. But she she wasn't giving up. She was wondering, 'What do I do now?' "

Barb wasn't sure what Ronda's financial situation was, but she assumed it wasn't that great. She was working in loss prevention for the Bon Marché (soon to be absorbed by Macy's department chain) and was still on a probational status, although that would end soon. She had told Barb earlier that she gave her paychecks to Ron and he handled all their money and paid the bills. He insisted on it, which wasn't shocking on the surface; Ronda wasn't good with budgeting.

"She told me many times that she never had enough money left out of her own paycheck," Barb said.

Ronda hadn't resented that at first, but within six or seven months of her wedding, she sensed a change in Ron, and suspected he might be seeing another woman. Then she found out it was his ex-wife! She had put everything she owned, including her Washington State Patrol retirement and her furniture, into the Twin Peaks Drive rambler, and she feared losing it all.

Although Ronda preferred living on the coast of Washington to inland Spokane, she was considering transferring to Macy's in Spokane when her provisional period ended. Barb crossed her fingers, hoping that would happen. If they lived close to each other again, Barb could always be sure that Ronda had backup—even though she wasn't wealthy herself. And it would give her such a sense of serenity to have *both* her children living near her again.

Ronda Reynolds was looking toward the future, rather than agonizing over the past. She was, after all, only thirty-three, pretty, smart, and capable, a woman who had come to see flaws in her school principal husband, small and large imperfections she hadn't recognized earlier. All newlyweds experience that, but Ron Reynolds's sins as a husband were egregious.

"Ronda was the kind of woman," Barb said, "who would pick herself up, dust herself off, and start all over again.

"She was anxious to come home, talk everything over with the people who loved her, probably lick her wounds, and then go on with her life. And we were so anxious to give her hugs and let her know we would support her decision to leave."

*   *   *

BUT RONDA HADN'T BEEN on either plane Barb met, and someone in the coroner's office over in Lewis County was telling her that her daughter was dead—that she was a suicide. Barb held the phone in her hand, and it was as heavy as stone. When she could speak again, she asked, "Is it being investigated?"

"Yes, ma'am, it is."

"By who?"

"The Lewis County Sheriff's Office. I have the name and number for the detective if you would like it."

"Yes, I would, please."

"I also have a number here for David Bell. He has asked me to please have you call him. He's waiting for you to call him."

Barb wrote down the numbers the almost disembodied

voice dictated and hung up the phone. She already knew Dave Bell's number but she wrote it down anyway.

"I was on automatic pilot," Barb remembers. "Not even sure if I was alive. But I had to be. My heart was pounding like a jackhammer. How could those few words—just a breath in time—shatter and forever change my life?

"Tears were rolling down my face. It seemed as if I was screaming, but I couldn't make a sound. The silence was deafening. The pain in my heart was like a thousand knives ripping and tearing, and my whole body was shaking uncontrollably. I wanted to die—but I knew I couldn't."

Shock had given way to grief, and then—like so many mothers who suffer the ultimate loss—Barb Thompson tried to bargain with God.

"Dear God, take me—not my child. Give me back my daughter and take me," she demanded. "I'll gladly give you my life—but not hers! Not my baby!

"Not Ronda . . ."

Barb had been through some incredibly tough times in her life, but she could not have imagined this. She had talked with Ronda in depth about her feelings for Ron, and realized that her daughter had suspected him of infidelity with his ex-wife for months. But Ronda had long since dealt with that. She knew her marriage was irretrievably broken. Last night, she had been more worried about what would happen to her beloved Rottweilers, which she had to leave behind at her house while she spent several days in Spokane. She loved those dogs like they were the babies she had never been able to carry to term. Would Ron or his sons feed them? Would they be warm enough in their outdoor pen? She feared more that her stepsons might hurt her dogs.

And Ronda wasn't alone. Her dearest, most trusted friend of more than a decade was helping her. Dave Bell and

Ronda had been lovers years before and talked about getting married. Although they loved each other back in those days, there were so many obstacles that blocked their wedding plan. Dave's divorce wasn't final, and he was going through a custody battle over his boys.

If he married Ronda too soon, his ex-wife might be granted total custody. He hadn't been able to face that.

So, a few years later, Ronda married Mark Liburdi, and she did love Mark when they married. Still, she and Dave Bell had never given up their platonic friendship. Months—even years—might go by without any contact between them, but both knew they would always be there for each other. Dave Bell had been helping her as much as he could as she prepared to leave Ron. Dave was single and Ronda soon would be.

"It wasn't as though she was going to leave one marriage and run to another man's arms," her mother recalled. "She wanted to get through her divorce and fight for those tangible things that were rightfully hers. Ron had told her she could take nothing with her when she left—except for her clothes and her dogs. And that wasn't fair; she had invested almost everything she had in the house she lived in with Ron. She even took some precious family things to that house—not heirlooms exactly, but sentimental items."

Barb Thompson felt it was quite possible that Ronda Reynolds and Dave Bell would marry one day—but not soon, and not in a hurry. Dave wanted to introduce her to his boys slowly—the right way. "I just hoped that his sons would be nicer to her than Ron's; the only one of the Reynolds boys who seemed to like her was Josh, the youngest. He was thrilled to have a 'mom' who made his school lunches and saw that he had clean clothes for school. He was still just a little boy."

Barb realized suddenly that Dave Bell must have gone to the house on Twin Peaks Drive early on this morning to pick Ronda up and drive her the seventy miles to the SeaTac Airport.

Oh my God, Barb thought. *Poor Dave. What he must have walked in on when he got there . . .*

Barb had to tell her mother that her cherished granddaughter would not be coming for a Christmas visit after all. Ronda was never coming home again. And then Freeman had to hear that his big sister had been shot to death. Barb herself had turned to ice. She had precious little time to cry. A single phone call galvanized her into action. Instantly, she became a woman with a mission. She was determined to find out what had *really* happened to Ronda, and to exact justice from anyone who might have hurt her.

She had no idea how long it was going to take. If it took the rest of her life, she didn't care.

Without Ronda, she no longer recognized her own life, but she realized there was no going back. Barb was the very epitome of a strong woman. At fifty-two, she had made her way through so many hard times and emerged—if not always victorious—in one piece, with the family she loved safe, too.

She was also a smart woman; Barb was determined not to let her emotions reveal her suspicions too early. Even though she knew it would eat at her like bitter poison, she would smile and pretend not to judge prematurely. She knew in her heart that her beautiful, kind—and, yes, stubborn—daughter hadn't committed suicide. But there were a number of people Barb suspected of doing harm to Ronda.

Somehow, she would prove who had done this. She had to.

*   *   *

BY THE TIME RONDA'S FAMILY learned of her sudden death, it was mid-afternoon, already growing dark. The temperature sank below freezing, and the roads were covered with black ice, the most dangerous condition of all because drivers often see the roads as wet when they are actually solid ice. If they misjudge and step on their brakes, they can easily spin out of control on the frozen roads.

Everything in Barb urged her to fly or drive over the mountains to the coast at once, but she forced herself to think rationally. She couldn't change anything now. It was far too late. She needed to pack, and to make arrangements for Ronda's burial. Or at least to begin to think about them. With that, anguish filled her heart; Ronda shouldn't be waiting to be buried or cremated; she should be sitting by the Christmas tree and talking to her Gramma Virginia.

What was going to happen to Ronda's dogs? One was Daisy's sister—Jewel—and the other two were rescues. Two of them were Rottweilers. A much older, injured Rottweiler had shown up at the Reynoldses' front door one night—never to leave. Ronda insisted on keeping her, and jokingly named her Old Daisy and nursed her back to health. Old Daisy seemed to know that it was Ronda who had saved her, and she adored her mistress.

And then there was feisty little Tuffy, the Jack Russell terrier.

Ron didn't like Ronda's Rottweilers, or any dogs for that matter. He had always insisted she keep them outside in their pen, even in the winter. When the temperature dropped below freezing at night and Ronda brought them inside, he complained that their shifting and snuffling woke him up as he was a "very light" sleeper. What if Ron forgot to feed them? If Barb drove her pickup truck over to Toledo, she could bring them back with her. But then, handling two big dogs and a hyperactive small one would be difficult as Barb tried to find out what had happened to her daughter. She didn't know where she'd be staying or if there were any motels that would allow the dogs to come in the room.

She worried about them; some of Ronda's stepsons were cruel to animals. One had shot a cat, and regularly threw rocks at the Rottweilers. Ronda was worried sick anytime she had to leave them for very long with Ron and his boys, particularly after her eight-year-old Rottweiler, Duchess, died while she was alone with Jonathan. Ron always said it was heatstroke, but Ronda hadn't believed it. She knew in her heart that her dog had been beaten to death. Barb kept Duchess's ashes in her trophy case.

Barb herself had been concerned for Ronda's own safety; the boys had never accepted her. The oldest son living with Ron and Ronda—Jonathan—was almost eighteen and Ronda told her mother that he delighted in sneaking into the master bathroom when she was taking a shower. Several times she had caught him peeping through the shower curtains at her. Ronda came to feel that she had no privacy in her own home.

The third time she saw Jonathan's face grinning through a crack in the shower curtain, Ronda took action. She had taught personal safety to rookies in the Patrol and many times she had had to overcome recalcitrant suspects when there was no backup available. Enough was enough. Ronda leapt out of the shower stall, pinned the teenager's wrists behind his back, and took him down, grinding his face into the bathroom floor.

And then she told Ron. She was even angrier when he pooh-poohed her concerns about his eighteen-year-old son.

"Jonathan hated Ronda after that," Barb told Dave Bell. "She humiliated him and she hurt him physically—but he had it coming. She told me he even threatened to kill her after that."

Ronda had reported Jonathan to the Lewis County Sheriff's Office, and deputies took her complaint that her life had been threatened. Jonathan was sent to live with his mother, Katie, for four months and court-ordered to take anger management classes.

But he never really forgave Ronda.

* * *

BARB KNEW MOST of the people who were—or had been—in the center of Ronda's life: Ron Reynolds, Dave Bell, Mark Liburdi, Cheryl Gilbert, who had come to the Twin Peaks Drive house to drive Ronda to Portland, myriad friends, and some of the people she worked with at Walmart and Macy's. Some Barb liked and others made her uneasy. She needed to know more about them.

Most of all, Barb Thompson needed sleep—if she could manage it without nightmares. She'd barely slept on Tuesday night; she'd been too excited about Ronda's arrival. They had talked late into the night, making plans. The last time Barb talked to Ronda was just before eleven. She thought Dave Bell had spoken to her at 11:45 and again at 12:30 A.M.

And then there had been the strange phone call waking Barb when she finally did get to sleep.

As crazy as it might sound to some people, Barb wondered if it had been Ronda, saying a last goodbye from somewhere in a misty place between earth and heaven where she could no longer talk. Maybe Ronda had died then at twenty minutes to 2 A.M. and not at five or six, as the deputies said Ron told them.

Barb *did* need sleep. In the morning, her head might be clearer. Whether that was good or bad was moot.

Every morning for the rest of her life, she knew she would always wake up thinking about Ronda.

*   *   *

ON THURSDAY MORNING, Barb Thompson rose in the frigid hours before dawn, prepared to fly to Seattle. It was an hour's flight, over the snow-tipped peaks of the Cascade Mountains, and even at that hour, the early planes were crowded. For the rest of the world, Christmas Eve was a week away, and families had begun to travel so they could be together for the holidays. Barb had forgotten about Christmas.

Dave Bell, Ronda's long-ago fiancé, had promised to meet Barb at SeaTac Airport in Seattle at a quarter after eight that Thursday morning and drive her the two hours to the Lewis County Sheriff's Office in Chehalis.

Barb trusted Dave, and she desperately needed a shoulder to lean on. Beyond Ron Reynolds and herself, Dave had probably been the last person to talk with Ronda. During their first phone call after Ronda's death, Barb had found Dave as shocked as she was. Maybe they could talk out some of their worries and preliminary conclusions as they drove south on I-5 toward where Ronda had lived. . . . and died.

CHAPTER FIVE

BARB THOMPSON STOOD ALONE on the curb outside the luggage area on the lower level of the SeaTac Airport. It had just begun to get light, and the wind cut through her like icy knives. The airport was decorated with evergreen trees, red, green, gold, and silver ornaments and displays, and she found herself wondering why. It didn't seem like Christmas. It had taken everything she had to get on the plane in Spokane and the sick feeling in her stomach hadn't lessened at all. She didn't care how she looked. When she couldn't bring herself to curl or fix her hair, she'd slapped on an old gray baseball cap that read "Classic Rope" on the bill. Some company must have given it to her when she bought horse training equipment. Her eyes were red and swollen and she tried to hide them with sunglasses.

"Still," she recalled, "I was afraid everyone who looked at me could see right through them—and me. They could surely tell that I was just an empty shell, a dead woman walking, going through the motions."

She knew that if anyone said a word to her, she would break down and start crying hysterically again. Did anyone scurrying around her know how close she was to losing it? And how she berated herself for thinking she had the right to break down?

Barb glanced around anxiously for Dave's green Dodge truck. He was always punctual. She dreaded facing him because she knew in her heart that he was in pain, too. She repeated a silent mantra, "I can do this, I *must* do this," for what seemed like a million times. But her watch said she'd been waiting for only three minutes. Finally, she spotted his familiar truck.

Dave grabbed her bags and loaded them in his truck and then gave her a quick hug. They had to move away from the curb and make room for other cars that were picking up arriving passengers.

They drove in silence for minutes as Dave turned left on 188th, the street bordering the south end of the huge airport, headed east, and then south, entering the on-ramp to I-5. They both knew they had to talk about what had happened, but neither was ready yet. Oddly, Barb had always thought of Dave as more of a son-in-law than either of Ronda's husbands. He was a compassionate man, and an honest cop. If she could talk to anyone, it would be Dave, but her questions stuck in her throat.

The drive south along the freeway was familiar to them both, and it would become much more so to Barb in the years ahead. They cleared the edges of Tacoma, passed the Fort Lewis army base and McChord Field, then Olympia, and headed toward Centralia and Lewis County, trying very hard to ignore the ubiquitous Christmas decorations.

Dave Bell began to tell Barb about the hours he'd spent with Ronda two days before—the last day of her life. Neither he nor Ronda had had any inkling then of what was to come. Or, if Ronda did, she didn't say it out loud.

Dave said he had helped Ronda pack many of her possessions and carry them to her Suzuki Tracker. David recalled that Ronda had said she might stay with a woman friend when she returned from her trip to Spokane. He thought it was Cheryl Gilbert.

"She was never again going to live in the house she shared with Ron," Dave told Barb Thompson. "She promised to give me a wake-up call on Wednesday so I could drive down and take her to the airport."

But there had been no call from Ronda. Dave said he'd driven to her house anyway. He had called her on the way down and been surprised when Ron Reynolds answered.

"I asked to speak to Ronda," Dave Bell told her mother. "But Ron came on the line."

Bell took a deep breath before he related that Ron had been "almost nonchalant" when he broke the news that Ronda had committed suicide. Stunned, Dave had continued on to Toledo to see what could possibly have happened.

Never once had Bell believed that Ronda had killed herself.

When he arrived at the house on Twin Peaks Drive, he identified himself as Ronda's friend and as a longtime police officer. A Lewis County deputy met him and questioned him after telling him only the most basic assumptions—that Ronda had shot herself in the right side of the head, using her left hand to fire the gun, and that she'd been found in the walk-in closet in the master bedroom, covered with an electric blanket that was plugged in and turned on.

"Evidently, Ron told them that he was sleeping less

than fifteen feet away—but he didn't hear the gunshot," Dave said.

Barb Thompson listened. Every word brought up more suspicions.

"We were packing her things Tuesday night in the bedroom," Dave said, "and Ronda took a revolver down from a closet shelf and she handed it to me. She said she wanted me to take care of it."

But Dave Bell asked who it belonged to, and Ronda answered, "Ron. It was his father's gun."

Bell said he couldn't take possession of a gun that belonged to someone else. He'd carefully unloaded the weapon, put it back in its holster, and placed it in a drawer under the waterbed in the master bedroom.

"I honestly can't recall," he told Barb, "whether I discarded the bullets on the bed or on the floor."

Dave Bell didn't know why Ronda wanted him to take the gun out of the house. She was very familiar with weapons; she'd been an instructor in gun safety when she was on the Washington State Patrol. She'd had a WSP-issued Beretta and a .357 Magnum Smith & Wesson that her uncle Bill Ramsey had given her. Mark, her first husband, had taken the S&W Model 66, and, of course, when she left the Patrol, she'd turned in the Beretta. As far as Dave knew, she no longer had any personal gun.

"Was Ronda afraid of something? Someone?" Barb Thompson asked.

Dave shook his head. "I don't think so. I'd say she was indecisive. She just wanted to come up to my house in Tukwila for the night, and fly to Spokane from there. But she was afraid if she left the house, and everything she'd put into it, everything she didn't take with her Tuesday night would be gone."

And there had been the problem of their pets. Ronda had three dogs and Dave had cats. How would they get along if they were suddenly thrust together? Not to mention Bell's sons, who were older now but really didn't know Ronda. He had hoped to introduce them gradually. He hadn't figured out how he could explain a pretty woman who was a virtual stranger to them—*and her dogs.*

Of course, if he'd felt she was in any danger at all, none of that would have mattered. "I would have dragged her out of there kicking and screaming if I had to," he told Barb.

Bell said he and Ronda had driven around Lewis County for a while, holding hands. That was only to comfort Ronda. Once again she had come to a crossroads in her life, one she hadn't foreseen. She was relieved to be getting out of her marriage to Ron Reynolds but she also felt somewhat embarrassed that she had failed at marriage—twice now. Ronda made several calls to friends on her cell phone, and then a short call to her estranged husband, Ron Reynolds. It had been a very brief conversation, and one without much emotion. From what Dave could hear, Ronda had focused on some specific details of their coming separation.

"We stopped and got a bite to eat," Dave recalled. "Ronda told me she had decided to stay one final night in her own house—because she wanted to confront Ron with what she was going to demand from him in their divorce."

They had also driven to Cheryl Gilbert's house. Ronda had been thinking of staying with Cheryl that night and possibly when she returned from her Christmas visit home, but she changed her mind. Ronda loved Cheryl's children, although sometimes she was overwhelmed because Cheryl's friendship was oppressive and somehow she seemed always to know where Ronda was.

"Ronda worried about that—and didn't want to encourage it."

Dave Bell watched as Ronda knocked on Cheryl's door. When no one answered, she tossed Cheryl's house keys in through the front door and flipped the lock.

When the two returned to the Twin Peaks Drive house, they saw that Ron's car was already there. Dave Bell had no desire to meet the man Ronda was married to—at least for the time being—and he needed to get back to his police department in Des Moines.

"We said our goodbyes," Dave said quietly, "and that was the last time I saw Ronda, although I did talk with her by phone later that night—twice—to make arrangements for me to pick her up the next morning and take her to SeaTac to catch her flight."

"When was that?" Barb asked. "I talked to her late Tuesday night, too."

"Around midnight. She was going to get reservations to fly out of Portland, but I told her that would make a really long drive for me—and it would be a lot easier if she could leave from Seattle. She said that was fine, and that she'd make her reservations to leave from SeaTac."

"Tell me the truth, Dave," Barb urged. "You've known Ronda for more than ten years. You may know her better than anyone. Did she *seem* distraught or suicidal?"

"No—not at all. You know me, Barb—I would never have left her there if I sensed anything like that. She seemed fine—tired, hoping she was doing the wisest thing, but she wasn't depressed and she certainly didn't seem like someone who was thinking of taking her own life. She was tough, and she liked to be in charge. Ronda would never have given up easily . . ."

Dave and Barb drove along in silence awhile. Once they

cleared Olympia, the countryside became more bucolic with farms instead of single houses.

They arrived at the Lewis County Sheriff's Office in Chehalis at 11 A.M. Detective Dave Neiser met them. Neiser explained that he had been one of the first investigators at the Reynolds's house, having been called out from home shortly after 7 A.M. the day before—Wednesday. He said that he was to have been the detective in charge of the investigation, but he had scheduled a week's vacation. So he had passed the case to Jerry Berry. He reassured Barb that Berry was "the best detective on the force."

And possibly he was right. Although Barb wouldn't know it for a long time, it had been Neiser who removed the death gun from its original position—for "safety's sake." He said that he didn't want the fire department EMTs to be hurt if the gun went off accidentally. After that huge mistake, there was no way to ever know for sure where it had actually been.

In this case, that mattered a lot.

Getting Jerry Berry to work on the mystery surrounding Ronda's death was one of the luckiest breaks Barb could have hoped for. Still, coming from her point of view, Barb was astounded and angry. How could the world go on as if nothing had happened? Who cared about Christmas vacations? She didn't know anything about Jerry Berry, and believed she was getting a fast shuffle.

"[With Neiser] I saw only a man whose demeanor was detached and unconcerned," Barb remembered. "As if David Bell and I were a bother and Neiser didn't have any time to spare for us. It took everything I had to keep from bursting out, 'Excuse me, but my daughter happens to be dead! Are you more concerned about your vacation than about a human life?' "

Dave Bell sensed her angry frustration and kept her from saying aloud what she was thinking He pinched her arm hard, and the resulting pain helped her keep her mouth closed.

"He knew what I was feeling, and how close I was to losing it. He wasn't doing much better, but at least he had roped in his anger and was able to snap me back to reality. I knew I had to remain calm and objective if we were to accomplish anything."

Barb Thompson was passing through the stages of grief rapidly. Things she had always believed in were crumbling; she knew that law enforcement agencies and judicial systems had their flaws, but she had always had faith and respect for them. Now her instincts told her to beware, and to keep her guard up. She honestly didn't know who it was she suspected of destroying Ronda, but her gut told her that she and Dave Bell had to think out what they did or said very carefully from this point on.

"We had to remain aware and cautious," she sighed later. "Dave at least had years of law enforcement experience, but I didn't. I had to learn fast, and keep my mouth shut, and not wear my emotions on my face.

"That I could do. It wouldn't be easy but for Ronda, I could do it."

* * *

LEWIS COUNTY DETECTIVE Jerry Berry greeted them. He wasn't an especially big man, but Barb found his presence "enormous." His blue eyes looked directly into her own, and she instinctively felt that she could trust him. He wasn't smiling but his eyes were kind and concerned. Berry had craggy, "down-home" features, a sun-weathered face, and dark hair that was beginning to recede. He wore black slacks, a white shirt without a tie, a sport coat, and cowboy boots.

Berry held out his hand and his grip was firm—but gentle. For the first time since Barb and Dave Bell had walked into the sheriff's office, she felt somehow comforted. This detective was a compassionate man, and his eyes never left hers as they talked.

"I felt God had given me a guardian angel," Barb recalled. "I was glad that he was now the lead detective because I knew somehow that he cared for her. Ronda was no longer just another body, but a human being who deserved to be treated with dignity. I knew Detective Berry would do everything in his power to uncover the truth about her death—whatever the truth might end up being."

Even so, Berry didn't give them much information. He couldn't. Barb understood that many facts had to be kept under wraps, even from a victim's survivors. In order to maintain control of a murder probe, investigators had to keep to themselves any information that only a killer might know. Although she was bursting with questions, she tried to hold back.

"Jerry Berry did tell us that Ron had called 911 at 6:20 A.M. on Wednesday, and that he'd managed to remain calm when he told the dispatcher that his wife had committed suicide. When the first deputies arrived, Ron, his three sons, and then two men from the school district were at the house."

She was appalled and she saw Dave Bell's jaw tighten when they heard that the boys were allowed to leave the death site without being questioned. Even most laymen knew that was one of the basic rules in Death Investigation 101.

"They had already left when I got there," Berry said quietly. "We can question them later."

"It's not the same," Barb mouthed under her breath. How many other mistakes had this small-county department made, omissions and blunders that would slow down the probe of Ronda's death?

Berry looked as if her questions had struck a nerve. He was angry, too, that the boys had been allowed to leave before anyone questioned them, but he couldn't say that. Barb sensed that he seemed to want to say more—but he was fighting back the impulse. She couldn't determine if he agreed with her or if he was being defensive.

"Mr. Reynolds told us he found your daughter in the closet—covered with an electric blanket," Berry said. "The entry wound was next to her right ear; she was lying on her left side. It appeared that both hands were under the blanket, and the gun was resting on top of the blanket. He said it was in her left hand."

"But Ronda was right-handed," Barb Thompson said. "It's Ron who is left-handed."

"How do you know that?"

"My mother and I had breakfast with Ron and Ronda in May when they came over for Mother's Day, and we talked about it then," she answered. "We joked about the fact that he and I are both lefties."

Jerry Berry was still looking into her eyes, but he was noncommittal about his reactions.

She plunged on. "Don't you find it strange that Ronda's husband asks for a divorce, Ronda makes plans to visit me in Spokane, she tells Ron that she wants financial compensation for what she contributed when they bought their new house, and she told me she refused to give him a divorce until six months had passed and she had a clean HIV test—

and *bang*!—she ends up dead? Doesn't all that raise any red flags for you?"

Berry looked up sharply, surprised. The HIV test was a new thread in an already complicated case. Barb explained that Ronda knew that Katie Huttula Reynolds had had problems with drugs off and on for years, and that Ron had been unfaithful with her. Ronda feared she might have been infected.

It was apparent that Ronda and her mother had been very close and had no secrets from one another, and Berry noted that in his brain, but outwardly, he remained frustratingly calm. "No, there was no 'suicide' note. There was a note on the mirror that read 'I love you. Call me,' and a phone number with a 509 area code."

"That makes no sense at all," Barb replied. "I don't believe my daughter killed herself. I want an investigation."

"And I plan on doing one, Ms. Thompson."

"Do you think she killed herself? Does it make any sense to you?" Barb persisted.

"There seem to be some discrepancies here that I find disturbing," Berry said. "I'm sorry—but I can't say more at this point. I assure you I'm going to work hard—it will be my priority."

She believed him but it seemed as though she wasn't really learning much about the details of what had happened.

Barb had another request. She asked to see Ronda's body. Neither Dave Bell nor Jerry Berry had expected this.

"I don't think that's a good idea," Berry said. "You need to remember her as the way she was—not the way she is now."

Dave Bell's look of distress mirrored Berry's. "He's right, Barb," Dave said quickly. "Trust me, you don't want to do that."

She hadn't allowed herself to visualize Ronda after a bullet had crashed into her head, and now an image pushed through her protective shield. Barb Thompson gulped back sobs, and feared she was going to vomit.

All she could think of was her daughter lying in a morgue somewhere on a cold metal tray. She wanted so much to go to Ronda and tell her everything was going to be all right. She had always done that—that's what mothers did.

"I was going to say, 'Mama's here,' " Barb remembered years later. " 'Mama will take care of you.' But I knew I couldn't think that way. I had to redirect my thinking. Inside my head, I began to say: 'Look hard. Look deep. See her smile? She's smiling at you. She's warm. She's okay. You can handle this. Settle down and focus on what you need to do.' "

Barb took a deep breath. "All right. If you don't want me to see my daughter—then I want to go and talk to her husband—to Ron."

Detective Berry warned her that that wasn't a good idea, either. But he could see going in that he wasn't going to dissuade this woman. She seemed to have an inner core of strength that overrode her sorrow and her shock. Most mothers would be basket cases only twenty-four hours after learning their child was dead. Inexplicably dead.

Sighing, Berry gave in. "I still don't think it's wise," he said. "I wouldn't advise it."

"I have to. I need to hear him explain what happened with my own ears," Barb said firmly. "Ron was the only one there with her yesterday morning—except for his sons."

"You're upset, and you're very angry, and we don't need any trouble."

"We already have trouble."

"Okay," Berry said. "If you feel you have to do this,

please control your temper and don't ask a lot of questions. But listen closely to everything he says, and then go to your car and write it down as close to word for word as you can get it. And after that, I would like for you to come back here and talk to me."

Barb nodded. She hated to ask Dave Bell to drive her back to what had been Ronda's home, knowing it would be difficult for him to relive what had happened a day earlier when he learned that Ronda was dead. It had been just a little more than a day, but it felt as if Ronda's death had been a week—even a month—ago. Everything was happening in slow motion, as if she were slogging through quicksand.

Barb offered to rent a car and drive herself, but Dave wouldn't let her do that.

"He was hurting, too," she recalled. "But he would be there for me. He wouldn't go in with me. I needed to talk to Ron alone, but Dave would wait nearby. Neither of us knew for sure what we were looking for, but we weren't nearly ready to agree with the coroner that Ronda had probably decided to commit suicide."

She and Dave headed back to his green pickup to travel ten miles south to Toledo.

Barb wondered what her son-in-law would say to her. Maybe he wasn't her son-in-law any longer.

She realized she hardly knew him.

Chapter Six

JERRY BERRY NEVER INTENDED to be a cop. He didn't have relatives in law enforcement, and he'd never been particularly fascinated with that kind of career. In fact, he'd spent the first twenty-two years of his working life in heavy construction—beginning at the age of seventeen. He enjoyed the work and the pay wasn't bad. He recalls feeling a sense of pride to finish a job and observe the results of his hard labor under a blistering sun or in driving rain.

At thirty-nine, he suddenly realized that a time would come when he wouldn't be able to lift the backbreaking loads he'd lifted at twenty. His muscles ached at the end of the day, and heavy construction wasn't nearly as appealing as it had been when he was a teenager.

"I wanted to do something else," he says. "But I really didn't know what I was going to do. Still, I knew I was going to find it."

He was living in Mossyrock at the time, a hamlet so tiny it doesn't get mentioned on most Washington maps. Not surprisingly, everyone knows everyone, and Berry was chatting with Knute*—who owned the Mossyrock Market— when their attention turned to the town marshal, who stood on the sidewalk across the street.

His name was Rufe* and he had become town marshal by appointment from the mayor.

Everyone in town viewed Rufe as a poor man's Barney Fife, but Barney got points for wearing a full uniform and keeping his one-bullet gun in its proper holster. Rufe wore his gun in a shabby holster and hung it around his neck on a leather shoestring. Fortunately, he had never shot himself or anyone else in the foot—or worse.

"What does it take to be a marshal?" Knute asked, trying to make conversation.

Jerry Berry wasn't positive, but he figured there would be a test, a background check, and attendance at the Washington State Criminal Justice Center in Burien, Washington. He couldn't imagine that Rufe would be able to go through all those obstacles and pass.

Half joking, Berry said, "I could do a better job than Rufe and I don't know anything about the law."

Knute then suggested that Berry go over to see the mayor and apply for the job.

James Roberts, the Mossyrock mayor, didn't have a regular office; the town wasn't big enough for that. The mayor was licensed to run the Washington State Liquor Store in Mossyrock, and Mayor Roberts conducted both liquor sales and political business from behind the counter of his store.

Berry walked over and automatically held his breath against the thick cigar smoke that seemed to curl around the bottles, ads, windows, and other displays. He'd never been in the liquor store without seeing it through a cigar-tinged haze.

He approached the mayor and announced that he wanted to apply for the job of marshal. Or as "chief of police" of Mossyrock, which seemed the correct term as they neared the millennium. "Marshal" sounded more like someone out of *Gunsmoke*.

Roberts looked him up and down, took the cigar out of his mouth, and asked, "You got any experience?"

"No," Berry said honestly, "but I'm in good shape and I can get through the academy."

After the Lewis County Sheriff's Office did a background check on him and found him clean, Mayor Roberts hired Berry and sent him to the academy.

He had no trouble with the curriculum or the physical strength and agility tests at the state Criminal Justice Training Center, but he was teased unmercifully; the last candidate from Mossyrock (not Rufe) had proved to be both dishonest and bizarre, and his background was all fake.

Jerry Berry *was* in good shape at forty, and even though the other trainees were only half his age and called him "the Old Man," he kept up just fine.

Disaster struck the day before the final fitness test required for graduation from the academy. He severely injured his left ankle, and even walking lightly on that foot brought pain. His teammates wanted to tell the academy staff and take him to the hospital, but he knew if he went he'd be barred from the next day's tests.

"I wanted to graduate with my class," he recalls. "I made them promise not to say anything."

The next morning, Berry wrapped his swollen ankle as tight as he could with Ace bandages, so it would move as little as possible. If he noticed that anyone was looking at him, he forced himself by sheer will to walk without a limp. The test required that each candidate take a quarter-mile lap around the track—as fast as he could go. Halfway down the back side of the track, he had to scale a six-foot wooden obstacle and keep running. Next there was a culvert to belly-crawl through, more running, and finally a ten-foot chain-link fence to scale and drop to the other side, with a final sprint to the finish line.

Berry did all right over the wooden wall, managing to land on his good foot, and it felt great to drop to his belly as he crawled through the culvert. But as he emerged, he made the mistake of starting to run on his left foot instead of his right.

"My ankle was on fire as I ran," he remembers. "The pain was like a burning rod being shoved into my ankle."

He was running as well as he could, but anyone watching could see that he was limping badly. The ten-foot fence rose between him and the finish line, and it seemed insurmountable. But he grabbed on and pulled himself hand over hand until he could swing his left leg over the top. Halfway down, he let go, managing to land on his right foot.

He hobbled, but he made it across the finish line before he collapsed. He graduated with his class and brought a modicum of respect back to Mossyrock. The town finally had someone who had beaten the Police Academy.

Berry hired one man—a twenty-one-year-old who had been in his graduating class: Erick Hendrickson. Erick was blond, six feet, two inches tall, and weighed 220. His nickname was "Baby Huey," which wasn't much better than "the Old Man." Maybe it was worse.

Berry was old enough to be Erick's father, but they made a great team. Together they set out to bring real law enforcement to Mossyrock. They began by staking out the town's two taverns, where most of the trouble began. Driving under the influence (DUI) was a regular pastime for a number of Mossyrock citizens. Arrests in that category rose 400 percent in the first year of the Berry-Hendrickson police force.

Berry had promised to stay for a year as marshal/police chief of Mossyrock. He knew it would be a self-limiting position, but he worked at it as hard as he had on any job in his life. He stayed there for nineteen months. During that time, he discovered that law enforcement was a perfect fit for him, and he wanted to learn more about it. When he was offered a job as a patrol deputy by Lewis County in 1991, he took it.

It seemed like a great opportunity, and he was enthusiastic about the future. Even as he drove out in the "tules" on foggy nights, ticketing speeders, more drunks, and writing citations for drivers without seat belts, Jerry Berry loved his job. He made a point of working just a little harder than he had to, and that didn't always sit well with some of the other officers in the sheriff's office. Berry tried to shrug off remarks about his age, although he was annoyed when a lieutenant, who was clearly as old—or older—than he was, asked him if he thought his age would hamper him on the job.

Jerry Berry had a goal: he wanted one day to be a detective, and the sooner the better. Berry was twenty years behind, and although he was only in his early forties, younger officers kept reminding him of it. He was always running to catch up with the two decades of experience he had missed when he was a construction worker.

With that in mind, he signed up for every training course he could, most of them useful in investigating homicides. John McCroskey, the Lewis County sheriff, agreed to fund some of Berry's tuition and he spent weeks studying interviewing and interrogation at FBI classes taught in Seattle. He also took an eleven-week Advanced Homicide Investigation class taught by Robert Keppel, one of the prime members of the Ted Bundy task force.

Berry drove once a week to Bellevue, Washington—a 160-mile round trip—to take classes that enhanced his skills as a homicide investigator. He learned about the secrets inherent in blood spatter from former Multnomah County sheriff's detective Rod Englert—who had become one of the top "blood pattern experts" in America. Berry also attended a class taught by Vernon Geberth, a genius in homicide investigation who had retired as commander of the homicide unit of the New York City Police Department's Bronx Division.

When the sheriff's office had no money to pay tuition for advanced criminal investigation classes, Berry was happy to pay for them himself.

Berry had no illusions about working in a big-city department; he wanted only to be the best investigator he could be right where he was.

Working with the U.S. Forest Service and the FBI, Berry helped break up a methamphetamine ring and recovered $150,000 in illicit drug money.

Sheriff McCroskey wrote him a letter of commendation, and he was named Officer of the Year.

Early on, Berry applied to be assigned to Lewis County's five-man detective unit. After two years, he got his wish. Between 1995—when he became a homicide detective—and 2001, he participated in twenty-three death investigations.

But Jerry Berry had never encountered a case like that of Ronda Reynolds. It would change his life and the lives of so many people in Lewis County, Washington. He refused to give up looking for the truth inherent in the mystery of Ronda's sudden, strange death.

As the years passed, Berry's dogged reluctance to go along with Coroner Terry Wilson's ever-changing opinions on the manner of Ronda's death, and his stubbornness about approving all the decisions made by his own department, made him enemies and annoyed his sergeant and others in high positions.

Maybe he was a little cocky. He prided himself on being thorough; he had never been a man to do things halfway and he expected as much from his fellow officers.

Berry would gradually become the "kicking boy" in a case that refused to go away. Many of his superiors felt he hindered their progress and procedures in investigating what a number of cops and laypersons felt was outright murder.

He was the one who encouraged Ronda's mother not to give up her continual criticisms of the Lewis County Sheriff's Office, and he supported her in her search for answers. But Barb Thompson would have done that with or without Jerry Berry.

Infighting behind the walls of any law enforcement agency is common, particularly when they are dealing with high-profile life-and-death crimes. Many departments refuse to exchange information with other agencies. In the Charles Manson cult murders, the Los Angeles County Sheriff's Office and the Los Angeles Police Department each guarded their secrets carefully, stubbornly refusing to share everything they knew. In a sense, a police department is much like a competitive business. The salesmen who make the most sales pit themselves against each other in the company. In law enforcement, he who brings in the most evidence against an infamous suspect wins.

His critics said Jerry Berry was a self-aggrandizer who

was determined to solve the Ronda Reynolds case all by himself. More likely, he was a truly dedicated detective who was showing compassion for a dead woman's mother. Detectives try to keep themselves emotionally separated from grieving families—but sometimes it isn't easy. The most sensitive humans make superior investigators, and that very sensitivity tends to make them let down their guards from time to time.

Barb Thompson was unaware of any of the backbiting and rustlings of suspicion and discontent in the sheriff's office. So far, Berry was playing by the book, and keeping whatever information he had sacrosanct within the Lewis County office.

Ronda Reynolds had been dead less than forty-eight hours, and the majority of the Lewis County sheriff's staff had already begun to believe Ron Reynold's emotionless statement that his wife had died a suicide.

Even so, there were endless avenues where the investigators might learn who Ronda really was.

CHAPTER SEVEN

DECEMBER 17 WAS A GRAY DAY, and it fit Barb Thompson's and Dave Bell's mood as they left the sheriff's office and their first meeting with Jerry Berry.

The last of the deciduous leaves had torn away from tree branches when the winds blew north from the Pacific Ocean and the Columbia River and only the fir, cedar, and pine trees added a muted green color as they bent toward the ground in the fierce wind. They drove in silence to what had once been Ronda's dream home. Barb realized she had never seen it outside of the snapshots Ronda had sent her.

At some point, they would have to talk in depth, but they each felt too much grief to begin. Barb had no doubt that Dave had been deeply in love with Ronda; the two of them had come in and out of each other's lives for years. If only they had managed to make their reunions last. Years ago, when Ronda was still a state trooper, she had made Barb promise that if anything ever happened to her, her mother would get in touch with Dave first—before she informed anyone else.

Barb had always suspected that Ronda had never really fallen out of love with Dave, even while she was married to two other men. She just thought Ronda had never acted on it. Dave wasn't available to her for most of the ten years they were apart. He was entrenched in an unhappy marriage, and even when he finally did divorce, the child custody battle between him and his ex-wife continued. He loved his boys, and he couldn't face the possibility of losing them. If he'd married Ronda back then, he was quite sure his ex-wife would have kept the boys away from him—not because he lacked anything as a father, but out of resentment. They meant too much to him to risk that.

By the time Dave was given custody of his sons, and was free to marry Ronda, they had maintained a close friendship for all the years in between. But it was too late. Ronda and Dave were like two trains on different tracks, never meeting at the same place and time.

*　*　*

IN THE INTERIM, Ronda had begun to date Mark Liburdi, thirty-two, a fellow Washington state trooper. Mark had reddish blond hair and a mustache, and he was very tall. He was an attractive man, especially in uniform, and Ronda quickly fell in love with him. Mark was eight years older than Ronda—and he had been married before. He had custody of his three children, two boys and a girl, but that was no obstacle to Ronda. She loved children and was happy to become a stepmother. They married in Spokane in June 1989.

Ronda wore a wedding gown reminiscent of the 1920s,

with a ruffled hat to match; she had designed it and Gramma Virginia had sewed it. Mark wore his full dress uniform.

Ronda's deepest hope was to have children of her own with Mark and build a large, blended family. The newlyweds and his children lived in Renton for a while, but they both wanted to move to a more rural locale.

Nine months later, Ronda and Mark were transferred to the Hoquiam WSP office on the Pacific Ocean coast in Grays Harbor County. The economy in that county had been hurting long before the rest of the country, and home prices reflected that. They bought a house on Stilson Road in McCleary with plenty of room for Mark's children and the children Ronda hoped to have with him.

It was the answer to Ronda's dreams. The gray rambler was surrounded by five acres of horse pasture, and they fenced their acreage in with electric wires topping the fences. There were stables for Ronda's horses. A creek burbled cheerfully behind the house, and there were plenty of blackberry bushes back there, too.

Mark fell in love with some adjoining property with a cabin hidden deep in the evergreen woods, and Ronda agreed that they should buy that, too.

Ronda was probably as happy as she had ever been in her life when she stepped outside her house to breathe the fresh air, and listen to the wind in the treetops. Her favorite shift in the Washington State Patrol was during the night and early morning watch, and her heart sang as she came home in the morning to this small ranch she loved so much.

She had other property, too, thanks to her mother's careful planning. Barb Thompson had owned thirty acres west of Dallas, which she sold to buy her horse ranch in Spokane. In her divorce from Hal Thompson, Freeman's father, it was decreed that Barb would put the Spokane acreage in Ronda's and Freeman's names. She did that, giving them joint ownership with rights of survivorship. Either could have borrowed money on the property at any time if they needed to.

"Ronda was always on my checking account," Barb recalls, "ever since she was fourteen, and she never took advantage of that."

Ronda loved Mark's three children, even though she and his thirteen-year-old daughter wrangled a bit, something to be expected with teenage girls and stepmothers. Although it was Ronda who took physical care of her and listened to her adolescent problems, Laurita* felt that her birth mother—a noncustodial parent—could do no wrong. Ronda understood that; she had no wish to speak badly of Mark's first wife.

Once, one of Mark's two sons stole something from a local store. Its value was negligible, but Ronda wanted the boy to learn a lesson. She "arrested" him and took him to jail. He stayed behind bars just long enough to understand the seriousness of what he had done, and she was happy to let him out and take him home.

Sadly, Ronda's dreams of having her own children were not to be. She miscarried several pregnancies. The losses may have hit her harder then they did Mark. Perhaps they did—he may have simply refused to talk about the lost babies, closing up and drawing inward because miscarriages and Ronda's grief were too painful for him to contemplate. He already had three children, and Ronda had none at all. She felt empty and inadequate as a woman.

By 1997, the Liburdis' marriage was not going well. They had married full of hope in 1989 but it looked as if their problems might be impossible to resolve. Ronda worried that she would never be able to give birth to a healthy baby. Mark apparently didn't grasp how devastating that was for her.

One miscarriage—or, rather, the premature birth of a male fetus—took place when she was in her fifth month. She had been so happy when she passed the three-month mark, believing that this was the child she could at last carry safely to term. She delivered at home in the bathroom, but her baby didn't cry and showed no signs of life. The placenta adhered tightly to the uterine wall, and she was in danger of critical hemorrhaging. As Mark drove her to the hospital, she was forced to carry her baby's pale body in her hands just above her knees, praying—but not really believing— that somehow doctors could make him breathe. She wasn't worried about herself; she wanted only to save her baby boy.

Mark checked her into the hospital's emergency room, and left. She thought he was only going to park his car, but he drove away, headed for his patrol shift. She was all alone.

Ronda and her best friend, Glenda Larson, never really forgave him for dropping her off at the hospital as if she only had flu or a sprained ankle. Why hadn't he seen how much she needed him during that tragic time? She was all by herself when the baby was declared dead.

Mark and Ronda fought often and separated frequently. Most of their disagreements were about finances. Ronda wasn't good at handling money; no one who knew her ever argued otherwise. If she forgot to pay a bill she knew Mark would be angry, so she didn't tell him. She realized that he'd find out eventually, but she avoided thinking about it. Once, he gave her the money to pay their property taxes and she forgot to do it. That became a huge bone of contention be- tween Mark and Ronda.

When Ronda saw that Mark's youngsters needed

clothes, she paid for them with her own money, rather than purchase them from a secondhand store as he suggested. She nurtured and tutored his two boys and his daughter, and they began to blossom under her care.

But the loss of her baby left Ronda with deep sorrow and shaky nerves. Where she had been able to brush off sexual harassment and reprimands by her Washington State Patrol superiors before, it was difficult for her now. Memories of the little boy who would never grow and thrive haunted her.

Ronda's state patrol file shows that she notified her sergeant that she was pregnant in March 1992, with an estimated delivery date of late October. At that time, her obstetrician recommended that she have no road-patrol duties, and shouldn't be lifting anything over twenty-five pounds for the duration of her pregnancy. She had to take several leaves of absence for medical reasons and, of course, again when she lost the baby.

For the old guard in the state patrol, she was living proof that women brought special problems when they set out to be troopers. Among themselves, they postulated that men were stronger, and they didn't have difficult pregnancies or cramps. Of course, no one said that out loud because it was officially forbidden, and considered prejudicial.

The one thing that Ronda never expected to happen was the continual sexual harassment and the steps superiors took to undermine her career as a Washington state trooper. She loved the job she had worked toward for half her life, and she planned to stay with the Patrol for many years.

Ronda had a fistful of commendations and she had captured some dangerous felons on her watch. Deputies from Lewis County and surrounding counties of Grays Harbor and Thurston liked her and trusted her. They knew they could count on her for backup if they ever needed someone in a hurry.

"She wasn't afraid to leave the freeway," one deputy commented. "If we needed her, she was there—backcountry dark roads or not."

And then, quite suddenly, Ronda began to feel ostracized in the State Patrol. She received two reprimands in one of her regular evaluations and that shocked her. The first chastised her for mishandling a collision: "The report was incomplete. Driver's statement, diagram, measurements, and witness statement were not taken. Incorrect codes were used. When corrected, you retaliated by making the report unprofessional in appearance . . . There was [*sic*] conflicting grammar errors . . ."

The writer unwittingly made his own grammatical mistakes as he castigated hers. Her superior went on to accuse Ronda of everything from handing in late reports to blaming everyone else for mistakes attributed to her. "You must be responsible for your own actions," the reprimand stated in conclusion.

Some might say they were piling it on. Although she had made mistakes, she was basically a most competent and courageous trooper. The report did not reflect Ronda's style.

Another reprimand accused her of damaging the undercarriage of her patrol unit when she crossed the I-5 median. Her superior officers declared that "preventable."

She once caught a murderer who had escaped from California, and arrested him all by herself, but that didn't seem to matter compared to her writing a report allegedly dotted with errors in grammar.

One of Ronda's supervising sergeants continually made inappropriate sexual comments to her. Like her mother, Ronda developed early and she had very full breasts. Her sergeant never looked into her eyes, but instead stared pointedly at her chest. When he asked her to strip down to the waist so he could check her bulletproof vest, she refused.

A major had actually squeezed her breast, and it was such a deliberate move that Ronda was angry. She had put up with "accidental" touching and pats that were too familiar for a long time, but she had had enough.

Her view of the Washington State Patrol as a bright, shining example of law enforcement where the "good guys" worked was rapidly growing tarnished, although she had many friends among the rank and file. As a starry-eyed teenage cadet, she had never imagined that senior male officers would be so blatant as they made comments about her breasts in front of her.

Ronda had missed a few court dates, or arrived late. Her sergeant went out of his way once to deliberately keep her from getting to a preliminary hearing. On another occasion, she got stuck on a traffic stop after an accident, and she simply could not leave. It happens when you're working in a job fraught with unexpected emergencies. But Ronda suspected that she had been set up deliberately and that she would be written up.

She grew tired of fighting, and, as much as she hated to consider it, she realized she might have to leave the Patrol. Only a small percentage of senior officers tormented her, and she knew that the vast majority of the Patrol officers were honest and decent—but the few who hounded Ronda were enough.

Several of Ronda's fellow troopers promised to stand up for her if she filed a sexual harassment complaint. That made her feel stronger. But there are others who won't even know about the harassment she endured until they read this.

Ronda expected to have some "backup" of her own

when she filed a complaint. But when her supporters realized it might mean their jobs, they backed down—and she
was left to fight alone.

She didn't win.

*   *   *

MARK AND RONDA continued to argue—mostly over finances.
In truth, she was abysmal when it came to balancing a bud-
get. She was almost foolishly generous, and she kept terrible
records. That irritated Mark, who was much more organized. They weren't the first couple who fought over money,
and they surely weren't the last—but it was a sure argument
starter for them when it came up.

When they fought, she often grabbed a blanket and pillow and found a spot on the floor where she could sleep
alone. "But, more often," Mark said, "I was the one who
had to sleep on the couch or somewhere else."

One thing they'd both agreed upon, and it happened
to have great impact on the investigation of her death. Neither of them liked electric blankets, and they wouldn't sleep
under one. They had none in their home, and if they were
visiting relatives and found electric blankets on their bed,
they would either unplug them or ask for some other covers. It was the idea of electricity running all over them while
they slept that gave them pause.

*Why then would Ronda have chosen an electric blanket
when she left her waterbed to sleep in the closet? There were
plenty of regular blankets available.*

Although the Liburdis had been deeply in love when
they married, their problems worsened as the years passed.
Sometimes Mark felt as if Ronda had a double life—but
that was only about money. She didn't cheat on him, but he

discovered she used a private post office box under another name for some of her bank mail.

And that was true, but there was nothing sinister about it. Ronda sold one of the horses she kept on her mother's ranch for a considerable sum. Many of Barb and Ronda's colts and yearlings sold for $10,000 to $20,000. Ronda opened a bank account with that money, but she didn't tell Mark about it; she wanted to have some money available to her without having to explain what it was for or have to beg for it. Still, she either signed her own name and her husband's on the account, or added Mark later so it would be in both their names.

Ronda continued to buy new brand-name clothes and toys for Mark's three children. She knew he would object to that and say they had enough already. But really they didn't. Mark bought expensive "toys" for himself—a new truck for hunting, guns, and other hunting gear. Ronda didn't want him to know how much she had salted away; she wanted to be able to buy Mark surprise presents, too.

With Cheryl Gilbert's urging, Ronda agreed to have her bank statements and checks sent to Cheryl's post office box. The more Cheryl could entwine herself in Ronda's life, the happier she was. She—and only she—still considered herself Ronda's "very best friend."

Following Cheryl's suggestion was a mistake. Before much time had passed, Cheryl got behind on her own bills. Without permission, she used the checks in Ronda's account—overdrawing it. By that time, Mark knew about the account, and he soon found out about the overdrafts.

Ronda didn't want to sue Cheryl or have her arrested, so she bartered with Cheryl instead. Cheryl agreed to clean Ronda's house, and Ronda would deduct her hours from the debt.

Barb Thompson tried to tell her daughter that that would take forever, but she knew it was useless to argue; Ronda would bend over backward to help almost anyone, and even though Cheryl continually tried to wriggle deeper into Ronda's life, Ronda felt sorry for her. She felt Cheryl was lonely and didn't want to just drop her.

Ronda had many close women friends, but if she had a real best friend, it was Glenda Larson, a fellow horse woman who was married to Steve Larson, a deputy with the Grays Harbor Sheriff's Office.

Ronda met Steve Larson first when she was on duty and someone threw a rock through her windshield. She called for backup and he arrived within minutes.

"I know some bad boys who live near here," Steve had said with a grin. "They're full of mischief. Let's just go knock on their door."

The rock throwers were there and quickly confessed. They were hauled off to juvenile detention, and Steve and Ronda started talking. His eyes lit up when she told him about her love for horses. He told her his wife was just as enthusiastic about her horses. From the time Glenda and Ronda met, they formed a tight bond, talking almost every day.

They lived close to one another in McCleary, and the Larsons had a big spread of land, stables, and, of course, several prize horses. Ronda and Glenda never ran out of things to talk about.

"We used to love being in my barn when it was raining," Glenda remembered a dozen years later. "We'd take care of the horses and listen to rain pattering on the tin roof."

*　*　*

DESPITE HER FEELINGS for Mark and his children, and her bliss living on their ranch in McCleary, Ronda couldn't deny the problems that kept cropping up. The time finally came when she knew she could no longer stay on as a trooper for the Washington State Patrol. Sometimes Ronda thought ruefully that it might have been better if she'd been flat-chested. Or homely as a mud fence. But she knew she couldn't take any more sexual harassment. And now the Patrol was asking her to pay back the shifts she had to take off when she miscarried and when she hurt her back in a high-speed chase. She had also collected money for her "injury on the job" from the state of Washington. As she made a U-turn at seventy miles an hour, the radar had flown off the dashboard of her police cruiser and hit her in the back.

Whether Ronda understood that she couldn't collect her regular salary and sick pay at the same time is now a moot question. Technically she had been double-dipping, and the Patrol wanted its money back.

On October 18, 1994, Ronda wrote her letter of resignation to WSP Chief Roger W. Bruett:

> *I can remember back to when I was sixteen and all I ever wanted to do was be a Washington State Trooper. This resignation is more painful than anything I can remember being faced with. The only other thing that comes close is the sexual harassment and discrimination that I have had to endure through my career with the department.*
>
> *The retaliatory investigation initiated against me in response to my claims of harassment and discrimination, the denial of necessary training, i.e.: first aid/ pr24/DUI and cultural diversity, premature removal of my mail receptacle, and locker, contents, and absence*

of transfer orders for an authorized transfer, are all evidence of the department's intent.

In order to protect my physical and psychological health—which has continued to deteriorate in response to the unfair and unprofessional treatment, ranging from a Major grabbing my breast to a hostile work environment, I resign from the position of trooper, effective immediately.

Ronda initialed the letter "R.L."

Her most important goal since she was a child had turned to ashes.

CHAPTER EIGHT

MARK WAS STILL A TROOPER, and that was often difficult for Ronda. She couldn't remove herself from reminders of the career she longed for and lost. Yet she certainly couldn't ask him to give up his job that he enjoyed so much.

Glenda Larson got Ronda a job in loss prevention (security) at the Walmart store in Aberdeen in the spring of 1996. Management there thanked Glenda for recommending someone so competent and dedicated to her job. It wasn't like working for the Patrol, but Ronda was a natural at spotting shoplifters, and she was enthusiastic about her new job.

She worked with Dan Pearson, both at Walmart and later at the Bon Marché. Glenda worked at Walmart, too, and so did Cheryl Gilbert—who often followed Ronda in her career moves. In their first store together, Ronda trained Pearson, who was younger than she was.

"She was very, very vibrant," Pearson recalled. "I was lucky to work with her."

By the time Ronda moved to the Bon, Dan had left Walmart and was already there.

He was glad to be working with her again. Ronda was always there to back him up, and she would tackle any thief without fear. "We fought together at both stores," Pearson said, "against violent shoplifters, and we usually had a fight at least once a week, most often when we were at Walmart.

"We had one guy," Pearson recalled, "who outweighed me by forty pounds, so you know he must have been a hundred pounds heavier than Ronda. He stole a pair of jeans, and Ronda spotted him. He tried to push her out of the way, and she hopped on his back and rode him like a bronco for forty or fifty yards out into the mall. It took both of us to handcuff the guy."

The two of them—Ronda and Pearson—played pranks on each other whenever they got a chance. One time at Walmart, Dan Pearson spotted a man wheeling a shopping cart full of cartons of cigarettes toward the doors without stopping at the checkout counter. Pearson took off after him as he carried half of the cartons out the door. The "shoplifter" code for the loss prevention department was "500," and Ronda responded to that announcement on the PA system.

"I told Ronda to watch the cart because I was sure the guy would be back for the rest of the cigarette cartons," Pearson recalled, "and she stood there watching it while I was out in the parking lot fighting with the shoplifter. She was so mad when I brought him back in and she realized she'd missed the fight. I'd left her there staring at a shopping cart. She said I'd insulted her integrity or intelligence or something, and I knew she was gunning for me."

Ronda coined her own term for Pearson—since he

wasn't fully trained yet. When she needed him, she called for "250" instead of "500," and soon everybody else in security called him that, too. He didn't mind; he thought it was funny. And he assumed Ronda had her revenge.

He was wrong.

It didn't happen right away, but just as Pearson was lulled into thinking that Ronda wasn't upset with him any longer, he was sitting in the break room when she dumped a whole Diet Coke with lots of ice into his lap.

"She did stuff like that," he said with a laugh. "She had a fun sense of humor. She put hand sanitizer on the phones just before I picked up the receiver, but she was a complete professional when she needed to be. Ronda always followed up on the people we caught. She ran the information and researched as far as she could."

Some of the thieves had long records, while others were amateurs. Ronda was a natural-born investigator, and she made the most out of her loss prevention career. Both she and Dan Pearson moved to the Bon Marché (now Macy's) in 1997. Wearing jeans and sweatshirts or raincoats—if the weather demanded them for shoppers—they faded into the background, expertly imitating actual customers.

Those trained in loss prevention must avoid many pitfalls, not the least of which is stopping and arresting someone in a minority group. They must decide instantly, and take a chance on repercussions. Ronda spotted a Hispanic man walking through the sports department who grabbed a twenty-dollar baseball cap, put it on his head, and kept going. She stopped him, and he filed a discrimination suit against her. She was moved temporarily to the jewelry department, because the store she was working in at the time wanted to avoid even a whisper of discrimination.

"She just couldn't let him steal that cap and walk away," Pearson said. "She wasn't looking at his color, race, religion or whatever. He was an ordinary thief."

On their break time, Dan Pearson and Ronda talked over personal problems. Theirs was a completely platonic friendship, and Ronda was happy when Pearson got married.

He wanted her to be happy, too.

* * *

AND THEN, suddenly, Ronda's marriage to Mark blew all to pieces. After eight years together, Ronda suspected that Mark had another woman waiting in the wings. The woman they had retained as a Realtor to sell Mark's mother's house seemed too familiar with him. Ronda tried to fight back her instinctive suspicions, telling herself that she was just being paranoid. She was sad to say goodbye to the small ranch she loved so much.

Ronda certainly wasn't cheating on her husband; when she was with a man, she was faithful. Still, she couldn't bear the suspicion that grew stronger and stronger that Mark and their Realtor had become intimate.

She was right. Women are seldom wrong about matters of the heart or of passion. Cheating was the one thing Ronda could not live with.

And so their marriage faltered, and then crashed. Their divorce was final in December 1997. It was a bleak Christmas for Ronda. But at least she had her family and a number of longtime friends to turn to. Particularly helpful were Ron Reynolds in her faith—Jehovah's Witnesses—who had counseled her for well over a year. In the latter years of the 1990s, the Liburdis and the Reynolds lived down the road from each other and the two couples were quite friendly.

Ron's wife, Katie, recalled that she was a very close friend of Ronda's and tried to give her advice during the time her marriage to Mark was crumbling.

The Reynoldses were some fifteen years older than Ronda and Mark. As time passed, Ron did a lot more than counsel Ronda. When her marriage ended in divorce, Ron and Katie's union did too. Ron had been an angel when Ronda needed someone to count on. He was always available and she'd often told Pearson how "pleasant" Ron was, especially when she compared him to Mark, who had a tendency to erupt into anger.

Ronda and her friend Glenda Larson both hated it when voices were raised in anger, and after one session of horseshoeing with Mark, neither woman wanted to endure another. There was no question that Mark and Ronda had loved each other on their wedding day; it was obvious in their wedding pictures. But in the end, their personalities grated on one another, and they each realized their marriage could not be mended.

Ronda had fallen in love with Ron Reynolds in 1997, and he with her. It seemed sudden to other people—but not to them—when Ron asked Ronda to marry him. They were engaged and planned to marry in January 1998.

Ronda was single for only a month; she felt she had found a safe harbor with Ron.

Dan Pearson was relieved during the first months of Ronda's marriage to Ron Reynolds; she seemed content and upbeat again despite their sudden marriage and their age differences.

There were some problems that cropped up, of course, but Ronda was confident that they could work those out. When he and Ronda moved out of McCleary in late summer 1998, Ron bought himself a "wedding present": a new candy-apple red Mustang convertible. But he soon totaled it when he ran into a Jersey barrier on the freeway. Undeterred, he bought his new pickup truck next.

Ronda told Dan Pearson that she was angry when she found out Ron had bailed his ex-wife, Katie, out of jail after she had been locked up on drug charges.

"Ronda was worried about her own bills," Dan recalled. "She said Ron wasn't paying them, even though she gave him all of her paychecks."

Ronda had also discovered that Katie Huttula Reynolds was using Ronda's Bon Marché credit card to purchase items she wanted.

"All Katie needed to know was the number," Pearson said. "And that was easy for her to get. For all I know, she was even taking the employee discount."

Dan Pearson did his best to back up Ronda in her personal life as he did in the store where they worked. A month before her death, she had called him from the freeway. "She was out of gas," Pearson said. "She said she'd had a fight with Ron and left the house in the middle of the night—so I went and got her."

Pearson was one of the last people Ronda ever spoke to. She called him on December 15 and asked to take a few days off while she was in Spokane visiting her family.

"I arranged that," he remembered. "Then she asked if she could come and stay with me and my then wife when she got back. She sounded a little upset—but not as if she was seriously worried. She told me she was leaving Ron and didn't want to go back to their house. Of course, I told her she could stay with us."

The next day, Pearson's boss came to his front door to

break the unbelievable news that Ronda had been shot to death.

"I started to cry," Pearson said, tearing up again at the memory of that day. "All of us who worked with her were broken up. So many people from the Bon Marché went to her funeral that the store rented buses to carry them all."

CHAPTER NINE

SADLY, WHAT SHOULD HAVE CLICKED into place perfectly in Ronda's life was out of synch again in December 1998. She was divorced from Mark Liburdi, and she soon would be divorced from Ron Reynolds.

And the man who had loved her all along was Dave Bell. Although she hadn't been in touch with him for months, he was finally free and his sons lived with him. He still loved Ronda, but she hadn't been aware of that as she leaned on Ron Reynolds for emotional and spiritual support.

If it wasn't so heartbreaking, it would have been like some Shakespearean comedy of errors: Ronda should have married David Bell and not Ron Reynolds. At the very least, she should have waited longer to even consider marrying either man so soon after her divorce.

But she was unable to see how strong and smart she was, or that she didn't need any man in her life to take care of her and make her feel whole and successful.

Barb Thompson saw that, and she too knew that Dave was the man who truly loved Ronda.

"It was as if God had opened a door to a life that Ronda only thought possible in her dreams," her mother said. "But that was a life she would never experience. Neither would Dave. It was too late for them."

*   *   *

NOW, ON DECEMBER 17, 1998, Dave Bell and Barb Thompson turned onto Twin Peaks Drive. Barb saw Dave's face turn pale as the brick and siding one-story house came into view. The fascia board's bright blue trim looked cheerful. That was Ronda's idea—she'd told her mother about it, and it was just right. With its multipaned and fan-shaped windows, it was an attractive medium-size home on a large lot.

On this day, an invisible pall seemed to hang over it. This was the second day in thirty-three years that Ronda wasn't alive.

Barb saw that the grass was yellow and flattened. She recalled a photo of the wave of pink annuals Ronda had planted between Pfitzer junipers and low barberry shrubs. The pink flowers were gone, leaving only brown stems. There were some large plants that had never left their nursery containers. They looked like chrysanthemums, bedraggled, rootbound, and probably frozen now.

Ronda had found out that Ron was betraying her with his ex-wife as far back as the prior spring, and she'd discussed her concerns with her mother by September. She wasn't ready to leave him then, because their finances were so intermingled—with Ronda turning over her paychecks to

Ron. He said he was paying her bills and her share of any communal bills. She hoped he really was.

Ronda had still hoped to save her marriage—until she discovered in late fall that Ron hadn't paid her bills at all. He had been lying to her about so many things. Barb's heart bled for her daughter when Ronda told her.

Maybe that's when Ronda just gave up caring about her lawn and garden. The neglected mums symbolized the time when Ronda knew her marriage was probably over.

Ronda's little cement statues of bunnies and wild creatures were right where they had been, frozen in concrete along the path to the front porch, and just inside the porch itself. Ronda had loved them, and the sight of them made Barb want to cry. She knew that Detective Berry wanted her to talk with Ron alone, although she wondered if she had the strength to do that.

But then she looked at Dave Bell. His eyes were filled with tears and his hands were shaking. Here was a man with over twenty years as a police sergeant, who was close to breaking down. He was doing his best, but his pain was obvious.

"I think I really do need to wait out here," Dave said.

She couldn't ask him to go inside the house. She couldn't begin to imagine what he was going through. Grief, of course, but she wondered if he was feeling guilt because he hadn't saved Ronda. It would be natural for a man like Dave to regret that he hadn't insisted that Ronda leave with him on the night before she died. Barb felt guilt, too, wondering if there wasn't something she should have seen, something she could have done.

They pulled into the driveway and noted which cars were parked there. The new pickup truck belonged to

Ron, and the Suzuki Tracker was Ronda's. The Ford Taurus parked there had belonged to Ron's father, and when he died the previous May, Ron had inherited it. Neither of them knew who owned the fourth vehicle.

Ronda's dogs began to bark from their pen on the right side of the house. Ronda would never have left them to fend for themselves, and that was a very strong argument against her killing herself.

Her feisty little Jack Russell terrier was in a section of the pen by himself, and her two Rottweilers were together in another pen—Jewel—one of the big dogs, was Barb's dog's sister, and the other Rottweiler, Old Daisy, was the crippled stray that had been hit by a car or beaten. Somehow the old dog had made her way to Ronda's door. Of course, she took in, tended to her wounds, and loved her. The cold of a mid-December day was hard on the elderly dog. But Barb knew that Ron never let the dogs in the house.

When Ronda adopted Old Daisy, it made him angry.

Ronda had tried her best to keep her dogs from bothering her new husband. She'd changed their feeding schedule and fed them at night so that they wouldn't get restless and make any noise that might wake Ron.

*   *   *

NOW BARB PROGRAMMED herself to keep her mind as open as possible—even to the point where she wondered if there was something horrible that happened to Ronda that might have driven her to suicide. At the same time, as she walked to the front door of what had been her daughter's house, she thought of herself as "The Mighty Avenger."

If someone had shot Ronda in the head, Barb felt herself capable of grabbing his throat (she pictured the killer as

Ronda Liburdi Reynolds was smart, kind, strong, and absolutely beautiful. She didn't look like a Washington State Patrol officer but she could hold her own with the male troopers. She died too young and her mother vowed to find justice for her.
Barb Thompson Collection.

Ronda was premature, a tiny baby who didn't grow eyelashes or fingernails for several months. She is about six months old here, living in California with Barb and her husband, Ron Scott. She was a happy baby whose young mother adored her. Barb Thompson Collection.

At age four, Ronda poses proudly in her Easter outfit. Ronda, Barb, and Gramma Virginia were living in Texas then, and Ronda started talking with a southern drawl.
Barb Thompson Collection.

Ronda graduating from the fourth grade. She was honored for her perfect attendance and for always making the honor roll.
Barb Thompson Collection.

Barb Ramsey Scott in her twenties. She was an exceptionally pretty young widow. She didn't have much time to date, as she always worked two or three jobs to support her mother, Virginia, and her little girl, Ronda. She probably knew Don Hennings during this time, but their relationship was complicated. Barb Thompson Collection.

Ronda, thirteen, now living in Spokane with Barb and her second husband, Hal Thompson, proudly shows off her white pony and full cowgirl garb. Since she was a baby she was consumed by everything equine and training to compete in horse shows. However, her dream of becoming a Washington state trooper began at this time, too. Barb Thompson Collection.

Ronda, fifteen, smiles for her junior high school yearbook. She was proud of her braces and grateful to have them. A schoolmate thought Ronda must be rich to have braces—but her mom worked hard to pay for them.
Barb Thompson Collection.

Ronda and Clabber Toe. She
loved all horses, but Clabber
Toe was her special horse.
Barb Thompson Collection.

Ronda, riding Clabber Toe, as they compete
in the American Quarter Horse Association,
Youth World Class horse show in Tulsa, Oklahoma.
Ronda was seventeen or eighteen and Spokane
horse aficionados believed she had the makings
of a champion. They paid for her trip to
compete. She came in twelfth out of 180.
Barb Thompson Collection.

Ronda was working toward her goal—and soon to enter the Washington State Patrol's training academy. When she graduated, she would be a trooper. She was the youngest female to be accepted, but she was very mature. Her family knew she would make it through the difficult academy. Barb Thompson Collection.

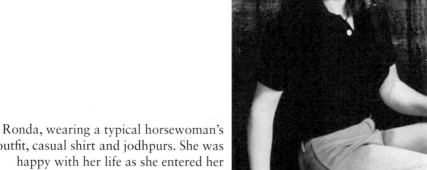

Ronda, wearing a typical horsewoman's outfit, casual shirt and jodhpurs. She was happy with her life as she entered her twenties. Barb Thompson Collection.

Barb Thompson in her late forties, still a most attractive woman. She divorced Hal Thompson because of his maniacal temper and jealousy when he'd been drinking. As always, she started over. She had gone from owning one horse to almost three dozen world class American quarter horses—Palominos and Paints. She was there when the mares foaled, and she raised the colts tenderly.
Barb Thompson Collection.

Barb's brother, Bill Ramsey. Their father treated his two daughters much better than he did Bill, so Barb protected him. He lived to fly, and she made it possible for him to attend the U.S. Naval Academy. He became a superior pilot and then a helicopter rescue pilot. He is always there to help Barb as she once helped him.
Barb Thompson Collection.

Ronda receiving her commission as a Washington State Patrol trooper and her badge. #954.
Barb Thompson Collection.

Ronda on a break from patrol. She worked all shifts, but preferred Third Watch, from 8 P.M. to 4 A.M. Local cops and deputies, as well as other troopers, remember they could count on her for backup.
Barb Thompson Collection.

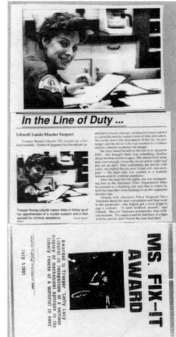

Ronda, writing up a report, was honored by a local paper for her work in catching a killer. Barb Thompson Collection.

Don Hennings, Ronda's "dad," hugs her. He was very proud to see her as a Washington state trooper. Ronda carried a gun on her hip, and taught gun safety in state patrol classes. Barb Thompson Collection.

Ronda stands beside her patrol unit. She worked a "one-man" car, although sometimes women friends did "ride-alongs." Claudia Self was with her the night she stopped a killer. Barb Thompson Collection.

Ronda with her fiancé, fellow trooper Mark Liburdi. They attended a Marine Corps Reserve formal dance. Gramma Virginia made Ronda's dress. Barb Thompson Collection.

Mark and Ronda rehearse their wedding vows on the evening before their wedding. Barb Thompson Collection.

Gramma Virginia and Ronda
collaborated on Ronda's wedding
gown and Virginia sewed it.
Barb Thompson Collection.

Mark and Ronda Liburdi smile after their lovely outdoor wedding.
Ronda looked forward to helping Mark raise his three children and
to having more of their own. Barb Thompson Collection.

A montage of Ronda's mom, "dad," and Ronda at her wedding.
Don Hennings gave her away, Gramma Virginia made her dress,
and Barb took care of the details like hanging balloons decorating
the hall for the reception. It was a happy day in June!
Barb Thompson Collection.

Barb Thompson and Ronda. The road ahead
looked bright. Ronda loved her new husband,
her law enforcement career, and she had just
told her mother that she was pregnant. Tragically,
this was the baby boy she lost at five months.
She loved Mark's children and the ranch she
and Mark bought in McCleary. But she was
devastated when she miscarried.

Barb Thompson Collection.

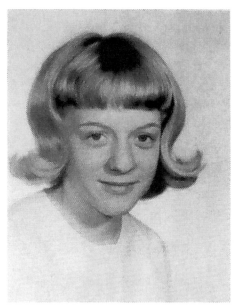

Catherine Huttula at fourteen.
Her family owned a profitable
pharmacy, and they lived in a large
home. She was a brilliant student who
would lose two siblings to death.

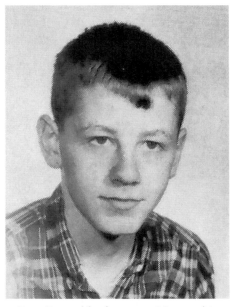

Ron Reynolds, fourteen. He was his
parents' pride and joy, and they were
indulgent. He got whatever he wanted.
His sisters and cousins found him
selfish and avoided him.

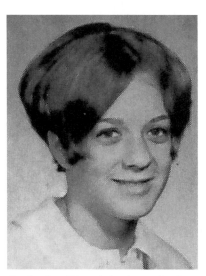

Catherine Huttula's photo for her
junior year yearbook at Elma High
School. Her personality drew fellow
students to her. She was extremely
popular with both male and
female students.

Ron Reynolds in the eleventh grade
at Elma High. He was a "brain" and
too thin to play sports. He and
Catherine both made the Honor
Society—but they didn't date. They did
attend church functions occasionally
with a group of other students.

Catherine Huttula with other members of the Elma High pep squad. She is the second cheerleader on the right. She was a rather plain teenager, but her personality more than made up for that.

Kelly, Catherine, Sharon, Connie, Cheryl

Pep Staff

Catherine Huttula
Duchess

Connie Valentine
Duchess

Cheryl Gowan
Duchess

Kelly Murphy
Duchess

Sharon Vansickdale
Queen

10

Catherine, left, laughs as the cheerleaders pose for yearbook pictures. She was one of four "duchesses" on the pep squad. She went to college in Arizona. But she came back to Washington State University and set out to win Ron Reynolds.

Ronda had been divorced only six weeks when she married Ron Reynolds in the first week of January 1998. A new year. A new marriage. A new life. She believed Ron truly loved her. Barb Thompson Collection.

Ronda wore a white satin suit for her wedding to Ron Reynolds. Barb couldn't attend the ceremony in January 1998 because she had horses foaling—but Gramma and Ronda's brother. Freeman, went. Barb Thompson Collection.

male) and "ripping the life out of his body. I could see his little round pig eyes bulging with fear as the life drained out of him."

Her rage and her grief warred with each other in her brain. She fought them both down as she tried to remain composed.

Barb knocked on the front door with her fist, and the sound echoed in her ears. She knocked again—harder.

Finally the door was flung open and she was looking at her son-in-law. He wore a T-shirt and sweat pants, and even though it was early afternoon, it was obvious that she'd dragged him out of bed. He looked surprised to see her, and confused.

"I need to talk with you, Ron," Barb said.

He invited her in and excused himself. She stepped into the hallway that led to the living room. A few feet beyond, another hallway angled off to the left and back to the bedrooms. There was a counter on the right that divided the kitchen and dining area from the living room. She looked around and felt a pang when she spotted one of Ronda's treasured western saddles.

All of the furniture in the living room was Ronda's— her couch, love seat, entertainment center with a large television set, end tables, lamps—everything. At first Barb was puzzled, but then she remembered that Ron's ex-wife, Katie, had gotten their house and all of their furniture when they divorced after more than twenty years. As Barb understood it, Katie Reynolds had also received a very large financial settlement, almost a hundred thousand dollars. And Ron had been furious. But two decades and five sons put the legal weight on Katie's side.

Barb peered into the dining room and saw Ronda's huge and impressive china cabinet in the far corner. It was virtually empty. She wondered where Ronda's precious things were, and where were the photographs that had hung on the walls? There were only faint outlines now that marked where they had been.

Of course, she thought. Ronda must have packed them up, preparing to move.

She heard footsteps and Ron walked into the room, buttoning his shirt. He offered to make coffee, and Barb said nothing.

"I need to know what happened, Ron," she began. "How could this terrible thing have come about?"

Her daughter's widower never looked up from filling the machine with water, filters, and freshly ground coffee, but, oddly, he began to talk. His thoughts burst from his mouth as if he had preprogrammed them into his brain, ready to spew forth when he was ready. He spoke almost in a robotic monotone.

"Ronda was a very troubled girl, you know," he began. "She was not a nice person. She had a lot of problems. She had no self-confidence. I had to counsel her constantly and build up her esteem enough to even go apply for a job. She would always say, 'I'm not good enough.' And there was a dark side to Ronda—a dark, ugly side that no one ever saw. But it was there. She was bad. She was a cruel, mean, manipulating person—a chronic liar and a manic depressive. She drove herself to this. She had no other way out."

Barb could barely breathe. Even if there was a fraction of truth in what he was saying, how could he be so cruel? He said Ronda was cruel, but he seemed to be enjoying listing dreadful things he believed—or purported to believe— about the daughter she had just lost. What could be crueler than that?

Barb forced herself to remember that Jerry Berry had

told her not to get angry, not to ask too many questions, but to remember everything.

"How did you find her?" she asked, trying to sound calm. She wanted to scream obscenities at him. She wanted to physically attack him. How dare he say such ugly things about her dead daughter?

But she didn't change expression.

"I kept her awake until about five A.M.," Ron Reynolds said. "I didn't want to leave her alone. I was worried she might do something to herself. Then I must have fallen asleep. The alarm woke me at six A.M., but she wasn't beside me in bed. I went looking for her. I thought she might be in the kitchen feeding the dogs."

But Barb knew Ronda routinely fed the dogs at night. There was always the possibility that she would feed them just before she left for Spokane, afraid Ron wouldn't feed them. No—Ronda would have asked one of her friends to feed the dogs. Barb said nothing.

Detective Berry had told her that Ron hadn't called 911 until twenty minutes after six. This house wasn't big enough to require someone to search for twenty minutes. And Ronda had been right there in the closet off the bathroom all along. Why hadn't he looked there first? Barb had also been told that Ronda's feet had made it impossible to close the closet door. How could Ron have missed her?

Barb had been staring at him, willing him to look at her, but Ron was definitely avoiding her eyes. He would not look at her. He focused on places in the room that were below his eye level: the kitchen counter, the wall, the couch, and even the floor.

But never at her.

She was practically burning holes in the side of his face, but he refused to meet her eyes.

Amazed at how calm her voice sounded, Barb Thompson asked, "Why would she do this? Had you been arguing?"

Ron seized another opportunity to damn Ronda's name. "Um," he mumbled. "We were talking about a separation. Um . . . we . . . she had lied to me, destroyed my trust. She had run up a huge number of charges on credit cards in my name. We had a discussion about it and I told her I couldn't trust her. I confronted her and told her it was a felony and she could go to jail."

"Did she give you any indication before that she was going to kill herself?" Barb asked. "Did she give you any indication that she was going to do this?"

"Ronda was going to leave," he replied. "We were going to separate for a while. I had been at a doctor's appointment in Olympia, and she called me on my cell phone on my way home and talked about forty-five minutes, telling me she was going to kill herself."

This was startling information. Had Ron been unaware that there was a witness—Dave Bell—to that phone conversation? Possibly not. Maybe there had been more than one phone call—a call before Dave got to Toledo on Tuesday. Phone records could straighten that out.

According to Dave, Ronda had called her husband from her cell phone while they drove around Lewis County on Tuesday afternoon. Dave had heard every word of her side of the conversation, and there'd been no mention of suicide. Nor had the call taken forty-five minutes. It had been a very brief call where she calmly discussed some details of their separation. Ron's version was diametrically opposed to Dave's recollection.

"If she was threatening suicide," Barb probed, "why didn't you call 911?"

His answer shocked her. "I thought about calling 911.

I guess I should have called them. But I decided if Ronda didn't kill herself then, she would only do it later. So I went and got a hamburger and went on to my school for the school Christmas play."

As Barb fought to absorb his words, she became aware of the sound of young voices someplace in the house—possibly some of Ron's sons. He and Katie had five sons as she understood it, two of them who were out on their own. The three younger sons had been living most of the time with Ron and Ronda. She thought they were at their mother's house.

Ron hastened to explain that after he came home from the school's Christmas play, he was with Ronda constantly. His lack of compassion for the inevitability of her suicide had apparently changed. "I stayed with her the rest of the night, and kept her right next to me," he said. "I held her all night and told her we would talk about it in the morning."

Barb Thompson saw someone moving in the hall, and she looked up, expecting to see one of Ron's sons. But it wasn't. It was a slender woman wearing a terry cloth robe, coming out of the same bedroom where Ron had gone to change his clothes.

Oh my God. Barb recognized the woman as Katie Huttula Reynolds, Ron's ex-wife and the mother of their five sons.

CHAPTER TEN

NEITHER RON REYNOLDS nor his former wife, Katie, seemed at all embarrassed to have Ronda's mother find them together in bed clothes, only thirty-five hours after Ronda died. They had obviously slept in the same bedroom right next to the closet where Ronda had breathed her last breath such a short time ago. Barb Thompson stared at Katie Reynolds, unable to speak. What they had done was akin to sleeping on a grave.

And why hadn't the police kept this house sealed until they were sure they had all the evidence they needed?

Katie Reynolds was a wisp of a woman, who was shockingly emaciated. She had good bone structure in her face, and might have been pretty years before, but now her eyes were hollow and her face stark white. She moved toward Barb Thompson, circling her waist in an awkward hug. She pressed a wrinkled piece of paper into Barb's hand.

"I should have felt sorry for her, I guess," Barb said,

"but I couldn't manage that. She seemed to be totally under Ron's control. That was natural—she'd lived with him for more than twenty years, and given him five sons."

"I wrote a poem for Ronda," Katie whispered, "that I want you to have. I loved her, you know."

Barb hadn't been able to believe her eyes, and now she didn't trust her ears. The two people in front of her were "beyond incredible."

She realized that she was gritting her teeth so hard that her jaws ached. Both of them seemed ready to sweep all memory of Ronda under the rug—although Ron wanted to keep her furniture.

"What about funeral arrangements?" Barb asked faintly. "Have you planned anything yet?"

"No," Ronda's widower said. He was irritated, obviously, at the very thought that he would be burdened with such an onerous responsibility.

"I believe that Ronda would want to be cremated," Barb said. "However, if you decide not to do that, may I have her body shipped back home for burial?"

Surely, at some point, he was going to show some humanity, some concern for how she was feeling.

"I don't care what you do with the body," he said with a shrug. "As long as I don't have to pay for it . . ."

And suddenly, despite the pain she felt, Barb felt the comfort of God's presence. She knew she could be strong enough to withstand anything—anything that might come her way as she fought to avenge Ronda. She had many questions to ask, many murky places in her daughter's life to learn about and to deal with.

On autopilot now, she pressed on. "What about her belongings? May I have those? Her dogs? Her jewelry?"

"Take her dogs," he said readily. "She would want you

to have them. She had a lot of fine, expensive jewelry, you know, and I can't let you have that. I will have to sell it to cover expenses. I'll box up her other things."

What expenses? Barb wondered. *He wasn't going to pay for Ronda's burial. He probably would inherit their house. She didn't care, but there were sentimental items she didn't want him to have, and there was the $15,000 she had loaned to Ronda to help pay for it. She suspected there might also be some evidentiary items that would answer some of her questions.*

And then Ron Reynolds blurted out something that he probably didn't realize sounded incriminating. "You know," he said, preparing to launch even more criticism of Ronda, "I found out where she had not paid her life insurance premium for December—so I had to make sure I got that paid and in the mail before the mailman picked the mail up at three-thirty yesterday. She lied to me about that, too."

For the first time, there was some emotion in her now ex-son-in-law. Anger. He seemed to want Ronda's insurance money very badly, indeed. Paying the premium after Ronda was dead wasn't remotely legal. But Ron had more grievances.

"She led me to believe that her life insurance was for three hundred thousand dollars, and it was only for fifty thousand. She never even signed the conversion form so it would follow her to her new job."

Actually, Ronda had signed a conversion form changing her policy to "self-pay" rather than having it paid by Walmart. She had also removed her brother, Freeman, as beneficiary, and named Ron instead. She had never, however, raised the pay amount on the policy. And even the third-party administrator for the insurance company looked at the signature on the conversion request and doubted it was Ronda's.

Ron was terribly concerned about money—seemingly far more than he was about Ronda's death. Barb bit her tongue to keep from saying that out loud. Was it possible that Ron was still in shock over her daughter's dying so suddenly? That would be a lot easier for Barb to accept. How could he be so cold and so ready to throw Ronda away? Ronda had loved him, and been optimistic about her new marriage. There must have been *something* there eleven months ago.

"May I have her car?" Barb Thompson thought she might be able to find some evidence—something—in Ronda's Suzuki Tracker that could help to explain what had happened.

"No," he said quickly. "I need to keep that. My name is on it."

"I flew here, Ron," she thought rapidly, trying to find a reason to convince him. "I don't have a car. I thought if I borrowed her car, I could take the dogs."

"Well, then—I guess you could. I'll get my boys to unload it."

Barb didn't want that. If the Reynolds boys cleaned out the car, removing Ronda's things, they might either accidentally or deliberately remove evidence, too. Maybe the sheriff's office could get a search warrant and execute it before that happened. She told Ron it might be better if they waited until she found a place where she could board the dogs first.

"May I have her china cabinet? Her grandmother gave her that." Surely he wouldn't be so greedy that he would keep that.

But Ron did refuse once again. "I have to keep that. Ronda and I bought that new dining room table to match it."

She didn't know how long she'd been in Ronda's house, but she did know that Ron Reynolds had never looked into

her eyes. She told his averted face that she would be in Toledo for a few more days, and that he could always call her
home phone and leave a message.

"I'll check on funeral arrangements and let you know,"
she said.

Barb turned toward Katie and gave her what she knew
was a contrived smile. Katie didn't seem to notice that.
Maybe Katie was sincere—but brainwashed.

Barb walked to Dave's truck and got in. She was curious about Katie's "poem," and she smoothed the wrinkled
paper out while Dave looked on.

It was dedicated to Ronda, and titled "Tragic Sadness."
In it, Katie painted herself as someone who had always
helped Ronda.

She ended:

Now I mourn her tragic death with many sad tears.
A troubled frantic girl
Yet filled with love and grace,
Her fine qualities
Would fill a large space.
I loved her as a sister
And I mourn that she is gone
I will put this good-bye
To a piano song . . .
Rest, dear Ronda—I will miss you.

Barb wondered how Katie had the audacity to hand her
the syrupy poem, professing how much she missed Ronda,
after she had slept with Ron in Ronda's own bed the night
after she died.

"He didn't say he had loved Ronda," she told Dave Bell.
"He didn't say he was sorry she is dead."

CHAPTER ELEVEN

AT ONE THAT AFTERNOON, Dave Bell and Barb Thompson went back to Jerry Berry's office. Still stunned by the odd reception she had received at Ronda's home, Barb read aloud the notes she had written down immediately after leaving. She described Ronda's widower as being not only unconcerned about her death, but derisive and insulting. He seemed interested only in his financial situation. He had made the insurance payment after Ronda was dead, and her son-in-law (if that was what he still was) said he had hired an attorney. He wanted to be sure he got Ronda's share of the proceeds from the McCleary house she owned with her former husband, Mark Liburdi. Berry made a note to check on that.

The Lewis County detective wasn't surprised to hear about Ron's attitude; he had noted the new widower's remarkably flat emotional affect the day before. He wasn't resistant to their investigation, and Reynolds had even let

Berry come back to the house on Twin Peaks Drive so he could measure all angles of the closet where Ronda died. But he sure didn't act as though he was in mourning.

"How long did Ronda know that Ron wanted to end their marriage?" Berry asked her mother.

"It wasn't a surprise—not on the day she died," Barb said tentatively. "When I talked to her on Sunday—December thirteenth—she told me Ron was definitely going back to Katie. And she said she'd known that for several days, but I'd known her marriage was in trouble for months. I urged her to check and be sure he was paying her bills with the paychecks she gave him."

Jerry Berry wanted to talk further with Barb, but he had an urgent appointment. He didn't tell her what it was because he was headed for the postmortem exam of Ronda's body, and he didn't want to remind her of that image.

That afternoon—Thursday, December 17—forensic pathologist Dr. Dan Selove stood ready to perform the autopsy on Ronda Reynold's body. He'd been called in from Snohomish County, which was north of Seattle and more than a hundred miles from Lewis County. He was a "traveling pathologist," often hired by smaller counties in Washington who needed an expert opinion. There was no one on the coroner's staff who could do it; Coroner Terry Wilson was not an M.D.—he was a physician's assistant.

Wilson did not attend Ronda Reynold's postmortem exam.

With Deputy Coroner Carmen Brunton and Lewis County detectives Sergeant Glade Austin and Jerry Berry observing, Dr. Selove looked at Ronda as she rested on the autopsy table. She was slightly shorter than five feet, seven inches tall, and he estimated her weight as being between 135 and 145 pounds. She was a lovely woman, the blood washed away from her ear and check, and from her hair, which he could now see was blond with brown roots. She wore purple bikini panties under her matching pajama top and bottom, and the top was stiffened where it was drenched in dried blood.

This was obviously a woman who had taken good care of herself; her hair was professionally cut, and her false nails were perfect—all but the middle fingernail on her left hand, which had a ragged tear along the tip. Had the bullet that killed her ripped her nail, too? Or had she struggled with someone as she fought for her life? There were few signs that she might have been involved in a physical struggle; beyond the torn nail, she had two pinkish, purple bruises on the knee and shin of her left leg. They might well have occurred hours before she died.

The forensic pathologist looked at the single bullet wound near Ronda's Reynolds's right ear. He quickly determined that it was an entrance wound that had no stippling of gunpowder fragments or soot on the skin. That was because all of the gunpowder was inside the wound track. This was a contact wound.

Either Ronda—or someone else—had placed the weapon tight against her skin. The resultant path of the slug was, according to Dr. Selove, from front to back, right to left, with a slight vertical downward angle. It had not crossed the midline of the brain.

The postmortem showed that, ironically, Ronda had been in excellent physical shape before the handgun's slug ripped through the right portion of her brain, ending in the back of the left side of her skull.

It was Dr. Selove's opinion that she had clinically died instantly as the bullet severed her spinal cord. He felt that she would have been unable to move any of her limbs.

Ronda's heart, lungs, liver, kidneys, urinary tract, and reproductive systems were all normal. Still, she had had a number of miscarriages, the biggest sorrow of her life. No doctor had ever been able to isolate the cause. Nor could Dr. Selove detect any blatant malformation or condition that might have prevented her from carrying a pregnancy to term.

Jerry Berry asked Dr. Selove to take oral, rectal, and vaginal swabs. He nodded, and asked his assistant to clip her fingernails, too. Somewhat surprisingly, the vaginal swab revealed a moderate number of active sperm, with attached tails. Ronda had had intercourse—or, perhaps, been raped—within hours before or after her death. That might explain the bruises on her leg. Since DNA matching was far from perfected in 1998, they could probably not match the semen to one particular man, although they could determine blood type if he had been a "secretor."

Rigor was already well established. There was no question about the cause of her death. There were myriad puzzles about "why," "when," and "by whose hand."

When the paper bags were removed from Ronda's hands, they observed hairlike fibers in her left hand, and a single identical fiber caught in her broken nail. Had she put up her hand in a vain attempt to fend off a bullet? If she was asleep—with her left hand beneath her head—the shattered nail couldn't have been hit by a slug; the path of the wound had not gone through her entire head.

The hair or blanket fibers caught in the nail might prove to be vital physical evidence, or they might mean nothing. Glade Austin and Berry did their best to preserve everything that might be useful to the case.

The two detectives carefully sealed and labeled everything that could be proved to be evidence of suicide—or of a manner of death that was anything but suicide.

Since Ronda's widower had told Barb Thompson that he didn't care what she did with her body, Barb made the arrangements to have Ronda cremated.

*   *   *

BARB THOMPSON CALLED HER MOTHER, although it was so hard to talk to her, knowing the grief that consumed her and not being able to give her any comforting news. Next she called Skeeter. She could tell by his voice that he was in a lot of physical pain. He had already done all the chores around the ranch without waiting for her son, Freeman, and he admitted his prescribed pain medication wasn't working.

Skeeter was not the love of Barb's life, but he was so considerate and he'd brought much-needed love and companionship to her. Without hesitation, without a second thought, he was there for her. He fought his own inner battles, struggling with the tragedy of his wife's death, alcohol, and his deteriorating health. But he was a stable haven where she could retreat, giving her strength to keep going.

Barb met Skeeter through her good friend Sandy. Sometime in the late 1980s, a woman and a small girl knocked on Barb's door. Sandy had an eighteen-year-old son who had suffered a devastating traumatic brain injury in an accident. He was left completely disabled, and his mom, Sandy, took full care of him and his little sister, Pauline. Later she would help care for Barb's mom, Virginia.

Like so many people who appeared at Barb's door, Sandy needed help with a horse. She had loaned Pauline's pony to a woman, and they needed someone to help them retrieve it. As always, Barb said, "Of course."

In 1991, Skeeter and his wife were in a violent car crash; an oncoming car had swerved into their lane and hit them head-on. Skeeter's wife was killed instantly, and he was taken by helicopter to Deaconess Hospital in Spokane in critical condition. He had a broken back and was in a coma for so long that he missed his wife's funeral.

Skeeter came out of his coma, although his broken back never healed completely and left him in constant pain.

"I didn't know him then," Barb recalled. "He was a mechanic, and he turned out to be the best mechanic I'd ever been around—he was a genius."

In 1992, Sandy and Skeeter were neighbors—and Sandy became very attached to his small daughter, Cheri-Lynn. She often brought Cheri-Lynn to Barb's ranch because the child loved horses, and Barb let her ride her Palomino stallion, Spokane Gold.

Barb sold a horse a year later and used the money to buy a new one-ton pickup truck. Three years later, her transmission froze and Sandy suggested she take it to Skeeter to get it fixed.

"You need to meet Skeeter anyway," Sandy urged. "He's single, loves horses, and he's a great mechanic."

Barb and her longtime friend, Don Hennings, had agreed to go their separate ways three years before. Although they were in love, they so often had problems getting their lives to mesh.

Despite the failure of their relationship, Don remained the father figure in Barb's family. He proudly shouldered the responsibility of being Barb's children's father. It worked for them.

"Don walked Ronda down the aisle for her wedding to Mark, and he went over to McCleary every six or eight weeks to work on Ronda's horse's feet and take her some hay. It was just that our romantic relationship seemed to die of its own weight in 1993."

Barb had been lonely, and so had Skeeter. She made an appointment to take her truck to his shop, and "the rest was history. We clicked immediately and the romance began. I already knew his daughter, Cheri-Lynn, and everything fell into place. She and Skeeter moved in with me."

*　*　*

BUT THEN RONDA was killed two years after Skeeter moved in with Barb, and Barb could think of nothing else. Fortunately, Cheri-Lynn was grown and on her own.

"Skeeter unselfishly put his own grief aside to nurture me through mine," she recalled.

When she called him from Toledo, Skeeter assured Barb that Daisy was okay at the boarding kennel and that he would visit the pup Ronda had given her the next day. She knew he would find time for Daisy. He loved the dog almost as much as Barb did, and knew how important it was that Daisy didn't feel she'd been abandoned.

"We said our 'I love you's' and 'goodbyes,' and I lay down to try to sleep in the motel. But sleep evaded me. Instead, I was haunted by thoughts and images of Ronda and different scenarios of what could possibly have happened at 114 Twin Peaks Drive."

Three days later, Barb was back in Chehalis. She and David Bell planned to meet with Detective Jerry Berry for dinner, and, hopefully, put together a plan. She knew she would have to talk to Ron Reynolds again, and that she would still have to continue her act to make it seem as if she didn't suspect him in Ronda's death.

Barb wanted to be sure that Jerry Berry knew that Jonathan Reynolds had threatened her daughter's life, about Ron's infidelity and his ongoing affair with Katie Huttula Reynolds, and that Ronda had mentioned her HIV fears on the evening of December 15 in their last phone call. Knowing of Katie's predilection for drugs, Ronda had been fearful that she might have contracted AIDS.

"I wanted to tell Detective Berry about Ronda's final realization of the kind of man Ron Reynolds really was, and let him know that my daughter put fifteen thousand dollars of her own money down on their house in Toledo. That she worked day and night—every spare minute she could find—to clean, paint, and remodel the home she shared with Ron. Maybe, taken individually, these things didn't mean so much, but together they formed a pattern of an evil, manipulative, money-hungry man."

Barb dreaded seeing Ron again, but she knew she had to. She vowed that she wouldn't let him make her cry—no matter what he said about Ronda.

"I wanted to see if he would tell me anything that would help me understand what happened that night. I had to make funeral arrangements, and I needed to be sure Ronda's dogs were okay."

Barb wasn't surprised to see Katie's car when she pulled into the driveway of what had been Ronda's home less than a week before. There was still frost on the windshield, indicating that it had been there all night.

"That didn't surprise me, either," she said. "I wondered how either one of them could sleep in Ronda's bedroom—in her bed—just twelve feet away from where she died, much less sleep together. It sickened me, especially remembering Katie's 'poem.' I forced my mind to turn to other things."

Barb heard the dogs bark, and walked to the side of the garage to look at them. They looked cold, but they had food and water, and it appeared that Ron had been leaving the heat lamp on in their doghouses.

"They also seemed sad and lonely, and I whispered my promise to them that it wouldn't be long before I got them out of there."

Ron's attitude toward Barb was surprisingly much warmer than it had been the previous Thursday. He assured her that he was having Katie and his sons box up some of Ronda's things for her, but he still couldn't let her have any of Ronda's jewelry.

"I'm afraid that might incriminate me, and make it look as if I had a motive to kill her," he said inexplicably.

She stared back at him. Why on earth would he think that?

"Ronda bought and collected a lot of fine jewelry," Ron said.

Barb knew that. Her daughter had treasured sentimental gifts of jewelry and saved up for other pieces. Did her widower think he could hide their value? (Later, she learned he had declared the value of Ronda's jewelry at a vastly underpriced $1,000.)

"I took a lie detector test," he told her, "and I didn't pass it. Jerry Berry told me that wasn't unusual under the circumstances, but my attorney told me not to talk to anyone. Do *you* know who's accusing me?"

Barb thought quickly. She suggested it might have been Ronda's paternal grandmother, Lavada, who lived in Oklahoma. Ron would have no idea how to contact Lavada, and it would seem—for a time—that Barb believed everything he was saying.

He repeated what he had told the detectives—that Ronda was alive at 5 A.M. on December 16, that he had talked to her and asked if she was okay.

"I kept her right beside me all night long, talking to her all the time to keep her awake—until she was so tired she would just fall asleep and not be able to hurt herself."

Barb could tell by his body language that he believed he had total control of the situation, and that he had convinced her of his innocence and even his power over her.

"I let him believe that," she said. "It would be better that way. If he thought I believed him, the more apt he'd be to make a mistake. Maybe his self-confidence was his worst enemy.

"No," she said emphatically as she recalled her second visit to Ron after her daughter's death. "*I* was his worst enemy. He just wasn't clever enough to know that."

He repeated a list of items he could not let her have because his attorney had told him to hang on to everything. Even Ronda's car. He said he couldn't help with any funeral arrangements because he was "too busy." He did offer to pay at least part of Ronda's funeral expenses, as he felt "somewhat responsible."

Barb bit the inside of her cheeks until she tasted blood to keep herself from striking back at him.

"He wanted me to take the dogs because they were almost out of food, and he didn't want to buy any. It was so hard to stand my ground and say I couldn't take them yet—when my heart was crying over leaving them. I knew if I took them, I would have no leverage to try to gain anything else personal that had belonged to Ronda."

She fought back the primal instinct that gripped her; she wanted nothing so much as to tear this man apart, limb by limb. She believed he had killed her child, and she wanted to see *his* eyes filled with fear. Still, she forced her features into a semblance of serenity so he wouldn't know.

Ron Reynolds finally agreed to call her and tell her

which items he would let her take and that he'd have them all boxed up and ready to go. He also said she could take Ronda's portable dog kennels so she could make a place for them. Surprisingly, he also said she could take Ronda's saddle, which was sitting in the living room.

It appalled Barb to think of Katie and her sons going through Ronda's things. But there was nothing she could do about that. She knew she had to keep her mouth shut, act timid, meek, and grateful, and walk away.

* * *

When they met with Jerry Berry that evening, David Bell and Barb Thompson verified each other's recall. David Bell told the detective that he had once had dinner with Ronda on her lunch break at Macy's. She had received a page from Ron and called him back. Bell had listened to Ronda's side of the conversation and could tell that Ron was trying to get her to stay in Olympia—since she was working late, he didn't want her to drive home.

"She asked Ron who was at their house," Bell said.

She was suspicious that Katie was there, and Ronda had also told Dave Bell that she wanted a clean bill of health—free of HIV—before she agreed to divorce Ron.

"Did she have a broken fingernail when you saw her last?" Berry asked Bell.

"No. None of her fingernails were broken Tuesday evening when I dropped her off at her house sometime between eight and eight-thirty. When we were driving around, Ronda sat next to me, with her left hand holding my right hand," Bell answered. "She was very, very particular with her nails, and if she had a broken nail, believe me, she would have mentioned it to me. I can definitely say she did not have a broken fingernail. She also talked about the fifteen thousand dollars of her money that she had put into the house that Ron wanted her to just walk away from."

The last conversation Dave Bell had with Ronda had been around 12:45 A.M. on December 16, when she called him to update him on her flight schedule. She told him she would be flying out of SeaTac in Seattle at 2:00 P.M. He would have to leave Des Moines by 10 A.M. in order to get to Toledo on time to pick her up and drive her back north to the airport.

"Ronda sounded good—happy—about going to Spokane then," Bell said. "She said she had gotten a little bit of sleep and felt much better. She sounded much calmer than she had been earlier—in the afternoon."

The sergeant from the Des Moines Police Department told Berry he was upset at Ron Reynolds's attitude when he called Ronda later on the morning of the sixteenth. Ron had been so matter-of-fact and emotionless when he said "Ronda committed suicide."

It was late in the evening when Barb and Dave Bell finished their meeting with Jerry Berry. They were even more convinced that Ronda had been murdered—although they could not get the detective to say that.

"Deep down, he knew it, too," Barb remembered. "He just didn't know how to correct the mistakes that had been made and find enough evidence to prove what we all believed. Once again, he told me he'd continue to work on the case, and to feel free to contact him at any time.

"I believed him. He was a sincere, dedicated man."

CHAPTER TWELVE

CHERYL GILBERT offered to help Barb Thompson in planning Ronda's funeral service. As she had told everyone, Ronda and herself had been very close friend. Now she was close to being the center of attention as she bonded with Barb. She even invited Barb to stay with her, an invitation Barb was grateful to accept.

Barb was a lot of help to Cheryl, and she needed to keep her mind occupied. Cheryl's water pipes had frozen in the bitter cold, and Barb crawled under her house and checked all the exposed pipe that was wrapped with electric warming wires. She found the short in the wires and they got the water running again.

Cheryl seemed sincere in her support. She accompanied Barb to the house on Twin Peaks Drive. Ron met them at the door and helped them load the chain-link dog pens and some rubber stall mats he no longer wanted. They didn't talk much, but he did agree to call the Lewis County Coroner's Office and officially release Ronda's body to Barb, who was responsible for the arrangements. Since Christmas was almost upon them, they decided to set Ronda's memorial services for January 4.

Ron gave in a little and allowed Barb to take Ronda's large framed photographs of her and Clabber Toe, and other miscellaneous pictures. Her pickup was stacked high with the kennels, stall mats, and more of Ronda's belongings—so she decided to drive back to Spokane and return with her large four-horse trailer to pick up whatever boxed items Ron was willing to give her. He had made it abundantly clear that he would not let go of anything "personal"—such as Ronda's jewelry, computer, or any cards or correspondence, but he had decided to give her Ronda's old furniture and some of her clothes. He was considering letting go of the antique china her father had left to her.

Barb knew that she had to act fast before he changed his mind. There was little intrinsic value in what Ron was offering, but it meant the world to Barb.

"I was hungry for any morsel he would toss me at this point," she said. "Even old soiled and discarded clothes. How sad, I thought to myself that these simple, meager, seemingly meaningless items would be all I would ever have to remember the vibrant, beautiful daughter I would never hold again."

Barb had already cried until she had no more tears. Her body was numb, and her heart was cold. She chose her words carefully when she spoke to Ron Reynolds, avoiding any mention of the events surrounding Ronda's death, focusing only on trying to soften and persuade Ron to let her have more of Ronda to hold.

"There was no softening this man," Barb wrote in her journal. "He could care less about anything except his need to get rid of what he considered trash, and conceal and withhold anything that might remotely have any material value—or might, in some way, connect him to Ronda's death."

*   *   *

CHERYL OFFERED HER FATHER'S CHURCH in Chehalis for Ronda's services and said he would officiate. The church was generous and offered to assist with the arrangements and prepare songs, flowers, whatever Barb and her family wanted. Ron sat next to her at the mortuary, flipping through cards to select one that suited him to pass out at the funeral.

Barb's need for revenge grew until she feared it would burst out of her, but she forced it down with prayer and determination. She didn't want to hurt her mother, her son, or Ronda's memory. She knew she had to let justice come for her daughter through the law, and not from her own rage.

"I was a walking, ticking time bomb," Barb said. "And not one person realized that but me."

She wondered how long she could maintain control before she gave in to her impulses.

"How long, I wondered. And the answer came: forever. I heard myself say out loud, 'If it takes forever, I will not falter and I will not take the law into my own hands.' I'd made my commitment to myself—and to God."

She drove back to Spokane, a six-hundred-mile round-trip over mountain passes, in the dead of winter, two nights before Christmas Eve. The roads were covered with snow, but the Department of Transportation's plows were out, leaving the roads bare with only the thinnest sheet of frozen glaze to cover the pavement—just enough to reflect the sparkle of oncoming lights, before they passed and the dark night came back.

"The freeway was quiet," she recalled a long time later. "The sky was clear and the stars bright. It was an eerie feeling to be warm and comfortable in my truck, being lulled by the whine of the diesel engine while I looked out at the frozen black night. I had already memorized every milepost, every curve, every fuel stop. I could not have known then how many cross-mountain trips I would take in the years to come."

Barb got home in the wee hours of the morning. She hardly got the front door open before Daisy was jumping on it from the inside, hysterically happy to see her. She got to the couch and lay down, and Daisy was right there, her eyes reflecting how much she'd been missed. Then a sad look came over her eyes as the dog turned away, lay down at Skeeter's feet, and averted her eyes. Barb doubted that she would be home long enough this time for Daisy to forgive her for leaving. It broke her heart.

Skeeter had waited up for her, too, dozing in his recliner. He and Freeman had already taken care of all the chores in the barn and with the horses.

"Skeeter had waited up to be sure I was home safe, and to talk. He needed to talk to me," Barb said with regret. "He wanted to hold me and comfort me and find out what had gone on over on the coast—but I couldn't talk. I didn't want to. I wanted to be left alone. Couldn't he understand? The only person I wanted to touch, to hold, to love, was my daughter. How could he even think he could take her place? I didn't realize that I was slowly breaking Skeeter's heart. I was being selfish and cold when all he wanted to do was help me and hold me. I had no idea how helpless and rejected he felt.

"It never entered my mind that I was casting aside a man who loved and cherished me, without a thought or a care. The more he tried to help, the more he tried to comfort, the more I pushed him away. I was too engrossed in my own agony and self-pity to care about his loneliness. That was the beginning of the end."

At that time, so soon after Ronda's death, Barb's emotions were sealed and she thought only about what she had lost. She wanted someone to take care of her home chores, to be there waiting for her when she came home after she did what she had to do.

"I wanted nothing or no one but my daughter," she admits. "And Daisy, the last gift I would ever receive from Ronda."

Daisy would forgive her, but her relationship with Skeeter would starve as she focused only on Ronda's death.

*   *   *

THE NEXT MORNING, Barb saw that Freeman had fueled up her truck and hooked up the horse trailer. It was spotless, and he had made sure there were ample tarps, boxes, and tools for her return trip. All she had to do was grab clean clothes and drive.

Ronda had been dead only a week but it felt like a year.

Barb returned to Lewis County, operating mostly on nerve. If she kept busy enough, she didn't have to let her mind wander into dark corridors full of pain.

She had a quiet Christmas dinner with Cheryl's family. Each evening the two women reminisced about Ronda.

They put together a list of songs for the funeral: "The Wind Beneath My Wings," was Cheryl's choice. "In the Sweet Bye and Bye" was for Gramma Virginia, as well as

"Peace in the Valley" by the Statler Brothers. For David Bell, they included "My One and Only Love." Barb, a country-western fan, picked Garth Brooks's "Against the Grain," and "Go Rest High" by Vince Gill.

It took Barb six evenings between Christmas and New Year's Day to put the whole service together, and she found herself consumed with it. Meticulously, she transferred photos from every phase of Ronda's life onto the screen of the church's modern computer setup, reliving the good years. They would show on the screen at her daughter's funeral, timed exactly to the music.

"I pieced together her life, and I noticed that she was always smiling, her eye always sparkling as if she were alive, in person right in front of me, and I felt as if her love surrounded me," Barb said. "I was in a different world every night, refusing to leave it, waking up the next morning to the sound of Cheryl getting ready for work and finding myself covered with my memories as my only warmth through the night."

Barb was in the denial stage of grief, afraid to let splinters of pain break through for fear they would crush her. Planning Ronda's memorial was the last thing she could do for her daughter, and she clung to the details. Barb was remarkably efficient as she meshed schedules, travel, and the script for Ronda's services.

Gramma Virginia would fly from Spokane on the morning of January 4, accompanied by two of Ronda's former classmates, who were like family. When Barb learned that Ron Reynolds was going to attend the memorial, she realized she couldn't let Freeman or Don Hennings attend; she feared they might try to kill Ron with their own rough justice. They both believed that he had brutally taken away someone they loved so much and had always tried to protect.

They would have another memorial service in Spokane—and Ron would not be in attendance. Freeman, Skeeter, and Don could come to that one.

Barb's brother Bill had flown immediately to Spokane to stand by her when he learned of Ronda's death—but he couldn't stay through January 4.

Barb had five important male figures in her life, and four could not be with her for Ronda's memorial. But David Bell would be there, even though he was as crippled by grief and shock as she was.

"I knew I could lean on him," she said, "and we'd make it through together."

*   *   *

A DAY OR SO before Ronda's services, Barb and Cheryl Gilbert drove to Toledo to pick up any remainders of Ronda's possessions that Ron would give up. Barb was surprised at the number of things he let her have. Ronda's cranberry-colored couch and love seat were somewhat worn, but her mother was glad to have them. Ron also released Ronda's entertainment center, her hope chest, some more photographs, and, surprisingly, all of his and Ronda's wedding pictures and her Bible. Cheryl wanted that, and Barb couldn't say no to her.

There were numerous pairs of Ronda's shoes neatly packed in Rubbermaid containers, but they weren't new. It was the the same with her clothes. There were a lot of them, but the two women saw that they were all old clothes. Ronda's wedding dress was there, her Patrol coveralls, and a number of coats.

There were blankets, comforters, and some worn-out pillows.

"I was pretty sure they had never belonged to Ronda,"

Barb guessed, "but simply trash he wanted to discard. He had told me I couldn't have her silver service, but I noticed one of the boys carrying out the dark cherry wood box where she always kept her silverware. I quietly and quickly packed it away without taking time to look inside. I suspected that some of the boxes contained her crystal, and her Elvis Presley plates, along with memorabilia from her father."

After Barb and Cheryl had carried out the couch and love seat—with no help from Ron Reynolds or his teenage sons—they weren't allowed back in the house, and were told to wait outside for the boys to bring things out to them. Beyond the old clothes, they could see that even dirty clothing had been dumped into bags. There was a five-foot ficus tree that Barb's best friend Don Hennings had given Ronda when it was small, and Ron permitted them to take that.

Ron didn't want the dog's leashes, clippers, medications, or other gear.

Cheryl and Barb put Ronda's things in a storage facility and then came back for the dogs.

As they drove away, it was clear that Ronda's presence at 114 Twin Peaks Drive had been obliterated—all but the really expensive furniture purchased since Ron and Ronda's marriage one year and two days before.

Ronda's funeral service took place on January 4, 1999, at a church in Lewis County. Before she had explored the tenets of the Jehovah's Witnesses, Ronda had attended church in Elma—where the pastor was Reverend Jacob Winters*. He presided over her funeral. He was Cheryl Gilbert's father, and Cheryl continued to assure Barb that she had been Ronda's dearest friend for many years. She seemed to espouse the beliefs that Barb had formed, and agreed that Ronda could not possibly have committed suicide.

Barb, Gramma Virginia, and David Bell stood together

to greet the throngs of people who walked into the church to celebrate Ronda's life. Barb knew some of them, but there were far more that she didn't recognize. There were the busloads of her daughter's fellow employees from the Bon Marché/Macy's, and dozens of friends from Grays Harbor and Lewis County, plus childhood friends of Ronda's. The mourners moved through the greeting room and stopped to study the pictures that Barb had assembled. She heard people comment that—as she had found—Ronda was smiling in every photo.

There was a wave of muted gasps when Ron Reynolds walked in. He arrived with his former wife, Katie Huttula, on his arm. The couple walked down the aisle and Ron took his seat in a pew near the front of the church on the right side of the aisle with one of his sons. Katie and another son sat directly behind him. A handful of Ron's coworkers sat near him and Katie, and Detectives Jerry Berry and Steve Burress sat in the last row on "Ron's side" of the church. Even the sheriff's investigators seemed surprised to view the obvious demarcation of loyalties taking place in the flower-bedecked church.

Barb Thompson rose on shaking legs to speak of the lost daughter she loved so much, ending with a hint of what her mission in life had become:

"She has been taken from us—so suddenly, so tragically—that I cannot find words to express the pain, the anger, and the injustice I feel. I do know one thing. I cannot, I will not, quit until I understand totally—until all my questions are answered and I know she can finally rest in peace!"

She could hardly see through her tears as she made her way back to her seat. One by one, people stood up to speak about Ronda's love, devotion, sense of humor, compassion, and zest for life.

Technically and legally, Ron was a newly bereaved widower, and yet he appeared to have swiftly moved on with his life. It was almost as if Ronda had been only a tiny blip in his path. While Katie Huttula looked shaken, Ron betrayed no emotion. There were no tears in his eyes, and he was not one of those who spoke before the crowd.

And then it was over. Jerry Berry walked up to Barb, gave her a quick hug, and whispered, "Hang in there, kid. I have to meet with some people who want to talk. We'll be in touch."

Ron Reynolds was suddenly standing in front of her.

"He walked up to me and began to speak," Barb remembers. "I had held my feelings in for so long—I couldn't do it any longer. Before he could say anything, I heard the words spewing from my mouth.

" 'How does it feel, Ron, to know you are the one person who could have prevented this? I hope God has no mercy on your soul.' "

Too late, David Bell grabbed Barb's shoulders, holding her and tugging her back. Two people she didn't recognize were pulling Ron away. She was livid that he had approached her, that he had brought Katie Huttula to Ronda's services. Barb was aflame with the memories of all the times she had bitten her tongue and pretended that his cruel accusations about Ronda didn't bother her.

"I had just destroyed any chance of getting any more information from him that might explain what happened, or that he would give me the rest of Ronda's possessions," Barb said later. "I said what I felt. Now he knew with no uncertainty that I believed he had killed my daughter."

* * *

JUDY AND LARRY SEMANKO spoke quietly to Virginia Ramsey after the service. They didn't want to say too much at such a sad moment, but both of them felt that something was wrong. It was the Semankos—Ron Reynolds's sister and her retired deputy husband—that Jerry Berry was going to talk to. They had gone to Ron Reynolds's home in Toledo at 9 A.M. on the morning Ronda died. "It was chaotic," Larry said. "Ron was making jokes with the men from the school district and wrapping Christmas presents. He'd been out of the Jehovah's Witnesses for some time by then, so he celebrated Christmas. He didn't appear to be grieving at all."

With Jerry Berry's permission, Larry had walked through his brother-in-law's home, and the hair stood up on the back of his neck. As a lawman for two decades himself, he had taken a number of courses on homicide investigation, and nothing seemed right.

"For one thing," he recalled, "the first thing I smelled when I walked in that house was freshly washed laundry. Someone had to have washed a load of clothes that morning."

Larry saw that the closet door could not have been shut because Ronda's legs protruded too far over the sill. He saw the lipstick writing on the bathroom mirror and knew it was no suicide note.

As a sheriff's deputy and as a coroner's deputy, Larry Semanko had seen many deceased people. And Ronda's death just didn't add up. He and Judy had decided they had to tell Ronda's family what they thought.

They would also share anything they knew with Jerry Berry.

*   *   *

RONDA'S SECOND SERVICE—a memorial—took place later at a Lutheran church in Spokane, the city where she had grown from a child to a woman. Ron Reynolds didn't attend; David Bell drove over from the coast. Over the years ahead, Barb would come to know he would always be there for her, never faltering or deserting her as she fought for the truth behind Ronda's death. Ronda's "dad," Don Hennings was there, too—standing beside Barb, Gramma Virginia, Skeeter, and Freeman. The church was overflowing with Ronda's friends from the Spokane area. Among those paying their respects were a contingent of Washington State Patrol officers.

Neither Barb nor Gramma Virginia nor Ronda's brother, Freeman, could bring themselves to bury the urn with her ashes. They vowed they would not—not until they had the answers to what had really happened to her. Instead Barb placed the urn in a glass case in her living room where she kept many of Ronda's trophies from the days she was a star equestrian.

Nineteen ninety-eight was over. It had begun with so much hope on Ronda's part, a tentative niggling of doubt for Barb, and, quite possibly, happy expectations for Ron Reynolds. They had made it through the first anniversary of Ronda's marriage to Ron, and her memorial services were over. It was almost harder for Barb, Gramma Virginia, and Freeman now because they had nothing more to do to honor their daughter, granddaughter, and sister. She was gone, and they were just beginning to grasp what "forever" meant.

Barb believed that the new year would surely bring some answers—and possibly an arrest. But, in truth, none of them could have predicted how 1998 had ended.

Nor could anyone say what lay ahead now or how many agonizing years would pass before many secrets would be revealed.

PART THREE

Barb

Chapter Thirteen

Jerry Berry had already pledged—if only to himself—that he would see this case through until the end—until there were answers that fit. He wasn't ready yet to make a promise to Barb Thompson. The poor woman was going through hell, and he didn't want to give his word when he might not be able to deliver.

He didn't know at that point that Barb would not only stay in close touch with him, she would haunt him. She knew in her bones that she had found at least one good man—a man who would find the truth—and she wasn't about to let him go.

Although Berry admired Barb, he had come to dread the sound of his phones ringing. Most of the things he suspected he could not tell her, and he hated to stall or evade the truth. But she was a pretty fair detective herself, and she soon found out all of his phone numbers: office, home, cell, police radio unit.

It wasn't that he minded talking to her, and she often came up with some good leads or paths to take—but he simply could not tell her everything he found out. Any homicide detective has to maintain certain secret things that only a killer knows in order to winnow out the "compulsive confessors" from actual suspects. Nor can they show their hands to anyone who might have guilty knowledge.

"I would get frustrated with Barb Thompson at first," Berry recalled. "And then I'd hide from her because I didn't have anything I could tell her. She memorized all my phone numbers, but I recognized her numbers on my caller ID and I wouldn't answer sometimes."

Berry had married recently—to Susan, who had worked for the Lewis County prosecutor's office until 2003 when she left to further her career in Seattle. Later, after Jerry's mother died, Susan stayed home to care for his disabled brother. Susan had a soft heart, and she frowned at Jerry when he failed to pick up the ringing phone at home. They both knew it was probably Barb Thompson.

"Why don't you talk to her?" Susan demanded. "Don't you feel sorry for her?"

And, of course, he did. But he couldn't give her much information or hope, and he wanted to be sure he didn't mess up this case. It seemed to Berry that he was the only one in the Lewis County Sheriff's Office who wasn't anxious to see a rapid and discreet closure of the Ronda Reynolds case. A final stamp on the suicide conclusion would make it all go away. Berry didn't care how long it took—just as long as they found out who had killed her.

He and other detectives had talked to a number of witnesses who spoke about how upset Ronda was to see her second marriage end within months. All but Berry felt that was adequate motivation for her to kill herself. It would be a convenient end to sweep her death under the rug and forget about it. But as the months went by, gossip multiplied in Lewis County.

There were so many more people who simply could not accept that Ronda would ever be self-destructive. When Berry talked with Mark Liburdi and his current wife, Krista, Mark, particularly, refused to describe Ronda as the kind of woman who would kill herself. They had ended their marriage with some bitterness, but Mark insisted that Ronda had been strong—not a quitter, no matter what.

She had called his house at 10:20 on the night she died. Mark said he'd listened to her talking on his answering machine. His impression was that she sounded as though she was in trouble. But he hadn't picked up his phone to talk with her.

"Was there anything unusual about her voice at that time?" Berry asked.

"I could tell she was upset because her voice wavered or quivered—"

"Something that was familiar to you?"

"Yes. The first thought that came to my mind was she and her current husband were arguing. I had nothing factual to base it on, other than just the tone of voice and I had heard it before."

It didn't occur to Mark Liburdi that Ronda might be afraid—particularly since she was leaving a message for his fiancée, Krista. She evidently wanted to talk about the sale of the McCleary ranch where she and Mark had lived.

"I've seen her at her worst—feeling her worst," Mark offered. "And she never mentioned suicide. Or did anything that would make me think she was even considering it."

The Liburdis were on good terms with Mark's ex-wife. Krista was handling the sale of Mark's mother's house, and their own house in McCleary was on the market. Ronda and Mark's funds were still somewhat entangled. They would split the equity they owned on their ranch. That would take a while—but Ron Reynolds was already asking for it. Krista told Berry that Ronda had told her she had a will that specified that money was to go to Barb. It wasn't much—about $5,000 to $7,000.

But it was complicated enough that they had all needed to retain an attorney to represent them.

"You told me, Krista, that Ron—after Ronda's death"— Jerry Berry began—"he talked to you a little bit and told you about Ronda being upset on the night before her death— and that he had to leave a doctor's appointment?"

She nodded, explaining that she had called Ronda at 8:19 on Wednesday morning, unaware that Mark's ex-wife had died.

"Ron answered, and told me what happened. I had to call him later in the day, and he started talking about what had happened on Tuesday. He said he was at a doctor's appointment and he had Ronda on the phone, and she was very upset and angry . . . He had to leave his appointment and drive, um, somewhere. He said he got there in forty-five minutes and he kept her on the phone the whole time to make sure she was okay. He said they fought all night and then he said he just couldn't stay up any longer and he fell asleep."

Ron had gone on, telling Krista the story pretty much as he'd told the Lewis County sheriff's men. "He said he looked all over the house for Ronda, and finally found her 'underneath clothes' in the closet," Krista said.

Ron's description, of discovering Ronda's death was void of emotion when he talked to Krista. Jerry Berry noted that each time Ron retold the story, he changed some slight detail—but no one he talked to recalled that he seemed overwhelmed, or even slightly disturbed, by the sudden death of his wife.

*   *   *

RONDA HAD MANY FRIENDS, several of them women involved in law enforcement. Years earlier, fellow female troopers and other women working in the justice system had made pacts to stand up for each other. One female officer in the State Patrol—who graduated from the academy several classes after Ronda—had committed suicide, and they were all shocked and saddened when they heard what she had done. They vowed that none of them would ever do that; they would call each other if they were depressed.

Ronda was one of the most vehement when she struck out about suicide, saying, "Suicide is never the right answer to problems. Life will always get better if you just hang around to see it happen."

No, none of Ronda's friends believed she had killed herself. They all agreed that that wasn't Ronda.

Ronda had taught many cadets and fledgling troopers gun safety and personal safety techniques while she was on the force. If anyone knew how to defend herself, she did. She could take down a man who weighed a hundred pounds more than she did.

But could she fight off two or more men?

Probably not.

*   *   *

ONE FEMALE RECRUIT, Lauren Sund*, who never met Ronda, remembers how she was inspired by Ronda even after she was dead.

Lauren was several years behind Ronda in the Patrol's ladder of employment. Being a cop of any kind had been the last thing in Lauren's mind when she was in her early twenties. In an almost eerie coincidence, she crossed paths with Ron Reynolds. And, in a sense, although the two women never met, Ronda Reynolds was the catalyst who caused Lauren to join the Washington State Patrol.

In late 1998, Lauren Sund was working as a bill collector and she also tracked down the "makers" of nonsufficient-funds checks.

"In Washington state," Lauren explained, "statutes gave collectors the right to make three calls to the debtor's residence and one to his work.

"Ron Reynolds—or someone signing his name—had written checks to a Lewis County grocery store. And they bounced. The total debt was $1,800."

Lauren Sund didn't know who Ron Reynolds was and she had no idea where he worked when she called him in the mid-December 1998. A man answered his home phone and abruptly hung up on her when she stated her reason for phoning him.

The next time she called, the voice that answered sounded like that of a twelve- or thirteen-year-old boy. Lauren used her acting ability, sounding younger than she was. She pretended that Ron had given her his work number, but she had lost it. The boy, Ron's youngest son, Josh, told her that his father worked at Toledo Elementary School and gave her his phone number.

When she called the school's main number on December 18, 1998, Lauren had never heard of Ronda Reynolds, and had no idea that she had died suddenly two days before. She asked for Ron Reynolds, wondering what his job was at the school. She thought that maybe he was a teacher or the janitor.

There was a pause and then Ron Reynolds came on the line. She was startled to learn that he was the principal. She explained who she was, and asked what plans he had to make good on the $1,800 worth of checks.

"Oh, he was so *mad*!" Lauren said. "But that phone call was the most chilling I've ever experienced. He told me that his wife had died 'unexpectedly' a few days before, and he'd moved his *ex*-wife in the same day! He didn't sound as if he was in mourning."

"She—Katie, my *ex*-wife—wrote those checks," he explained, as if that was the most natural thing in the world. He didn't seem at all angry at his ex-spouse for writing the rubber checks.

Shocked, but trying not to show it, Lauren gave him a week to come up with the money to reimburse the grocery store and pay penalties. He did pay the collection company—she didn't know where he got the money; that wasn't part of her job. Nor did she feel that she had enough to go on yet to report his attitude and statements to the sheriff's office. She did, however, look up the news coverage of the death of Ronda Reynolds.

Lauren Sund found the process of tracking down Ron Reynolds and further investigating the story he told her (all of which turned out to be true) so interesting that she signed up for classes in criminal justice at a nearby community college.

"In 2002, one of my professors wanted us to do a paper with examples of investigations, and I chose the situation with Ronda Reynolds," Lauren recalled. "I didn't know quite where to start, and my professor told me to call the sheriff's office and talk to them about my experience with Ron—what he said to me two days after his wife died. I talked to one of the detectives and he sounded totally bored. He kept saying, 'Umhmm, umhmm,' but I could tell he didn't care. He told me he'd call me, but I knew he wouldn't because he didn't even ask my name or phone number. He just didn't care."

Undeterred by the investigator's attitude, Lauren Sund applied to become a trooper with the Washington State Patrol. She has worked there ever since, and loves her job. And she, like Ronda, has had contact with all kinds of dangerous offenders.

When she learned some years later that Barb Thompson was seeking information about Ronda's death, Lauren contacted her and offered to do whatever she could do to solve what she believed to be Ronda's murder. Even though the Lewis County detective had shown no interest in her information, Lauren hadn't forgotten Ronda and the cavalier attitude of her widower.

*   *   *

BARB WAS MOVING in a whole new world, one that had pitfalls, detours, and resistance from the people she had believed would help her find out the truth.

But she had faced almost impossible odds before in her life, and she would meet whatever anyone threw at her.

Chapter Fourteen

Barb Thompson had dealt with every challenge that life brought to her, and, until now, she had survived. Sometimes she even thrived. But Ronda's violent death brought her to her knees.

Barb was a caretaker, a woman who forgave many who didn't really deserve it. She was born on May 4, 1945, just as World War II was ending. Her family was living in San Diego then. She was the last of three children; her sister was several years older, and her brother, Bill, was two years older than she was.

"I was my father's spoiled little darling," she says ruefully. "He was absolutely wonderful to my sister, and especially to me. My brother didn't fare so well. Like my mother, he was the brunt of my father's abuse."

Warren Ramsey was not quite half Cherokee Indian and he was an alcoholic. Virginia Ramsey, Barb's mother, suffered both physical and verbal abuse from him, and she and the children moved constantly, whenever he wanted to. From San Diego they moved to Oregon, Nebraska, Illinois, and finally to Utah. Barb attended several different schools between Salt Lake City and Murray, Utah.

When she was three, they lived on a farm in Oregon, and her father worked at a brick factory. They raised leghorn chickens for their eggs and meat, and they also raised rabbits.

Their living conditions offered few luxuries. Barb and her sister dreaded going to the outhouse because they had to get past a goose, "a mean old gander" that nipped at them. Warren often made her brother catch the goose by the neck and hold him whenever the girls had to go down the path. Barb knew that if her brother Bill didn't catch the wicked gander, her father would take his leather belt to Bill.

"One day, after Bill had to catch that old gander about five times, my brother had had enough," she recalls. "I got about halfway to the outhouse and Bill turned him loose. The gander got me. He didn't really hurt me, but he pecked me good and beat me with his wings. When I told my dad—because I was his spoiled little princess—he took his belt to my brother unmercifully."

She vowed never, ever, to do anything or tattle about anything that would cause their father to do that again to Bill. She loved her brother a lot, and she didn't want to see him hurt so badly again.

They moved into town and her father found a job driving dump trucks. Although she was still a little girl, she remembers seeing her mother sitting in her bedroom crying as she tried to soak toast in milk so she could eat it.

"My dad had beaten her, too," Barb recalls. "Her face and mouth were so swollen and black and blue that she could hardly talk—much less eat."

Little Barbara was rapidly growing a social conscience, and she designated herself as the protector of her family. One night, her father came in the kitchen angry because he had found a cigarette butt in the coal shed.

"Which one of you has been smoking?" he demanded.

Barb knew it wasn't her or her brother. She suspected it might have been her sister—or even a neighbor boy who was older. But her father's belt came off and he began to beat them all.

"He barely tapped me; he was maybe a little harder on my sister—but he was brutal to my brother. I knew he wasn't the smoker, but I couldn't bear to watch Bill get spanked, so I confessed, knowing Dad wouldn't punish me. He didn't. I got away with everything and got anything I wanted—*if* we could afford it, which wasn't often."

Barb's heart ached when she watched her mother fix dinner and then wait until her children had eaten. Only then would she eat—and just what was left. "If we had chicken on Sunday, we kids got what we wanted, then Dad, and I look back and remember my mother chewing on the neck, and if she was lucky, she got the back of the chicken.

"She never complained. We children never went hungry. I know, looking back, she did—but we never did."

Warren Ramsey continued to control his family viciously. Why he treated his son so cruelly, no one knew. But he resented it when Bill collected "airplane cards" and Barb would flash the cards for him to test him as he named all the planes accurately. Ramsey demanded that Bill help him as he worked on cars or junked out those that no longer ran. Bill never had any spending money and he wasn't allowed to go to school functions.

Bill was obsessed with flying and his one goal was to join the Civil Air Patrol, but his father wouldn't let him.

Barb found a way around that, too. Although she hadn't the slightest interest in the CAP, she piped up and said that she really wanted to join, knowing that her father would insist that she had a protector in the group. That, of course, would be Bill.

"I hated the Civil Air Patrol, but I loved watching Bill be so happy. It was worth it to see him finally get something that meant so much to him."

Bill Ramsey was a genius. "He was a straight-A student" Barb said. "He won an appointment to the U.S. Naval Academy when a Utah state senator learned of his academic achievements. But he might not be able to go. He had to pay for his own transportation from Utah to the academy in Maryland, and my dad wouldn't help him."

Her father had given Barb an old gray mare, and she delivered a little filly that Barb adored. Barb was about fifteen then and already in love with horses. She taught the pretty little filly how to do tricks and doted on her. But her brother had finally found a way to get away from their father's abuse and learn to fly. That seemed to be the answer to a prayer for both of them. Barb didn't think twice before she sold her filly for enough money to buy Bill a plane ticket.

"Except for the time he sicced that ornery goose on me," she laughed, "Bill was always there for me, and he deserved a chance."

Bill Ramsey flew helicopter rescue missions in Vietnam. When he retired from the Navy, he flew for private companies looking for mineral deposits or setting power lines or rescuing mountain climbers who had been stranded by avalanches. To this day, he flies helicopters fighting forest fires. It takes highly trained pilots to maneuver over flames and downdrafts and pinpoint where to dump massive containers of water and/or chemicals.

"I idolized Bill," Barb recalls. "I still do. But the two men I married were more like my father. When you grow up watching your mother let a man abuse her—and watch her go on loving him—you begin to believe that abuse is what love is. I learned, and I married the same type. Ronda learned from me."

It is a familiar progression to anyone who works or volunteers in women's shelters in America. Although Barb vowed she would never marry a man who shared characteristics with her father, she did.

Her older sister left home to get married when Barb was in her mid-teen years, and now her brother was gone. Nothing had changed at home, but she thought her mother might find life easier, seeing all of her children out on their own. Barb moved to California to live with her sister.

During her senior year in high school in San Diego, Barb struggled to get her high school degree. But then something happened that no one expected. In 1963, her father suddenly left her mother for a much younger woman after twenty-two years of marriage. He drove Virginia Ramsey to California and "dumped" her close to where Barb and her sister lived. She called her daughters and they hurried to pick her up.

Virginia had never really held a job outside her marriage, paid bills, or done anything that would have prepared her to be on her own. She was crushed and humiliated that her husband would abandon her.

Barb had been so close to graduating from high school that she figured she could finish up in California. But she realized too late that even though she had enough credits to graduate, she lacked the required history credits to do so in her new state. She was smart, and she had worked hard to get through school, but family was the most important thing. It would take her mother, sister, and herself working together to make it through. She swallowed her disappointment and figured she could catch up later with her education.

Virginia and Barb rented a tiny apartment. Together they could make the rent. Virginia worked nights as a waitress and Barb worked days as a policy typist for an insurance company. Barb was eighteen and Virginia was still a relatively young woman, but they spent almost all of their time working. Virginia was discouraged by the turn her life had taken. Mean as he was, Warren Ramsey was the only man she had ever really dated, the only man she'd loved, and he had left her in the cruelest way possible.

As the next few years passed, both women worked on learning new skills. Barb worked in payroll departments, both in accounts receivable and accounts payable. At night, she tended bar four or five times a week. Virginia went to a power sewing machine school and learned to do factory work. Work was plentiful, and they weren't afraid to do men's work if they had to. Barb had a job once for one of the first companies in the country to rent out heavy construction equipment: RENT-IT-SERVICE in San Diego.

San Diego was a beautiful place to live with its temperate climate, access to the Gulf of Santa Catalina and the Pacific Ocean, and its bountiful flowers year round. Traffic wasn't nearly as congested in the 1960s as it is now.

As beautiful as any Hollywood starlet, Barb dated often, married very young, and became pregnant in the early months of 1965. She gave birth to Ronda on September 16 that year, but Ronda's father, Ronnie Scott, wasn't nearly ready to settle down with a family.

"It was a very rocky relationship," Barb recalls. "Ronnie's uncle offered him a job in Dallas, Texas, and he and I and the baby moved to Texas in 1966. My mom followed a few months later to help me take care of Ronda. She loved that baby girl."

Barb always held down two jobs. In Texas, she became the collection manager for Wales Transportation, a manufacturer of prestressed concrete beams. She had developed a strong, efficient work ethic. She was organized, able to juggle many tasks. She kept meticulous records. One day she would need all those skills—and more.

Barbara had, however, married a man who was cut from the same cloth as her father. Ronnie Scott drank too much, and when he drank, jealousy washed over him—even though she had never given him any reason at all to think she cared about other men.

During one of the times when she tried to leave him, Barb realized how trapped she was. She was horrified when he tied her up and gagged her—and then left to buy film for his camera. She wasn't sure what he meant to do to her next, but she knew it wouldn't be good, and she was afraid. When Ronnie was drinking, he was another person entirely.

She tried unsuccessfully to wriggle out of her bonds, and she finally managed to roll over to the bedroom window, where she threw herself out. It wasn't that far to the ground, and luckily a neighbor saw her.

Barb didn't want to report Ronnie for rape; he was her legal husband, even though they were estranged. This was years before it became legally possible to charge a husband with rape, but her terror during the time she was helpless didn't make her want to stay with Ronnie.

Barb's time with Ronnie Scott was not only difficult—it was brief. They broke up in 1968, when Ronda was three. Ronnie was fatally injured four years later in a June 1972 automobile accident. Now Barb was the only breadwinner.

She thanked God that Virginia Ramsey was there to care for Ronda, then six years old. She trusted her mother completely, and Ronda was happy to have her grandmother living with them.

Ronda was a lovely child with a face like a rose, something that would never change. She was Virginia's first grandchild, and her "gramma" often said she was pure joy.

"She never caused us any trouble," Barb Thompson said. "She had perfect attendance and straight A's all the way through the ninth grade. She was never rebellious, and she never touched drugs or alcohol. Gramma taught her to sew and cook and do all the girly stuff, and if she got in trouble for not doing her homework or chores, she went to Gramma for comfort. My mother was there to share her dreams and plans and her crushes with. She was Ronda's 'safe place.' "

*   *   *

RONDA HAD MANY DREAMS, and she managed to fulfill a lot of them. She loved dogs and horses, and she was a champion equestrian before she was a teenager, winning ribbons and trophies from many shows. She shared her love of horses with her mother.

Barb married for the second time. She met Hal Thompson in Texas in the 1970s, and married him in March 1974. Hal and Barb's son, Freeman, was born in Dallas on July 2, 1975.

*   *   *

WHEN HAL GOT A JOB in Spokane, Washington, they all moved to the Northwest in June 1976. Finally, Barb Thompson put down roots. She loved the Eastern Washington acreage with room for horses, dogs, and kids to run. Thirty-four years later, she still lives in the same house, and Virginia's house used to be right next door, although a few years ago her health problems demanded that she have full-time personal care from Barb.

Ronda started the fifth grade at the Airway Heights Elementary School, which was close to Fairchild Air Force Base. She missed Texas some, and she put on an exaggerated Texas drawl. For some reason, this angered the other ten-year-old girls in her class. All but one of them. One day, Rahma Starret saw that the mean girls had someone down on the ground, and they were all kicking at whoever it was.

"It was Ronda," Rahma recalls. "There were five or six girls beating up on her—so I just waded in and saved her."

They were both farm girls. Ronda had her horses that she adored, and Rahma was attached to the cows on her farm. They soon spent a lot of time together.

"She was always upbeat," Rahma recalls. "She was very nice, but very strong, too. She believed in women's rights, and she stood up for girls who were being treated badly."

Ronda got braces in junior high, and Rahma envied her. "Only the rich girls had braces. I asked my mother for some, too, but she laughed and said that I didn't *need* braces so there was no point in spending money on them."

The two girls went to Cheney High School, located fifteen miles west of Spokane, and they rode the bus together.

"In our senior year," Rahma remembered, "Ronda talked about wanting to be a police officer, and I thought she would be good at that. She was fair, understanding, and honest."

Rahma didn't see Ronda for several years after they graduated, and then she was invited to Ronda's first wedding. "When I heard she was dead, I thought that she was still married to Mark Liburdi. I remember she was very nice to his kids."

*   *   *

OVER THE YEARS, Barb tried never to say anything negative to either of her children about their fathers. She suffered abuse, both emotional and physical, but she never complained to Ronda or Freeman. It was essential that they respected their fathers. Because they were the best part of their fathers.

Hal Thompson was a great guy—except when he drank. Then he was an entirely different person. One night while he was out, Barb noticed that one of his horses was sick, and she loaded the gelding into the horse trailer and took him to the vet. After he was treated, she brought him back to their ranch and put him safely in his stable.

"Suddenly," Barb recalled, "Hal was standing outside my open driver's window, and he had a loaded .357, cocked, only an inch or so from my head. He kept saying I'd stolen his horse, and he wouldn't listen to any sense. I really thought that was the end of me."

Once again a neighbor saved her. As he drove by, he saw that Hal was holding the gun against Barb's head, and he called the police. Hal was horrified when he sobered up, and apologized over and over.

But she knew it could happen again, if he drank. And there would always come a time when he would drink. Barb wondered if she could ever hope for a trusting relationship with a man.

For the moment, Barb's hands were full—raising Ronda and Freeman, and supporting her mother, too.

Although Don Hennings had gone on to another relationship just as she had, she thought of him often. She had met Don Hennings some years before, long before she met Hal Thompson, and they kept track of each other. Don was as nice to all of them as Warren Ramsey and Ronnie Scott had been mean. He adored Ronda and became, according to Barb, "really the only father she ever knew."

Don was a John Wayne sort of man, broad-shouldered and ruggedly handsome. He was born to wear the ten-gallon hat he often affected, a good man with callused hands and skin weathered by the Eastern Washington heat.

Don's relatives in his hometown of Ritzville, Washington, never questioned their love for one another, but often fate and change tore Don and Barb apart. As much as they cared about each other, they had diverse interests and different goals. With the wisdom of time, experience, and hindsight, Barb would one day realize that Don was the one man she had really loved. That may have been the reason she hated it so much when she saw her daughter follow the same path with David Bell. Both of them took tragic detours when it came to love, and both of them missed out on lasting happiness. Barb has never said where she met Don or when. He traveled a lot, and he was away from Ritzville and Washington state during most of 1964 through 1965. "Let your readers figure out our story," she said reluctantly. "This really isn't my story—it's Ronda's."

But of course this is Barb's story, too.

"Don and I never lied to each other, never did mean things to each other—we were just different with different goals and ideas," Barb recalled. "We never denied our love for each other. What Don did—what *we* did—was show Ronda and Freeman that just because two people can't share their lives, doesn't mean they can't still be friends, and share their children, and have a good, respectful family relationship."

There were people in Ritzville who believed Don was Ronda's biological father. Barb recalled the rumor mill of a small town. "Don's own mother would only smile that wise old smile if she was approached by inquisitive neighbors," Barb said. "Don's parents loved both of my children as their own grandchildren and were brokenhearted when Don's and my relationship didn't mature into marriage."

Barb had never lived with Don Hennings. "I never—*never*—had a man in my bedroom except my husbands after we were married," Barb explains. "My children never had an inkling that I ever had sex after Hal and I divorced. The men in my life were presented to my children as friends and were expected to act just that way when my children were present."

*   *   *

IF ANYTHING, Barb Thompson was far stricter than most parents. Because she spent so many years as a single mother, she was super vigilant. She believed that children learned what they lived. Gramma Virginia and Barb made sure that Ronda and Freeman always had a good breakfast after they did their morning chores. Dinner was on the kitchen table with all present and accounted for, and the TV off. It stayed off until they finished their homework.

When Ronda was seventeen, she had her own quarter horse, the gelding she named Clabber Toe. She and Clabber Toe managed to travel to the 1984 Quarter Horse Youth World Show in Tulsa, Oklahoma, where they cleared jumps as easily as if Clabber Toe had wings. Ronda had saved her money, and two local trainers in Spokane helped. They had recognized Ronda's innate talent and admired her devotion, how she would practice for hours.

Barb wouldn't let Ronda wear shorts to school, low-cut jeans, show her bare midriff, or wear even slightly low-cut blouses. She stressed over and over that they were responsible for their own behavior, and they must not give in to peer pressure.

By the time Ronda and Freeman each reached their twenties, they thanked Barb for being so "annoying"—they were grateful that she had gone out of her way to protect them. Neither had ever delved into drugs or alcohol, and they spent much of their youthful energy riding and showing horses.

It would have been easier, surely, for Barb to look the other way—especially when she was working two jobs. But she heaved a sigh of relief to see they had come through the dangerous teen years safely.

Barb had done all the right things in raising her children—if, indeed, there are "right things." What is right for one child may not be right for another. She had not realized that the parts of her life that she hadn't been able to control had imprinted on her children. As much as she'd tried to make their home a loving, soft landing spot, Freeman and Ronda had grown up aware that their family didn't have much money. They'd had no permanent father, and their grandmother was the "hands-on" mother figure who cared for them while Barb worked long hours. They seemed content, and probably were, and being children of divorce didn't make them any different than half the kids in their classes.

"I didn't believe Ronda had any idea of the verbal and emotional abuse I absorbed from some of the men in my life," Barb said regretfully, "But from the time she was eighteen, we talked about the kind of men she was drawn to. My heart sank when I realized that she favored 'punishing men'; she had watched me and my reactions, and she thought that's what love was."

Ronda had tried to work it out in her own head. "I don't understand—I've tried to break the cycle," she once told her mother. "Maybe the challenge is to change them. Maybe that's what has made me fall in love."

"I'm here to tell you," Barb said to me recently. "My daughter felt everything I did from the time she was crawling."

PART FOUR

The Investigation

Continues

CHAPTER FIFTEEN

CHRISTMAS EVE 1998 arrived eight days after Ronda was found dead. On that religious night, Lewis County Coroner Terry Wilson declared Ronda's death "Undetermined." His office gave no information about how long it might take for them to actually make a determination.

There were enough loose ends emanating from Ronda Reynolds's "undetermined death" to weave into a potholder. Each time Lewis County's investigators thought they were done with it, each time they attempted to package it up neatly and put it away, a few strands crept out again.

Detective Jerry Berry had inherited the job as lead investigator, simply by default: Dave Neiser was on vacation. At the time, Berry was regarded as a superior investigator by the Lewis County Sheriff's Office. He had gone along with the department's position, but he soon wished he hadn't—not in the Reynolds case. Now he regretted mightily that there were things that should have been done at Ronda's death scene, procedures that could never be accomplished with optimum accuracy weeks later.

Later on December 16—a few hours after Ronda's body was removed—Berry had returned to the house on Twin Peaks Drive. He had needed to take measurements, especially in the closet off the bathroom. He didn't know how much he might find. When Berry had arrived earlier that morning, the scene had already been contaminated, crucial evidence moved, and there were too many people walking through the house—both investigators and laymen.

When he came back for the second time some hours later, Berry found the closet's dimensions quite small, only five feet by six feet. He could see that Ronda's lower legs and feet would have protruded out over the sill so that the door could not possibly be closed.

He shuddered to think what evidence might have vanished already. And most of the Reynoldes' neighbors were not even questioned. Nor would they be.

*   *   *

THE SEMEN FOUND in Ronda's vaginal vault on autopsy, and in the female contraceptive in the bathroom's wastebasket, was gone, and it had apparently never been tested for blood type. Even if the last man who had been with Ronda was a non-secretor, they could have tried to find out who he was.

Dave Bell denied that he and Ronda had been intimate that last day. Ron Reynolds had seemed pleased to say that they had intercourse sometime during the night when he watched Ronda to be sure she wasn't going to kill herself. That seemed suspicious to Berry: a woman as upset as Reynolds described wasn't likely to feel romantic. It seemed more probable that she had been raped.

By someone.

While he was at the Reynoldses' house for the second time, Jerry Berry took more photographs.

"Red flags kept popping up for me," Berry recalled. "The only person who said Ronda was suicidal was her husband, Ron. He told me how he had forced himself to stay awake all night so she wouldn't kill herself. The only person who said she ever drank hard liquor was Ron. The Black Velvet bottle we found in the bedroom was empty— but he said there was enough in it earlier in the evening for two or three drinks. There were two glasses and a Pepsi can next to it."

That became a moot point; on autopsy and through lab tests, Ronda had absolutely no smell of alcohol on her breath or in her blood or urine. Who had emptied the Black Velvet bottle? Ron hadn't been tested for the percentage of alcohol or drugs in his blood.

Nor had his sons.

And then there was the curious condition of the family bathroom in the Reynolds home. When the first responders arrived in answer to Ron Reynold's 911 call, Bob Bishop, one of the deputies had noted that the walls and mirrors in the main bathroom were steamed up—as if someone had taken a shower shortly before deputies and EMTs got there. Ron's wedding ring had still rested on the edge of the sink in the master bathroom off Ron and Ronda's bedroom, and deputies had seen the pale band of skin on his third finger, left hand.

Why on earth would a man who had just found his wife dead of a gunshot wound to the head pause to take a shower? To wash away blood spatter or gunshot residue— or because he was in shock?

Gunshot residue (GSR) found on the hands, skin, or

clothing of a suspect was once considered an essential part of an investigation when someone perished by gunshot. Mystery novelists swear by it. But some forensic labs don't even bother to test for it anymore. So many other things can leave traces of gunpowder elements (barium, antimony, and lead). Even using toilet tissue can leave similar amounts.

Reynold's attorney argued that Ronda had traces of possible gunshot residue on her hand. Ron was not tested for gunshot residue. Sergeant Glade Austin said it would be useless anyway—that the court wouldn't allow the results into evidence.

Almost from the beginning, Jerry Berry felt that Ronda's death was "a staged suicide." And he worked the case with that in mind.

That did not sit well with Sheriff John McCroskey and the rest of the brass at the Lewis County Sheriff's Office.

*   *   *

THE WASHINGTON STATE PATROL'S crime lab had worked on the ballistics report of the gun and single bullet that had killed Ronda Reynolds. The gun was a .32 Rossi, Smith & Wesson long revolver, and the cartridges—five of them unfired—were .32 S&W long bullets.

Raymond Kusumi, a forensic scientist at the WSP lab, test-fired the weapon. The revolver was operational and he noted no malfunctions. The trigger pull took three and a quarter pounds for single action, and approximately eleven pounds double action. The bullet casing from the one shot fired had extractor and ejector marks that were identical to the lab-fired bullet.

There was no question that this was the gun that killed Ronda.

To fire a gun requiring considerable power to pull the trigger would have been impossible for Ronda to do considering the position in which her body was found.

And what could explain the fact that the gun had allegedly landed on Ronda's forehead rather than recoiling and tumbling down and away? Several ballistics experts would be puzzled by this as the investigation stretched out. The wound was next to Ronda's ear, but the gun's position defied the basic rules of impact and motion.

Add to that the fact that both Ronda's hands were beneath the blanket when she was found, and suicide seemed the least likely choice for the manner of her death.

While Lewis County families enjoyed the holiday season with trees and lights and presents, Jerry Berry struggled to explain to himself—if no one else—why the physical aspects of the death scene didn't line up.

Things simply could not have happened the way Ron Reynolds had explained them.

*   *   *

ONE PERSON WHO HAD shown up at Ronda's house early on the morning of December 16 was Cheryl Gilbert, forty-one. Jerry Berry had noticed that she was eager—almost overly eager—to help with the investigation. Despite whatever pain she felt at Ronda's death, she appeared to enjoy being the center of attention when anyone asked her a question.

On December 18, Berry had taped a formal interview with Cheryl.

Berry asked, "Cheryl, can you tell me what your relationship was to Ronda Reynolds?"

Cheryl answered, "We met in November of 1991 at my parents' house at a Thanksgiving dinner, and since then, we've been best friends. We—there's hardly been a day go by that we don't talk."

"When was the last time you talked to her?"

"Ten-thirty at night on Tuesday, the fifteenth. She called me at home. I saw her in person, um, between—I left her house about three-thirty in the afternoon on the fifteenth. I was there probably an hour."

Okay. During that visit, what was her demeanor? Can you tell me what you guys talked about?"

Berry had opened the floodgates, and words rushed out of Cheryl's mouth.

"She was extremely upset," Cheryl began, "and she said on the phone that, preceding my visit, she said her husband had told her that he loved her [and] loved his ex-wife, but he had chosen to go back to his ex-wife and he wanted her out. Um, we talked. I offered my home for her to come stay at and we had lived together prior, um, probably around 1991–1992 down in Elma for a while and she knew she had a place to come to at my house. Um, we discussed— she was extremely upset and she was telling me that she felt like she was in the dark, you know, just so down. And I told her I understood because previous to that, I mean seven years ago, I had gone through a divorce, and she was there to help me through that and knew I understood. I looked at her kind of sideways and she knew that I was concerned that she might do something drastic, and she looked me right in the eyes and said, 'No, I would never do that.' And we both knew that we were talking about suicide and, I mean, it was just a given that she would never do that."

Cheryl had been a reserve officer in the town of Elma and she recalled how she, Ronda, and several other female officers had made their "no suicide" pact. "Whether we saw each other yesterday or ten years ago, just give any of us a call. We would never do that. And Ronda was adamant against it."

Cheryl expanded on her earlier statement that Ronda had emptied the waterbed she and Ron had shared. That had happened when Cheryl visited on December fifteenth.

"I watched her get a hose out of the garage, and she said, 'I'm gonna empty this waterbed. I don't want his ex-wife sleeping in *my* bed!' "

The two women had proceeded to do just that.

Cheryl Gilbert was animated and dramatic. She said Ronda had asked her if she would drive her to Portland the next morning so she could fly to Spokane and a reunion with her family.

"Had she started packing yet?" Jerry Berry asked Cheryl Gilbert.

"Kind of. She was gathering things together, yeah. But she told me on the phone that night, um, she asked me to go to the school and talk to Ron and try to talk him out of it, I guess. I said, 'Well, do you want me to come over after I'm done at the school?' and she said, 'Yeah that would be fine—you can help me pack and we'll go to the airport.' "

With every question from Berry, Cheryl was becoming more important in Ronda's life—at least in her own mind. She spoke of two of Ron's younger sons, and said she had seen them in the house during her afternoon visit.

"Did she call you or did you call her—during your conversation at ten-thirty Tuesday night?"

"She'd called me [earlier] and I wasn't home. She asked my daughter if it was okay if she moved in with us and my daughter said she always had a place with us. Ronda was making plans to get a single bed and, um, get it moved up to my house 'cause I have four bedrooms and she was just gonna take the fourth bedroom. And then she called me back at ten-thirty P.M. I asked her where she was. She said she was in bed . . . she had refilled the waterbed."

Cheryl said she'd asked where Ron was, and Ronda said he was in the other room. "I assumed it was the living room 'cause that's usually where he was. They were watching two different TV shows most of the time."

Cheryl said she'd repeated her offer to pick up Ronda and take her to the Portland airport the next morning, and Ronda said she'd take her up on it.

She wasn't sure why Ronda had changed her plans to stay at her house that night. "She just left my keys up there and then went back home."

Cheryl didn't say why she hadn't mentioned that to Ronda in the ten-thirty call.

Ever the peacemaker, Cheryl said she'd taken her children to school and then swung by the elementary school in Toledo to talk to Ron. But his truck wasn't in the teachers' parking lot.

"So I headed up toward their house and I saw all the county cars, um, sitting in the driveway, and I didn't knock—I walked right in. One of the deputies was standing there and I said, 'Is Ronda here?' He just looked at me and he said, 'No.' And then Ron came around the corner . . . and he told me Ronda had shot herself."

"When was the last time you talked to Ron?" Berry asked her.

"I talked to him, um, Thursday morning, the, uh, seventeenth. He called me."

"He called you?" Berry asked, surprise in his voice. "Why did he call you? Do you know?"

"He called to find out if I had talked to her mom and grandma in Spokane, and he wanted her mom's phone number. He said he hadn't contacted them because he didn't know if they had been informed or not."

"Did he ask you any questions . . . about what the family said?"

"Yeah, I said I talked to them Wednesday night and he said, 'Are they blaming me?' and I said, 'I don't know,' which wasn't really the truth."

"Did Ron, at any time, say anything to you about his financial situation?"

"He did," Cheryl responded. "I said, 'Ron, what happened? I know that you told her yesterday morning that you wanted to go back to your ex-wife,' and he said, 'Well, that's not the whole story.' He said she [Ronda] had charged on his credit cards . . . to the tune of twenty-five thousand dollars. I can't—I mean there weren't that many new things in the house. I know thirteen hundred dollars fixed her car, and they bought a new dining room set. Other than that, she didn't—there was no new jewelry. There was not a lot of clothing. She worked at the Bon and she had to weary baggy sweaters and sweatshirts— she had a couple of the Bon Marché brand sweatshirts— but there wasn't anything elaborate that showed up at the house."

(At this juncture, no one but the collection agency knew of the $1,800 in groceries that Katie Huttula had written rubber checks to buy.)

Cheryl Gilbert said that Ron told her he was looking all over for Ronda's life insurance policy. When she told him that Virginia Ramsey would like to have Ronda's jewelry back, and also the china cabinet Virginia had given her, he said, "I'm not letting go of the jewelry until I sell it to pay off some of these bills."

Jerry Berry was about at the end of his questions. "Did

Ron Reynolds ever show any remorse to you or say anything about how much he was gonna miss her or anything?"

Cheryl shook her head. "I told him on the phone, 'She really did love you, Ron.' And he goes, 'I know that.' And when I was out at their house, as I was leaving, I hugged him, and he just said he was 'sorry,' and that was it."

"Okay. Cheryl, is there anything you can think of that I might need to be aware of?"

"Not that I can think of right now, but it just doesn't feel right. I just can't imagine Ronda killing herself."

Nor could Barb Thompson. As close as Cheryl Gilbert claimed to be to Ronda, it was her mother who knew her best. Not everything. Nobody knows everything about someone else. Not even mothers.

"No parent, whether they will admit it or not, knows her child in every explicit way," Barb Thompson allowed. "A parent knows her child in a way that only a parent can know—but only in certain areas of their lives. Their mate knows them in another area, a very special, very intimate, private way. Close friends know that person in a different—similar—way."

Barb tried to deal with the gossip that Ronda had killed herself, and with Coroner Terry Wilson's validation of that, but she could not equate the Ronda she knew with someone who would take her own life. As far back as Barb could remember, Ronda's motto had been "No fear!" Both on the job as a state cop and in her daily life, Ronda had waded in with all flags flying.

"I believe I could go on with my life if Ronda had been killed in an accident. It would have been final and I could have accepted it. I could even have accepted suicide if I knew she had chosen to take her own life, I could have accepted that. There would have been a finality to that, too.

But I needed to know the truth, and I wasn't finding it. I was finding just the opposite."

As kind as Cheryl had been to Barb Thompson during the week before Ronda's funeral, Barb was puzzled when she learned of Cheryl Gilbert's statements to Jerry Berry about Ronda's last few days. She doubted that Ronda would have asked Cheryl to intercede with Ron. "Ronda took care of her own problems," she told Berry, "and Ron didn't even like Cheryl. Why on earth would Ronda have asked Cheryl to go to his school and plead for Ronda's marriage?"

Barb Thompson returned to Spokane, but she commuted between there and Lewis County regularly, believing still that it would be only a matter of months before the truth about Ronda's death would come out.

Barb found a home with Cheryl for Tuffy, the Jack Russell terrier, but she took Jewels and Old Daisy home with her. The Rottweiler that Ronda had nursed back to health seemed inconsolable without her and paced back and forth looking for her.

"Finally, Old Daisy found one of the bags of Ronda's old clothes," Barb said, "and she pulled out one of her nightgowns and carried it back to her dog bed. After that, she could sleep."

The loss of Ronda had left so many creatures with empty places in their hearts: humans, and even dogs and horses.

CHAPTER SIXTEEN

JERRY BERRY'S WORK ENVIRONMENT became more and more difficult. He had become far from the fair-haired boy in the detective division. His superiors and the investigators he worked beside were treating him like a pariah. Nevertheless, he kept working, trying to unravel the mystery of Ronda Reynolds's death.

On February 11, 1999, Berry was driving his sheriff's car northbound on I-5 shortly before 4 P.M. when he spotted Katie Huttula just ahead of him. He touched his siren lightly, and she recognized him and pulled over. She smiled at him, and agreed readily to do an interview with him. They pulled off a safe distance from the freeway, and Berry asked if she minded if he taped their conversation.

"That's okay," she said.

"We were talking about an incident—a death investigation—involving Ronda Reynolds. Can you tell me what your relationship was to Ronda and how you knew her?"

"Before she married Ron, I was real close friends with her—had been for several years. Then she married Ron—who is my ex-husband of twenty-four years, who I have five children with. We were very close friends, and even to the time when they were married, we maintained a fairly good relationship."

"You mentioned that Ron called you on the fifteenth from school?"

"Yes."

"Do you remember the gist of that conversation?"

"Yes, sure. Over the last four months, Ron and Ronda had been having marital problems, and they evidently had been talking about a divorce for quite some time. Last summer, Ron called me and asked if I would consider reconciliation. We started having some verbal communication over the phone over the last few months about our reconciling if and when they ever were divorced. I encouraged him to try to work out his marriage—if possible."

Katie said Ron had called her from school on Tuesday, December 15, and told her Ronda was leaving him and going to Spokane and they were getting a divorce.

"He asked me if after the Christmas music concert—it was going to be over at nine or nine-thirty—if I would come to Toledo from Tumwater, where I was residing, and talk with him about possibly starting some counseling, with the possibility of reconciliation of our prior marriage and the future."

She said Ron had called her that afternoon, but he hadn't been at school then; he had been at his cardiologist's office.

"Then you called Ron back that evening of the fifteenth?"

Katie stumbled a bit over her words. She recalled getting home between ten and eleven, but she hadn't checked her message machine.

"I was negligent to do that," she said. "He had left a message that Ronda had decided to stay and for me not to come down. I'd promised the kids I'd be down, so I quick got on the phone and Ronda answered. She told me they weren't gonna get a divorce—she didn't want a divorce—so I just told her: 'Work—just work on your marriage,' and I wasn't gonna interfere, and to try to get some sleep."

Katie said that Ronda had called her back within minutes and asked her to talk to Ron. She hadn't wanted to, but Ronda had allegedly put him on the phone. Once again, she suggested her ex-husband and his new wife get some sleep, calm down, and unplug the phone. She portrayed herself as the voice of reason that last night, a person just trying to help out.

Katie said she had befriended Ronda shortly after Ronda lost a half sister to death. Ronda hadn't met her half sister until they were both adults. The sisters got along extremely well, and Ronda found her—only to lose her too soon.

"She was very despondent over that, but she wasn't suicidal at that point. She did mention suicide to me over the years that I knew her."

"Did she ever say how she would commit suicide?"

"I've been trying to think of that, but I don't recall that she ever mentioned how."

Jerry Berry asked Katie if she knew anything about life insurance policies Ronda might have had.

"Ron says he thinks there's a life insurance policy, but he doesn't know if it covers suicide because most of 'em don't."

Ron had already made a claim against Ronda's insurance, but Katie either didn't know that or was pretending she didn't know.

"Is there anything else, Katie," Berry said, "that you can think of that might help me with this investigation?"

". . . The kind of woman that Ronda was, and you know, what I loved about her was she has such dignity and grace. At the same time, she was very forceful, and I think it was a hard world for her to live in . . . dealing with people . . . I definitely saw lots of tears and crying and depression [over] her breakup with Mark and her problems with Mark. She was really down with a lot of mental depression and she did not want to take her Lithium, and she didn't like being labeled a manic-depressive, but there's lots of people that are."

That struck Jerry Berry as odd. Katie Huttula herself had been diagnosed as being bipolar, but there was absolutely no record of Ronda being manic-depressive, and he knew from the investigators' follow-up report that Ronda had never been prescribed Lithium. The woman who sat beside him in his police car and pontificated on what was wrong with Ronda seemed to be describing herself. Katie was the one with a long history of instability and drug use. If forced to choose, Berry would have thought Katie was more likely to take her own life. But here she was animatedly telling him how neurotic Ronda had been.

Now, there were two people who were vocal about Ronda's alleged penchant for suicidal thoughts: her widower and his ex-wife.

And they were living together, and had been since the day Ronda died.

*   *   *

BERRY'S FELLOW OFFICERS were taking potshots at him. Dave Neiser said, "Leave it to Jerry Berry to make this into a murder," and it was clear that that opinion was shared by others.

"I was butting heads with them, and I found myself working in a more and more hostile environment," Berry recalled. "You don't do that in Lewis County. You follow orders and go along with the program."

He couldn't do that.

On May 26, 1999, Berry's sergeant, Glade Austin, representing the sheriff's office, distributed a message to the department that he was officially closing the case of Ronda Reynolds's death, declaring it a suicide. Sheriff John McCroskey's force wasn't interested in Berry's theories on the case. It was over; it was suicide and that was that.

According to Austin, anyone who read through the case file, looked at the photographs, and based his opinion on the totality of the information available would agree that Ronda Reynolds's death was probably a suicide.

The detective sergeant also stated that Rod Englert, a former Multnomah County, Oregon, homicide detective and one of America's top half-dozen blood-spatter experts, had concurred.

(In truth, Englert a longtime friend of mine, instructed him to go back and re-create the crime scene, and deduce what they could from that. He did not do an in-depth study of the Reynolds's case. When I mentioned the case to him, he said he had not "concurred" with Sergeant Austin, and that he had been told nothing of the circumstantial evidence surrounding Ronda Reynolds's death.)

Glade Austin had been with the Lewis County Sheriff's Office for twenty-seven years. He had viewed Ronda's death as a suicide from day one.

Two days later, Jerry Berry sent his own message:

> As the primary investigating officer, I do not agree
> with this conclusion and at this time, I still do not be-
> lieve this was a suicide. I base my opinion on the fact
> that those who reviewed the case have only looked at
> the photographs and the case report. They have not
> had close contact with the suspect in this case, nor have
> any of them been directly involved in this investigation.
> There remains an incredible amount of inconsistencies
> and circumstantial evidence that I feel make it impos-
> sible to rule this case a suicide at this time.
>
> Therefore the best I can do is express my concern
> and opinion that this case should not be closed—but
> suspended.

Jerry Berry continued to work from his own notes, so
he was unaware that much of the evidence in the Reynolds
case had been either returned or destroyed. He assumed it
was still being held safely in an evidence locker in the sheriff's office on the off chance that new information would
come in.

He had taken a number of photographs inside the Twin
Peaks Drive house during the first few days after Ronda's
death. He believed they were all in the Reynolds file at the
Lewis County Sheriff's Office, and he counted on using them
in his investigation.

Jerry Berry's conclusion that Ronda's case should not
be closed was filed away and no one acted on it. Its official
status in the spring of 1999 was "Case Closed," and not
"Case Suspended."

Since the sheriff's office considered the Reynolds's case
to be over, they acceded to Barb Thompson's requests under

the Public Information Act for copies of their probe. Could she read it and understand it without any background in criminal investigations? Case files connected to unexpected deaths—no matter if they are murder, suicide, accidental, or natural—can be thick and unwieldy. They are also full of codes, abbreviations, medical conclusions, and the results of various tests. Barb tackled it, making it a point to look up anything she didn't grasp.

"This would not preclude the case being reopened," Glade Austin wrote, giving Barb Thompson a small sliver of hope: "If significant information should come before us at a later date, indicating otherwise."

But Sheriff John McCroskey pointed out in a written statement, "The case remains unsolved because there is no conclusive piece of evidence or information that points in one direction to the exclusion of all others. It is possible the case could remain unsolved and open indefinitely."

Jerry Berry saw no problem with that. All he was asking for was to have the investigation marked "Suspended—Inconclusive." He had been loyal to the Lewis County Sheriff's Office for years, and he wanted to continue that allegiance. There was no tearing hurry to close the case; they weren't in a race or trying to set a closure record on cases. They were looking for the truth, and that could take time.

He feared that the case would never be resurrected, despite what Sheriff McCroskey had said. The passage of time would only put it deeper in dusty files. Barb Thompson showed Berry the photographs of the "crime scene" that Lewis County detectives had given to her. He looked, did a double take, and looked again.

"My God, Barbara!" he burst out. "Most of these aren't the crime scene photos. These were taken two years later!"

He ran his finger down the evidence listed on the case file

copy that Barb Thompson had and found numerous codes that meant documents had been "returned" or "destroyed."

"Wow," he breathed in exasperation. "They destroyed all this evidence. They'll never make an arrest now."

* * *

IN JANUARY 2001, when the frustrated detective became too insistent about reopening the investigation of Ronda's death, Jerry Berry was reassigned to patrol. Being sent back out on patrol was a step down for Berry. The sheriff said this was "standard procedure," and all deputies and detectives were rotated regularly. But going from a detective to a deputy who patrolled Lewis County out in the countryside felt like a slap in the face to Berry.

And it proved to be more physically dangerous than working out of the detective division. Although it hurt at the time, Berry found one of the few light spots in his profession when he returned to patrol. "I got spurred by an angry rooster while I was handcuffing a suspect," he recalled with a chuckle. "It would have been better to get a dog bite, I guess, because that rooster didn't want to let go of me!"

Berry worked all his official shifts on patrol, but he kept investigating Ronda Reynolds's death in his spare time, adding to the long list of events that simply did not jibe with the county's position of death by suicide.

Perhaps Jerry Berry's most unforgivable mistake happened when he went to Chief Criminal Deputy Joe Doench and asked that the Reynolds file be sent to famed homicide detective Vernon Geberth for evaluation and possible suggestions. Doench had initially felt that there were some things that didn't line up in Ronda's death, and he agreed to send the file to Geberth.

Geberth, whose book *Practical Homicide Investigation: Tactics, Procedures and Forensic Techniques* is one of of the bibles detectives turn to, is retired as the commander of the Bronx Homicide Division of the New York Police Department. He has participated in over eight thousand homicide probes, and he currently teaches classes to detectives all over the country. Apparently he became the first expert consultant to review the entire Reynolds file.

Jerry Berry had once taken a course taught by Geberth and been impressed. He felt that if anyone outside his department could shed new light on the Reynolds case, it would be Vernon Geberth. While Geberth is considered one of the most skilled and experienced experts on homicide in America, he says exactly what thinks, and he is not particularly known for his tact.

Geberth gave his opinion on what he saw as a flawed investigation, and his report was scathing. He called the Lewis County Sheriff's Office's handling of Ronda's death "a major police malfeasance. There are very few cases [where] I can state with such strength and conviction that 'This was a homicide.' "

"In my professional opinion," Geberth wrote, "Deceased [Ronda Reynolds] was a victim of a homicide. She did not commit suicide as reported by her husband. Deceased did not fit any 'Suicide Profile' that I'm familiar with. In fact, only her husband contends that she committed suicide. Everyone else who was interviewed stated emphatically that this could not be the case. Those who were close to Deceased are adamant that she was not suicidal, loved life, and would never consider killing herself.

"She had made both short and long term plans. The evening before her death, she had made airline reservations. Her best friend and former boyfriend, a sergeant in the Des

Moines, Washington Police Department, had helped her pack her belongings . . . Later that evening, she had called him around midnight. She seemed calm and had a definite plan of action, which was for him to pick her up and bring her to the airport.

"The facts and circumstances of her death are highly suspicious and not consistent with suicide cases the consultant has reviewed. There were many inconsistent statements made by her husband that the police were not able to pursue. Furthermore, his total lack of concern and remorse throughout this investigation are troublesome and raise the level of suspicion as to his involvement in his wife's death."

Geberth softened that opinion just a little when he said it was not uncommon for law enforcement agencies to "short change" investigations of apparent suicides.

Geberth also wrote, "He [Berry] is a good man who put his career on the line to do the right thing. He did an excellent job."

The New York homicide expert's report infuriated the Lewis County detectives. Joe Doench exploded: "He made us look like Keystone Kops."

As a result of Geberth's negative and humiliating report on their procedures followed—and not followed—as they worked Ronda Reynolds's case, Doench, with Sheriff McCroskey's approval, forbade Jerry Berry to work on the Reynolds case—even in his spare time. "Furthermore," the edict went on. "if anyone in the department mentions it, you are to come to me immediately!"

From that point on, every report Berry filed was criticized. He was sent to "counseling."

"I went from being a stellar employee to one who couldn't do anything right," Berry said grimly. "One day in December 2001, I just came in and quit . . ."

Jerry Berry had taken all the derision and harassment he could. But just because he handed in his badge didn't mean he was quitting his search for the answers about what had *really* happened to Ronda on the night of December 16 three years before. He assured Barb Thompson he would continue. He would take yet another look at every facet of Ronda's death and find the so-far indefinable elements that eluded them.

Barb Thompson and Jerry Berry had long since become friends, and they worked together to create a wedge that would force the sheriff's office to re-open the probe. Jerry and his wife Susan had become two of Barb's strongest supporters. They believed that she was absolutely correct as she continued her fight to get the bleak word "suicide" off Ronda's death certificate.

Jerry Berry kept his promise to Barb that he would not charge her even a penny for his private detective work. She was grateful, but she wondered how Jerry could do that. He no longer had a job—although his wife, Susan, did. He told her he would be obtaining his private investigator's license and pick up whatever jobs he could.

"But I don't want you to worry about that," Jerry said gently. "I'll manage and I'm not going to let go of justice for Ronda."

CHAPTER SEVENTEEN

JERRY BERRY STARTED BACK at the beginning of the case, marking every thing that struck him as odd. He was still unaware how much of the evidence and some photos had vanished from the major case file in the sheriff's office. He interviewed witnesses and backtracked on his own investigations.

In the first six months after Ronda died of a gunshot wound to her head, Berry had written down all the inconsistencies he had noted in witnesses' and survivors' actions. Looking at it again—as he had done frequently over the years—he could not fathom why the case had been closed.

Was no prosecuting attorney willing to bring charges? It was true that come election time, prosecutors relied on their winning cases, and a chancy case could lower their percentages. But if someone had the guts to take this one on—and win—Ronda's case could make his or her career.

Berry came up with twenty-one questions:

1. When Mr. Reynolds was asked at the scene if his wife was left-handed or right-handed, he didn't know. It would be reasonable to assume that a person would know if their mate was right- or left-handed. Likely a left-handed person would place the weapon in the victim's left hand, a subconscious act possibly explaining Mr. Reynolds's reaction when he was asked this question.

2. Mr. Reynolds stated that there had been about two shots of liquor in the Black Velvet bottle and that Ronda had consumed it during the night. The toxicology report indicates there was *no alcohol* in her system.

3. If Mr. Reynolds tried to talk Ronda out of committing suicide for 45 minutes on the cell phone, why did he choose to stop, eat, and then go to a school play before going home? Certainly not consistent with a husband worried about the welfare of his wife.

4. Mr. Reynolds stated that he went to bed with Ronda at 10 P.M. and never let her out of his sight until he fell asleep at 5 A.M. Witness statements and phone records show that Ronda was in the bedroom alone and talking to friends until about 12:45 A.M. Ronda allegedly told a friend that Ron was in the other room. This was partially confirmed by his youngest child.

5. Mr. Reynolds stated that the closet door was closed when he opened it and found Ronda. We know that due to the position of the body that this could not be true. The door was open and could not be closed due to the lower portion of her body and

legs being in the way. This can still be clearly seen in the photographs.

6. Ronda was covered with an electric blanket with *both* hands underneath, yet the gun was on the outside of the blanket and appeared to have been pushed into her left hand. That is—the blanket was between her skin and the gun.

7. There was fixed lividity, which usually takes eight to twelve hours.

8. There was pronounced rigor mortis, more than normally expected for a body that had been down for such a short period of time. (5 A.M. to 6 A.M. We acknowledge that the electric blanket may have affected the postmortem changes to some degree.)

9. Medical experts tell us that (brain) death was instant and no movement would have occurred, thus indicating that even if she had shot herself, there would have been no conscious movement to get her hands back under the blanket.

10. Ronda's hair was pushed upward as it would be if someone examined the wound.

11. Ronda had a damaged fingernail, indicative of a struggle.

12. The message on the bathroom mirror was inconsistent with a suicide note. It simply said the victim loved Mr. Reynolds and she wanted him to call her at her grandmother's house in Spokane.

13. It took almost a half hour for Mr. Reynolds to call 9-1-1, after he awoke at 6 A.M. (Not a very rapid response.)

14. Mr. Reynolds stated that he had checked for a

pulse behind Ronda's ear with his fingers, yet the blood pattern behind her ear showed no signs of interruption or disturbance.

15. Witnesses' and his own statements indicate Mr. Reynolds is a very light sleeper—yet he didn't hear the gunshot less than twelve feet away.

16. A gunshot residue test on Ronda's hands could not determine conclusively that the gun had been in her hands.

17. There were no prints on the gun.

18. The three boys did not see Dave Bell hand Ronda a gun. Ronda gave the gun to Bell, which he unloaded and placed in a location indicated by Ronda—a location where Mr. Reynolds routinely kept the gun.

19. I checked the drawer beneath the waterbed where Dave Bell placed the gun. Due to the difficulty of getting to that drawer under Mr. Reynolds's side of the bed, I don't believe she could have removed the gun without waking him up.

20. I was never able to locate the "brown holster" the gun was reported to have been in.

21. The very evident lack of remorse during his call to 911, and during the investigation, makes Mr. Reynolds suspect.

All twenty-one red flags were as true in 2001 as they were in December 1998, and Berry had other questions he didn't note.

But he would as the months and years passed.

PART FIVE

Life Goes On

in Lewis County

Chapter Eighteen

RON REYNOLDS DIDN'T LIVE with his ex-wife Katie for good. Although she moved into the Twin Peaks Drive house only hours after Ronda died there, he seemed to consider her an interim person—someone who would care for their younger boys and do the housework. Katie stayed through May 1999, but they couldn't revive their marriage.

Ron had become a hot commodity on the market in a small town—a widower, tall, and not bad to look at, and who earned close to $60,000 a year as a school principal. Any suspicions that he hadn't told the whole truth about Ronda's death were soft-pedaled in the community. He was much beloved by the students in his school, who found him funny and appreciated that he knew all their names—even long after they moved on to high school and beyond.

Many people felt sorry for him in the tragic loss of his bride.

One of the women in town who was attracted to Ron

was Blair Connery*. Her younger son attended Toledo Elementary School and spoke highly of "Mr. Reynolds." Recently divorced and raising two boys on her own, Blair attended most school functions, including sports events. In the fall of 1999, about nine months after Ronda died, Blair noticed Ron Reynolds standing alone at the sidelines of a football game. "I went up to him and introduced myself," she remembers. "I acted on impulse."

If opposites attract, they did. Blair is a striking woman, full-bosomed with masses of blond hair, sparkling eyes, and a lively sense of humor. She chatted with Reynolds for a short time, explaining that her son was one of his students.

"I didn't expect anything from that meeting," she says, "but he called me up a few days later and asked me for a date. I said 'Yes,' and that was the beginning of my almost three years with him."

Blair believed completely in Ron's innocence regarding Ronda's suspicious death, and she felt sorry for his boys—Jonathan, David, and Josh—who had been left virtually without a mother. Their birth mother, Katie Huttula, loved all her five sons devotedly, but events in her scattered life often made it impossible for her to care for them. Sometimes she would disappear and no one knew where she was. Blair knew she hadn't been living with Ron and the boys for several months.

If her family knew where Katie was, they weren't telling anyone.

Blair vowed to step in and make it easier for both Ron and his three younger boys. She knew he had two older sons, and at least one ex-wife in his past, but he seemed somehow lost. She even had visions of their respective sons becoming close friends. At first, that seemed possible as the boys were all close in age.

"We did all the family things together," Blair recalled. "There were events at school, holidays, sports—where it was good to have a father figure and at least a substitute mom. It wasn't long before I found myself falling in love with Ron."

When Blair began spending time at Ron's house, she confirmed that Katie Huttula Reynolds had moved out—but she had left many of her possessions there, as if she might move back in at any moment.

That didn't bother Blair, especially as the months passed and there was no sign of Katie. Blair had always felt Ron was honest with her. He'd told her on their very first date that he "couldn't make love," and as it worked with Ronda—although Blair knew nothing of that—it was akin to throwing down the gauntlet. She figured he had been through such a traumatic period that his impotency was to be expected.

Blair was happy when she was able to make him feel secure enough to succeed in bed. She took it as a personal accomplishment and a sign that he trusted her as much as she believed in him. Indeed, they had intercourse every day, although Blair was disappointed to find he was a selfish lover who seemed to lack concern for her needs. Maybe he just didn't know any better. Their lovemaking was over almost before it began, and he rolled over and went to sleep.

But sex wasn't the most important thing in the world, and they settled into a comfortable relationship over Christmas, 1999. Blair had a good job and some family money, and she went all out buying presents for Ron and his boys. He now spent two or three nights a week at her house. She bought bunk beds so that Josh, his youngest boy, could stay over, too. And she was at the Twin Peaks Drive house every weekend, looking after them all.

"I did Ron's ironing for him," she said with a rueful expression. "And then I cooked dinner for him. I made enough so they could freeze it and have it later in the week. I even bought the groceries. I felt so sorry for those three boys. I did everything I could for them—cooking, cleaning, laundry, pulling weeds, introducing Ron to my friends, and his sons to my own boys."

Somehow, though, Ron and Blair's sons never formed much of a connection; their interests were completely different. Ron had virtually no close friends, and the only people he and Blair visited were Ron's mother, Laura, and her boyfriend, Tom Reed. Laura Reynolds adored her only son and believed everything he told her. He had a way of explaining things that made more sense to her than the rumors that rumbled around Lewis County.

While Laura doted on Ron, Blair sensed that Tom Reed wasn't initially very supportive of him. Sometimes she caught him studying Ron with a strange look on his face. On one occasion when they were alone, Tom asked Blair if she thought Ron had "done it," inferring that he might actually have shot Ronda.

Blair shook her head and answered. *"No!"*

She was shocked that Tom would even ask such a question.

Because she was obviously a woman with a giving nature, it took months before Blair began to realize that she had become more of a convenience than a lover. She was a very handy—and unpaid—housekeeper. Ron took it for granted that she would make his house run smoothly, just as she did her own.

When the glow of Christmas wore off in January 2000, so did Ron's passion for her. It was like switching off a light.

"He turned completely cold," she recalled, mystified

that he could change so quickly. Still, she wanted to keep believing he was an innocent man, and she brushed aside her doubts. He was troubled, and had so much on his mind. And he wasn't well. He saw a cardiologist regularly, and took Coumadin to thin his blood and avoid clots.

Once, he jumped off the tailgate of his pickup truck and cut his leg, and he began to bleed heavily. Blair was there and managed to stop the bleeding with a tourniquet until he was stitched up. She was a woman for all seasons.

Her sons came first with Blair, and Ron's method of child-raising disturbed her. Ron left his two older teenage sons alone when he stayed at her house, and they were allowed to watch pornographic movies whenever they wanted; their rooms were stacked with sex magazines. They gravitated to grunge music, and she sometimes suspected they were into drugs, but Ron didn't seem concerned. She wondered if she coddled her boys, but she needed to be sure they were safe and that drugs and alcohol and seamy sex didn't affect them. Lewis County had its problems with drugs like methamphetamines, so she had always been extra cautious.

One night, Blair and Jonathan Reynolds, who was about nineteen, were in the kitchen alone. There was a sudden lull in their conversation, and uncomfortable moment when neither had anything much to say. Jonathan lifted his head and stared straight into her eyes.

Then he said, *"I did not kill Ronda!"*

She felt a chill run through her body when she heard that. She hadn't even suggested that he had, or started a conversation with him about his late stepmother. She had long known that both Jonathan and David were fascinated with death. David was more overt about it. He spoke of death and of killing animals a lot. She was particularly disturbed when she saw David's room. He had saved the yellow police tape left behind after the sheriff's investigation into Ronda's death, and he draped it all over his room.

"I wondered how he could do that," Blair said. "It had to remind him of what happened to Ronda."

There was no question that the boys were brilliant—just as Ron and Katie were. They got A's in school without really trying, and had inherited much of Katie's exceptional musical talent.

Blair had heard the stories about how much Jonathan and David hated Ronda. One of the boys was the only person present when Ronda's beloved Rottweiler, Duchess, died suddenly at the age of seven. Ronda had evidently been worried whenever her dogs were alone with Ron's sons. When one of her Rottweilers was just a puppy, Jonathan had kicked it across the kitchen.

Blair knew that when Duchess died, Ronda called her mother and said Ron told her that Duchess had died of heatstroke, but when Ronda got home, she could tell Duchess had been viciously beaten. Not long after, Ronda's German shepherd disappeared. Barb asked if Ron's sons had "killed him, too?" but Ronda avoided answering. She didn't want "trouble."

"I even heard that one of the boys threatened to kill Ronda," Blair said, long after she had left Ron. "They just didn't like her bossing them . . ."

Blair hadn't known Ronda, and, at some point Blair Connery realized how little she knew about Ron himself, despite all the time she spent with him. "He never showed emotion," she said. "He never got really happy or angry. The most emotion I ever saw was when he was jealous of an old boyfriend of mine who was dying of cancer. He didn't want me to maintain a friendship with him. He was jealous—which was ridiculous."

But most of all, Ron never talked about his childhood. "He preferred to let the past take care of itself," Blair said.

"You could tell there was a secret in that house," Blair commented, "but I never found out what it was."

*   *   *

PERHAPS THERE WERE SECRETS in Ron's parents' household, too. When Laura Reynolds gave birth at the age of thirty to their third child on May 30, 1951, Ron was his parents' first boy. He was two and a half months premature and weighed around three pounds. They told stories of having to put him in a warmed oven to keep his body temperature up. This was the son Laura and Leslie had hoped for, someone to carry on the family name. But he was so tiny that he wasn't expected to live. They vowed that he would.

Baby Ronnie was coddled and protected, and he did, of course, live. But he grew up very spoiled because he seldom heard the word *no*. His parents gave him everything he asked for. He wanted a pony when he was four, and he got one—but his older sister Judy ended up taking care of it. A few years later, it was the same scenario with a horse. Ron lost interest in the things he wanted so rapidly, and he hated chores or responsibility.

"He really never cared about pets," Judy recalled.

Judy, five and a half years older than Ronnie, did most of the outside work at their McCleary home that a son might be expected to do. She didn't mind; she hated housework, and she much preferred carrying in firewood to doing dishes or making beds.

Leslie Reynolds was not a wealthy man. Far from it. He was a millwright for the Simpson Lumber Company in McCleary, and always on call if any of the machines there broke down. But he provided well for his family, possibly because he was a natural-born workaholic. Sometimes it seemed as if he spent more time at the lumber mill than he did at home.

The Reynolds family participated in very few family-oriented activities, mostly because Leslie was always working. Laura Church Reynolds came from a well-known family in Lewis County. She had nine sisters and almost all of them had at least three children. Holidays could have been happy and riotous occasions, but Ron shut his cousins out. When they visited his house, they weren't allowed to play with any of his toys, although on the rare occasions he went to their houses, he played with theirs.

Decades later, they remember that Ronnie was a tattletale. If they didn't want to play what he chose, he ran to his mother to complain. And he usually got his way.

As a boy, Ronnie asked for a lock on the door to his bedroom. None of his cousins or friends were allowed to go in there after that.

It wasn't long before he was unanimously disliked by all the cousins in the family, many of whom who say he is still selfish, inconsiderate, manipulative, and has no interest in other people's feelings.

"One thing," his cousin Julie Colbert said. "He is all about the buck. There was a time when I was eighteen and we drove to Arizona—and took Ronnie along. Somewhere along the way, we stopped in a place that had slot machines. Ronnie was putting quarters into it, but he didn't win anything, and he quit. I walked by it on my way to the ladies' room, and put in a quarter, and I hit the jackpot. All those quarters came pouring out."

Ronnie had been furious, and he sulked. She offered him

half the money she had won, but he refused. He thought he deserved it all.

"That was Ronnie," she sighed. "He never had any empathy or any caring about anyone else."

At some point, his cousins and siblings simply shut him out of their lives, and they no longer considered him a relative—or even a friend.

He didn't mind.

Judy always struggled with her weight, and Ron teased her, calling her "Fatty," and worse names, and it hurt her feelings.

As soon as they were able to, Judy and Phyllis had to work to buy their own clothes, but Ron didn't. Judy recalled a time when Ron wanted a jacket that cost a hundred dollars. "My parents bought it for him," she said. "But we girls got nothing unless we earned the money ourselves."

Sister Phyllis was six years Judy's senior and almost a dozen years older than Ron. She married young and moved to South Carolina, and after that, she had little personal interaction with her family in McCleary, Washington.

Ron's sister, Judy, married Larry Semanko—who would serve twenty years with the Lewis County Sheriff's Office and four years as a deputy coroner under Terry Wilson. They were both quite young, but their marriage was a very happy union, destined to last. The Semankos were often asked to "babysit" with Ronnie, as his parents didn't like to leave him alone. Sitting with her little brother was usually a harrowing experience, because Judy's parents forbade them to discipline him.

There were times when the Semankos couldn't resist because Ronnie was incorrigible. One time he kicked Judy with his cowboy boots and left purple bruises but the elder

Reynoldses were angry with her—not their precious Ronnie. Judy couldn't even get a word in to tell her parents what Ronnie had done.

When Larry once gave Ronnie a very light spanking, he tattled to his mother about it and both Leslie and Laura were furious.

Still apprehensive because they had almost lost their only son at birth, the Reynolds never really got over worrying about him. They continued to give him everything he asked for, even though he grew to be a robust boy with no sign that hinted at his premature arrival.

It was generally accepted that Ron had an intensely acquisitive nature, even as a child. He wanted things and money and he got them. When he was in high school in Elma, Washington, he and his best friend got drunk, Ron missed a turn, went off the road, and wrecked the car his parents had recently bought him. It wasn't new—but it had been in very good shape.

Leslie and Laura Reynolds simply could not accept that their son might possibly have been intoxicated enough to cause an accident, so they were all too anxious to believe the lies he told them. He said emphatically that he never drove if he had had anything to drink. For that matter, he assured them that he just didn't drink. Period. They trusted him and Ron got another car right away. This time his mother had a protective "cage" installed in case he ever had another accident.

Other students at Elma High called him "Roll-Bar Ron" after that.

Ron was highly intelligent, and he always got good grades. He had his share of friends in the Class of 1969 of Elma High School, although he was never a jock. Academically, he was in the top ten of his class at graduation. His parents were extremely proud of him. They focused their lives around their son.

In the 1960s, the Elma High Eagles were tightly knit, and they would remain so. For their fortieth reunion in August 2009, more than a hundred graduates showed up.

Ron met Catherine Huttula in high school, and they went to the same church youth group together, but no one is sure if they dated. He was dating Donna Daniels, and Katie was far more sought after than Ron was.

"Katie was very, very popular," a man who went to high school with her remembers. "She was a cheerleader, and very attractive to the boys. She was always a class officer."

Ron appeared in the senior high play *He Thinks He's a Rabbit*. Some of his fellow students knew that Ron had a wild side, but one boy said, "I always thought of Ron Reynolds as white-bread and pure."

Even then, he had a chameleon-like personality. He could be anything he perceived someone wanted him to be—if he wanted something from them. Otherwise, he ignored them.

Ron married very young, shortly after he graduated from high school. His first wife was Donna Daniels, who was a devout Christian, and very naïve. Many of her classmates recall Donna as "the sweetest girl in the world."

The newlyweds moved to Pullman, Washington, to attend college at Washington State University. The baby Donna conceived died in utero, and their marriage didn't last long. Often Ron Reynolds doesn't even list Donna as one of his wives. She has been happily married for decades and has a son and a daughter with her second husband.

Many people believe that Catherine Huttula was Ron

Reynolds's first wife, and the only wife he had before he met Ronda Liburdi, but that isn't true.

Both Catherine and Ron dabbled in drugs in their college years, but she was the one who got hooked. According to relatives, schoolmates, and friends, Katie's affair with both illegal and prescription drugs would continue off and on for the next forty years.

There had been halcyon years for both Katie and Ron and the other elementary school kids in McCleary and Elma. The children belonged to everyone in the two small towns, ran free, and seemed to have nothing to fear. Katie and her siblings and friends played kick-the-can, hopscotch, and even enjoyed hide-and-seek in the morgue of the local funeral home.

Catherine and a fellow Elma High graduate attended nursing school in Arizona immediately after high school. Katie's problems with drugs grew worse there and she was asked to leave college.

The Huttula family was well-to-do, and owned a pharmacy in Elma, but their family had suffered—and would suffer in the future—a number of tragedies. Mrs. Huttula bore five children; there were three older siblings: Carl, Janice, and Catherine, and two younger—Tom and Mary. Carl died in Vietnam in 1967 when he was a door gunner on a helicopter. The aircraft was hovering over wounded soldiers they had gone in to medevac when Carl was shot and killed. One classmate who was in Carl's unit remembers that the entire helicopter exploded in midair. Carl was buried in a closed coffin from the funeral home whose morgue he once scampered around.

He hadn't wanted to go to Vietnam. One of his friends recalls finding Carl crawling in the snow, dead drunk, a few days before his unit was set to leave. He was trying to get across the street to the Huttulas' house.

"He wasn't making any headway, so I took him in my house and sobered him up before I took him home," his friend said.

Catherine was sixteen, two years younger than Carl, and she had been especially close to her brother. His death devastated her. Although she maintained a bubbly façade, some who knew her say that she was never the same after Carl died.

Janice became a schoolteacher, but never married, and Katie eventually became a registered nurse. But she lost her job at at least one hospital when drugs were found missing from locked cabinets. Tom Huttula would one day take over the family pharmacy but he was forced to bar Katie from coming in the store after the count of drugs and other items didn't tally with the amount delivered to the drugstore.

Mary suffered from bipolar disorder and committed suicide in the fall of 2004. She may have been living with Katie at the time, although opinions vary on that.

Mrs. Huttula was often ill, with headaches and vague complaints, and Katie's school friends were used to seeing her lying on the couch, sometimes waiting for meds from the family pharmacy. That was one image Catherine's friends had of her mother.

"When I think of it," she said, "Catherine was a lot like her mother. She was always complaining of sickness, too. Her father was a sweet, wonderful man, though."

Other memories of Katie's mother weren't very positive. Mrs. Huttula taught "nurse's aid" classes at Elma High School, and many of her students found her "mean." One girl—who happened to be related to Ron Reynolds in the vast network of cousins on his mother's side—became pregnant and desperately tried to hide it.

"Mrs. Huttula told the whole class about it, and I was so embarrassed," the woman said forty years later. "She brought it up several times—using it as a kind of 'teaching aid' on what happened to girls who weren't virgins. Finally, I told the principal and she stopped."

*   *   *

JUDY SEMANKO WAS aware that although her parents had been married over thirty years, her mother wasn't really happy. Laura never complained, but Judy sensed that her father loved her mother far more than she loved him. They never fought, and their three children weren't subject to harsh words, but Judy knew. Even so, she expected them to stay together.

After Ron Reynolds's divorce from Donna Daniels, Catherine Huttula hooked up with him at Washington State University. Although they hadn't really dated at Elma High, suddenly it was almost as if they wore magnets that kept pulling them together.

Ron earned his bachelor's degree at WSU in education, and years later got his master's degree, which made him eligible to be a school principal.

Ron's college grades were even better than those he'd earned at Elma High School. He explained his technique to friends. He would "think ahead" on any given chapter, read the summary of that chapter, and then write down what he thought questions on a test would probably be. Then he would search for the answers in the chapter itself. It saved him a lot of reading and improved his grades at WSU.

Although she didn't seem to be ideal wife material, Ron married Katie Huttula and fathered five sons: Simeon, Micah, Jonathan, David, and Joshua. They had biblical names, possibly because Ron and Katie had become deeply involved in the Jehovah's Witnesses.

"My brother forbade his sons to play with our children for fifteen years," Judy Semanko said. "There were all these cousins in our extended family, but Ron considered them—and us—'heathens' after he joined Jehovah's Witnesses."

Shortly after Ron graduated from college, Leslie and Laura Reynolds got a divorce. Although she knew they weren't happy together, it was a shock for Judy and it hurt a lot to see her family break up. She vowed to remain close to both of them.

Neither ever married again, although at eighty-nine, Laura has lived with Tom Reed for thirty-one years. Tom is a kind man who would like to be friendly with everyone.

Ron's father later moved to a house adjacent to his own.

As Blair Connery suspected, there were some secrets in Ron's childhood home, but mostly they came from the effort it took to maintain the image of a perfect family. Ron's parents were far happier apart than they had ever been together. Nevertheless, he remained their shining child, their brilliant son, and they both believed in him. Even Tom Reed—after his early doubts—had come to believe that Ron was incapable of doing anything immoral or illegal. He now considered Ron his best friend.

The longer they were together, the more Blair Connery began to wonder if some of the rumors about Ron's possible part in Ronda's sudden death could possibly be true. Still, that wasn't why she thought about breaking up with him; she simply grew weary with caring for what were, essentially, two households and two families. And the flatness of Ron's emotions made it impossible for her to break through the invisible wall that surrounded him.

CHAPTER NINETEEN

LESLIE REYNOLDS'S HEALTH declined in the mid-1990s. Ron and Katie convinced him that he shouldn't be living alone in his house next door to theirs. What their reasoning was is obscure; his house was far more comfortable than the used camping trailer they bought and put behind their house. They moved the elderly man into that. Katie promised to cook for him and do his laundry, and assured him that she and Ron would look after him. They would also see to paying his bills so he wouldn't have to worry about that. Nearly eighty, Leslie Reynolds had cancer and the early signs of Alzheimer's disease.

He turned his assets over to Ron, his trusted son.

His daughter Phyllis was in South Carolina and Judy was sixty-five miles away; she tried to keep in touch with her father, but Ron didn't encourage it. He was concerned that she might try to go after their father's money. That was the furthest thing from her mind. She just wanted to be sure her dad was doing okay.

The camping trailer was cramped. It had bunks because there was no room for a comfortable bed. Leslie couldn't cook anything hot for himself, and he was lonely in the camper. Leslie told Judy that he had been told he wasn't allowed to go into Katie and Ron's house.

Leslie Reynolds had given Ron money for all of his life. He wasn't poor; he had a pension, Social Security, and savings. He'd even given Ron money for lawyers in a custody hearing.

Judy Semanko found out how bad it was for her dad when one of her aunts—Edna Arnot, who worked for the county, checking on senior citizens—called her. She had visited Leslie and found there were no groceries in his cupboards, and nothing at all in the refrigerator.

"Buy him what he needs," Judy said. "I'm sending you money right now, and I'm heading over there."

When Judy got to McCleary, she found her father terribly thin and barely able to walk. She told Ron she wanted to take him home with her for a visit, but her brother said the doctor felt that wouldn't be a good idea.

Katie Huttula Reynolds was an unlikely caretaker. She continued to be addicted to all manner of drugs—from prescriptions to crystal meth to marijuana. Indeed, her drug use was usually the first thing people mentioned when they attempted to describe her. She didn't stop using—not even when she was pregnant with some of her sons. Her friends and relatives had long since learned to hide their prescriptions, since almost all of them had found pills and capsules missing after visits from Katie.

Judy saw that Katie hadn't been taking care of her father. At the very least, Leslie Reynolds was undernourished.

Once Leslie called Judy in desperation. "Katie told me that I don't have any money left," he said. "She says I'll have to go into a home—"

"You have money, Dad," she told him. "Don't worry. I'll straighten it out." And she did. He had money, but not nearly as much as he had had before he was moved into Ron's travel trailer.

Judy finally managed to take Leslie to his doctor, but not before she bought some decent clothes for him. Everything he had was old and threadbare. She asked Ron for three hundred dollars to buy shoes, shirts, and trousers for the old man, but Ron insisted on taking him shopping and buying the clothes himself.

At this point, Leslie Reynolds could no longer walk. He was clearly afraid of angering Katie. One of his arms was bruised, and the bicep hung below his upper arm where it had been torn. Someone—Judy never determined who—had appeared to have grabbed him roughly.

Judy was prepared to prove to the doctor that her father should be able to go home with her for a long visit. She was concerned about his health and nutrition, and she had discovered that neither Ron nor Katie was doling out his medications to him in the proper quantity and at the right time.

"They just gave him the bottles and let him figure out when to take them. He's taking way too many at a time," she told the doctor.

She was shocked when her dad's physician said there was no reason she couldn't take her father to her house, and that that might be a good idea.

At Judy and Larry Semanko's house, Leslie Reynolds grew much better physically—but his Alzheimer's symptoms remained. He forgot things, and grew confused easily.

On his birthday, he was relaxing in a recliner after dinner when he kept asking the same question: "How old am I?"

Finally Judy said, "Dad—today you will be eighty!"

"Damn! I'm old!"

And they all laughed. It was one of the few humorous moments they'd shared since her father began to decline. With Judy and Larry, Leslie continued to improve enough to move back with Ron.

When Ron married Ronda, life at home in McCleary was much better for the old man. She cooked Leslie good meals and took care of him. But he was ill—both from the Alzheimer's and cancer—and it became clear that he needed to be in some kind of assisted-living facility. Judy found a comfortable nursing home for him, but the staff called her a week later and told her they could not care for him; his needs were too great.

And then Judy couldn't find her father at all. Ron had moved him out of the nursing home, but she had no idea where he'd taken the old man. She finally found him in a hospital annex in Centralia. Shortly thereafter, he was taken to a hospital in Olympia, where he died in May 1998.

Ron inherited his father's house and assets. His divorce from Katie had cost him dearly, and he felt all of his father's possessions should go to him. Neither of his sisters fought him for his dad's house and car and now much-diminished savings. He gave the car to either Jonathan or Micah.

*   *   *

BY THE FIRST YEARS of the millennium, Blair slowly begin to wonder if Ron might be cheating on her. It hadn't even occurred to her during the early days of their relationship. His job as principal kept him so busy, and there were always after-school meetings and teachers' conferences to explain his absences from home.

"Finally, I began to suspect that he was seeing Katie again," Blair said. "I found his Visa bill and there were charges for dinners out for two during this time."

Like Ronda, Blair had failed to understand why Ron continued to help Katie out. She knew that Ron had paid off Katie's car. Whatever the attachment was between him and his ex-wife, it seemed never to have been completely severed. Katie might have been attractive once, but at close to fifty, she was bone-thin and worn looking. With any other man, Blair might have thought Ron felt sorry for Katie, but she'd learned he had precious little empathy for anyone else's problems—even her own. Katie had some hold over him, but Blair didn't know what it was.

And then Blair began to doubt what the real quarry was in Ron's "hunting trips" in the woods down near Aberdeen "He wanted to put a mattress in the back of his pickup truck, so it would be handy while he was hunting," Blair laughed. "I accused him of cheating with Katie, but he denied it."

Blair stayed in the relationship longer than she might have, because she concerned for Ron's sons. But she was increasingly turned off by his preoccupation with money—her money.

"He had plenty of money coming in after Ronda died. He collected the fifty thousand dollars on Ronda's work insurance, and his salary was up to seventy thousand dollars. He had a low house payment—but he still wanted me to get a credit card so he could put all of his bills on it. I could see no reason for that. We weren't even married. I refused to do it."

Was it for money to help Katie? Blair doubted that.

Maybe Ron simply wanted to build up his savings so he wouldn't have to worry about money when he retired.

Blair hadn't thought about *other* other women—beyond Katie. Her older son was getting married, and she was caught up in his wedding plans. She didn't have time to keep track of Ron. Quite honestly, she found herself less interested in a long-term relationship with him.

"Frankly, I was never quite sure where Ron was," Blair said. "We had drifted apart, and I didn't have time to take care of all his chores."

One evening, Blair called Ron and said she had some things that she needed to drop off at his house. He sounded nervous when he said, "It's not a good time."

She asked if someone was there, and he mumbled something. Blair figured he was entertaining Katie. She found out later that it hadn't been Katie who shared the restaurant meals with him; it was Sandra*, a woman who taught in the Toledo School District. There were others, too, women she never knew of, and Blair realized the concept of fidelity had never filtered into Ron's brain.

"I liked Sandra," Blair Connery said. "What I knew of her. She was a Lewis County girl, too. She had lovely hair, a nice figure, and she had overcome a lot. She married when she was very young—in her teens—and had a baby. She could have given up because her marriage failed soon after. They were both too young. But she studied and got her GED and then more education and became a teacher."

Sandra had a large piece of property, one of the things she had in common with Ronda and Blair—Katie, too. They either had money or property in their families or they had worked hard for it. Sandra came from a family with a solid financial background.

But Blair was curious. Her government job allowed

her to view certain property transactions, and she found that Sandra had changed the deed on her land within a few months of her marriage to Ron, and he became half owner of Sandra's acreage, a not insubstantial addition to his net worth.

Indeed, every liaison Reynolds had had with a woman as an adult man had enriched him financially. He had the house that Ronda had helped pay for, the benefit of all her painting and decorating skill, and Barb Thompson never got any of Ronda's expensive furniture or good jewelry back. Katie Huttula had come to him from a well-to-do family, Blair had contributed money, groceries, and her own labor in cooking, gardening, laundry, and cleaning, and she came from money, too.

*   *   *

KATIE HAD LEFT RON'S HOUSE at his request in the spring of 1999. Shortly after she moved out, Katie Huttula bragged to old high school friends that she was "living with Vince Parkins*," another Elma High classmate.

One day, Parkins became violently ill in the Olympia apartment where the pair was living. He told Katie he had to go to the emergency room. She drove him there and seemed considerate as he slowly got better.

Puzzled by his ailment, which seemed far more serious than his initial diagnosis of stomach flu, his doctors ordered tests and found that he had ingested arsenic. Almost all people have a small percentage of arsenic in their systems, and those who live near the various waterways and beaches in Washington state have more than average.

But Vince Parkins had enough arsenic in his system to threaten his life.

He told Katie what the doctors had found. When he was released from the hospital, he couldn't get in touch with her to drive him home, and when he finally got there, he saw that she had packed all of her belongings and disappeared.

Bewildered, he told friends and relatives, "I don't know why—but I wonder if Katie was trying to kill me."

Another man told mutual classmates that Katie had surprised him. "They [the Huttulas] have one weird daughter," he said. "I dated her twice and I'll never go out with her again!"

He didn't go into the details of what had turned him off.

* * *

BARB THOMPSON WONDERED how Ron had managed to collect on Ronda's insurance policy with Walmart. She wrote to the insurance company in Iowa, and although they wouldn't share information with her, they agreed to send paperwork to the Lewis County Sheriff's Office. They sent the following information to Detective Dave Neiser: Ronda had become eligible for death benefits through Walmart in the amount of $50,000 on September 12, 1998—three months before she died. The Walmart coverage could have been converted as Ronda paid the premiums and she could increase the amount, too, as it was "always open enrollment." The monthly premium for the $50,000 payoff was $6.50. That amount had arrived in the insurance office on December 18 and was posted to her account on December 22—six days after Ronda's death.

When Ron Reynolds filed his claim for the $50,000, he identified himself as the "Executor" and "Beneficiary." It was all very civilized and pleasant, although he didn't get the money until September 1999.

The company wrote: "Mr. Reynolds, your insurance proceeds have been deposited into a Resource Manager Account in your name. This is a flexible account designed to accommodate both your immediate and long term financial needs. Because we understand you may need time to make decisions about your funds, you are welcome to keep your balance in this account as long as you like. While you do, it earns an attractive rate of interest."

Both Ron Reynolds and Katie Huttula Reynolds were extraordinarily covetous about money. Katie had been awarded almost $100,000 when Ron divorced her, and that left a bitter taste in his mouth. Especially since she had spent almost all of it in a year.

He had fully expected to realize $300,000 from Ronda's insurance, and Barbara was the first to see how upset he was about that when she confronted him the day after Ronda's death—far more upset than he seemed to be about the loss of Ronda.

Ron took the $50,000 as soon as it was available.

CHAPTER TWENTY

IN THE LATE SUMMER and fall of 2001, the Lewis County detectives had began to look at Ronda's manner of death again. Barb Thompson was heartened when she heard there were slight stirrings in the sheriff's office of new interest in the case. She hoped that it was true.

By Christmas season 2001, Ronda had been dead for three years, and Jerry Berry had resigned from the sheriff's office. Apparently Ronda's widower had expected that the past should be old news by then. He was tired of the questions, the suspicions, and the way some people stared at him.

He must have known that he remained the prime "person of interest" in Ronda's death. Sheriff McCroskey had written a letter to Barb Thompson on July 26, 2000 in which he offered his condolences. Then he added, "As happens in any investigation, some mistakes were made— but none of them changed the facts we have to work with. . . . Unfortunately, the only suspect in this case invoked his rights and has an attorney."

Rayburn Dudenbostel, a civil attorney in Elma, and Brett Ballew were representing Ron Reynolds now. Dudenbostel had been Laura and Leslie Reynolds's lawyer for years. He described Ron as a "gentle man, who has suffered a great tragedy and is upset."

Ron's attorney said that the sheriff's men asking questions more than two years later had opened up a lot of wounds. "You can imagine how upset you would be if you woke up and your spouse had committed suicide, and then be accused of killing her, and finding out law enforcement didn't follow procedures."

Because Ronda's death investigation was about to be reopened, he declined to tell *The Chronicle* reporter Sharyn Decker any information he had that would exonerate Ron Reynolds—in case it might be used against him.

Dudenbostel said he had no doubts that Ron was innocent, and pointed out that that could have been established if detectives had only swabbed his hands for gunshot residue. He added that Ron had passed a second polygraph, submitted to interviews, given DNA and handwriting samples, and handed over telephone and credit card records.

Dudenbostel and Ballew insisted on being present during any questioning of their client. That should not have scared Sheriff McCroskey's office into dropping the case; virtually every suspect in a homicide case retains an attorney. That doesn't mean "hands off."

On December 14, 2001, Reynolds prepared to submit to his last "cooperative" interview, this time with Sergeant Glade Austin. Blair felt he wasn't very concerned about it, because he'd gone through "practice" interviews with his attorneys to prepare him for the questioning. Blair went with

him, and she recalled that Jonathan Reynolds was also instructed by the attorneys on what to do and say when the
sheriff's detectives interviewed him. This was standard practice, although legal clients are admonished to tell the truth.

This pre-Christmas interview was almost three years to
the day from when Ronda died. It was a very long questioning period—almost two hours on the tapes that silently
recorded it. It began at 6:12 P.M. and ended at 7:48. Blair
Connery waited in Dudenbostel's outer office, not privy to
the statements Ron was making.

Austin began by asking Ron basic questions—birthday,
occupation, address—before he plunged into the more difficult queries. The detective sergeant first thanked Ron for
his continued cooperation.

"Going back several years, when did you first meet
Ronda?" Austin asked Ron

"I met her several years before we got married. At the
time I was one of Jehovah's Witnesses, and she was attending and she was a friend of my ex-wife's. So that's how I
met her."

The detective and the suspect agreed that that was probably about 1996.

Ron said that his first wife was Catherine Huttula.

She was not. He simply skipped any mention of his actual first wife, Donna.

After his divorce from Katie, he said he had become a
much closer friend of Ronda's. They married on January 2,
1998, and lived first in McCleary on Elma-Hickland Road.

"How long did you live there?" Austin asked.

"Um . . . well, we got married in January, and I signed
papers on my house in Toledo in August of '98."

"How, in general, would you describe your relationship
with Ronda from the time you got married?"

"We had a good relationship. Um, you know, we didn't fight. We didn't have problems that much—I mean, um, you know, some kid problems once in a while, you know, but, uh, we got along. The only thing that, uh, came to mar our relationship was, you know, some of the dishonest things that Ronda started doing."

"Is it safe to say it's difficult for a stepmother to have three boys in the house at times?"

"Yeah. I think that was somewhat hard on Ronda because she wasn't used to it."

This was inaccurate. Mark Liburdi had two sons and a daughter, and Ronda had been a mother to them for eight years.

"Was it difficult at times for the boys, too, having a stepmom in the house?"

"Uh—probably, yeah."

"Okay. What led up in a progression-type fashion to a point that you decided that you were going to separate or get divorced?"

"Well, I started getting more and more information, um, about Ronda running up credit cards, and you know there was one that was over six thousand dollars that I paid for when I closed my house deal. And, uh, there were some others that I was starting to get notifications in the mail about, and when I questioned her about this, she wasn't truthful and she'd say, 'Well, that's Mark's account. This is a mistake having—getting it sent to you,' and, you know, she just kept . . . um making excuses and not telling me the truth, so gradually I grew to not be trusting her. It was like a breach of trust—"

"Do you remember when that would have started?" Glade Austin cut in.

"Well, I was probably starting to get suspicious some

in August, between August and November [of 1998]. I was getting more suspicious all the time, 'cause I kept getting phone calls and things."

"Now, were these credit cards you were aware of?"

"No," Reynolds said. "Every time I'd try to get accurate information, she was not honest about it. She'd tell me things like: 'I'm taking care of that. That's a mistake.' "

Ronda, of course, was no longer present to defend herself. And Ron had spent those summer to winter months in an affair with his ex-wife, so he himself wasn't a prime example of honesty.

Someone had falsified information in order to get a credit card—or several—in the name Mrs. Ronald Reynolds. But *which* one of his most recent wives had done that?

Katie Huttula had written $1,800 worth of bad checks to a supermarket without Ronda's knowledge. Was it possible that *she* was the wife who kept getting new credit cards?

Glade Austin focused only on Ronda, however, and he appeared to be phrasing his questions in a way that validated his own opinion that Ronda was dishonest, rather than focusing on anyone else. Ron was quick to oblige.

"I went through ... um ... After she passed away, I started going through papers and things and I uncovered evidence and I found out they [credit cards] were in my name and I called the companies and I got copies of the applications and things and I realized that she had forged my name and signatures and things."

"You probably didn't have those cards in your wallet?"

"No, I didn't."

"When did you finally reach a point where you decided that it wasn't going to work, and you were talking with her about splitting or separating or divorcing?"

"I took some time to think about it ahead of time—

probably through the month of November—but, you know, it was like . . . um . . . it was like the day before the night of her suicide that I talked to her about it and told her I wanted her to leave because I felt our trust was broken."

"So that was the day that you actually, for the first time, said, 'It's over, move out, get out, or—' "

Ron shook his head. "Well, I didn't say it like that. I—I tried to be kind. I mean, you know, I—I cared a lot about Ronda and it broke my heart that she did that. But I was at a point where, for the good of the future of myself and my boys, I couldn't have her doing that."

For a man who was capable of giving charismatic speeches at educational conferences, Ron Reynolds's answers to Austin's questions were halting, stumbling, and dotted with "ums" and "you knows."

The longer the interview continued, the worse his memory grew. He thought that December 15, 1998, was the first time he'd actually told Ronda it was over between them. He could not remember what time of day that happened. He thought that conversation had happened before she took the waterbed apart, but he wasn't sure. They had talked about separating in their home, and no one was around. At this point in this interview, he didn't mention his doctor's appointment that day in Olympia.

"Did you and Ronda and the rest of the family celebrate Christmas?" Austin asked.

"I was getting ready to celebrate Christmas. Ronda did not want to celebrate Christmas because of her beliefs as a Jehovah's Witness, but I was preparing stuff to celebrate it with my boys and we were just gonna spend it at home."

"You were no longer a Jehovah's Witness?"

"No."

"Okay. Now on the fifteenth, you had a doctor's appointment? And some time near that appointment, you and Ronda talked for an extensive amount of time. Do you recall where you were at when that phone call started?"

"I was in the parking lot of the Olympia Multi-Specialty Clinic, where I go see my cardiologist. And I'd completed my appointment with him, and when I got in my pickup, Ronda had left at least one message on my cell phone, and I returned the call to her and started talking to her there in the parking lot."

"I think the conversation lasted about eighty-four minutes?" Austin asked.

"I didn't know that until later, but we did talk a long time . . . At times, she was saying some things that kinda worried me, so I just kept talking to her. I noticed it was getting late so I started driving home, and I continued to talk to her . . . uh, until I got pretty close to home and—"

"Okay," Austin interrupted. "Can you be somewhat specific on what she was saying that bothered you or worried you?"

"Well, she was really depressed over us separating and . . . she started talking about things that led me to believe she had suicidal thoughts. And she was talking about one of her friends in the Patrol who had committed suicide and she said: 'I never used to understand why she did that, but I understand that now because it would be so peaceful.' Or something like that. So, you know, I'm not an expert on those kind of things, but when somebody's talking like that, I know it's serious, so I just kept talking to her and trying to calm her and tell her, 'Look, things are gonna look better, and uh, and uh, I was fully planning on going home and talking to her, but as I got close to Toledo, she, um, said, 'Don't come home now. I'm fine' and—"

Once again, Austin interrupted his subject, but Reynolds's voice overrode his.

"—and I'm gonna be okay . . ."

"Were there other things she said during that conversation?" the detective sergeant asked. "Other than that—that led you to be concerned?"

Derailed from his rapid string of words, Reynolds wilted a little.

"Well, I can't remember conversations that well. I—I'm not good at that, but . . . um—Just her whole tone sounded depressed."

"At that point was she threatening suicide or saying she was going to commit suicide?"

"No. Talking about it. She was having ideations, you know, you know. It had me concerned."

Reynolds was, indeed, not good at remembering details, examples, and even whole conversations. He faltered often. He couldn't recall if it had been during the phone call or later on the night of the fifteenth when Ronda said she didn't want to go on without him.

"So you drove back to Toledo [from the clinic in Olympia] and I believe that you were going home, but she told you—"

"She told me basically, 'I'm okay now. You don't need to come home.' So the time was getting close for me to be down to the school for my program, and I grabbed a quick bite to eat and went there because, you know, I thought she was stable."

Ron said he'd stopped at Betty's Place in Toledo for a hamburger, after deciding it wasn't necessary for him to go home to check on Ronda.

His reactions on the last afternoon of Ronda's life appeared to have been mercurial. He was terribly worried for

Ronda when she called him in Olympia; he was fearful that she was suicidal. But he called no one else, and as he drove into Toledo, he had apparently felt serene in his belief that she was no longer in danger.

He explained that a school principal was expected to be at the various plays and musical programs—so he showed up at seven for the school Christmas program and stayed until at least nine-thirty.

"I'm usually the last one out, making sure all the doors are locked and the building is clear."

When he arrived home, he'd seen Dave Bell there, with his truck backed up in the driveway. The Des Moines police sergeant and Ronda were apparently unloading the truck and carrying things back into the house.

"I think she was taking stuff back in her room. I didn't stay out there to watch what they were doing," Reynolds said. "I didn't interfere with that. I went in the house and talked to my boys 'cause they were kinda upset, saying, 'Ronda's taking things out of the house,' and I told them, you know, 'It's okay. She's gonna be leaving—it'll be all right.' "

Ron said he hadn't talked to Dave Bell at all. He'd been too busy talking to his sons. "They were okay with it. I mean they weren't upset or anything. Nobody was really upset."

"Did you have any conversations with the boys about David Bell and a gun at that point?" Galde Austin asked.

"No, I never knew anything about it. The boys saw him give it back to her, but *I* never knew about that until after her death."

Reynolds said he'd helped Ronda put the waterbed back together, and they'd begun to refill it. "We were just talking while we were doing that."

"Was [*sic*] there conversations about what her plans had been before Dave Bell brought her back?"

"She didn't go into what her plans had been. She just said she decided to stay home and try to work it out . . . I kept telling her I've made my mind up, you know. I didn't give her any false hopes."

Reynolds said that his boys had gone to bed later than they usually did—Josh at the end of the hall, his wall backing up to the master bathroom closet, Jonathan in the first room beyond the front door. It had French doors and had been designed as a family room. David's room was on the corner of the house.

Perhaps seeing Ronda with another man had made Ron jealous, and she became—at least temporarily—more attractive to him. At any rate, he told Glade Austin that they'd been intimate. "We had intercourse, and then she got back up to make some phone calls in the bathroom—we have a phone jack there. But then, after she came to bed, she was beside me, and when I went to sleep, she was beside me."

Asked about the bottle of whiskey detectives had found in the master bedroom, Ron still couldn't explain that.

"Do you know if Ronda had anything to drink that evening—alcoholic-type drinks?" Austin asked.

"Well," Reynolds began slowly, "there was a bottle of—we'd had a partial bot—you know, maybe a fourth full or something of Black Velvet in the house. I noticed that that was in the bedroom, and um . . . so she could have been drinking, but I don't know. I didn't see her drink . . . But I know the bottle was in there and that wasn't a normal thing . . . I don't think it was there that morning."

Any hard alcohol was usually kept in a cabinet above the refrigerator in the kitchen. Reynolds didn't recall the can of Pepsi and some glasses on the bedroom floor. He seemed completely baffled about who might have emptied the bottle of Black Velvet.

Ron didn't know what time he'd gone to bed. He'd been in bed when Ronda joined him after making some calls. He did remember that she had made one call to his ex-wife, Katie. That was *before* they had sex, he thought, and he was fairly confident that he had gone to sleep before Ronda did.

"What time did you wake up?" Austin asked.

"I recall waking up briefly sometime around five to five-thirty A.M. 'cause I remember looking at my alarm clock. I didn't check [on her] or anything, but I had the feeling that Ronda was there, and I fell back asleep until my alarm started going off."

"After that, what time did you wake up with the alarm clock?"

"My alarm goes off at six, but I didn't—I was really tired and didn't wake up on the first ring, and it goes on at nine-minute intervals. I wasn't sure what time I woke up— um . . . I also set my alarm clock five minutes fast—"

Austin waited, and Ron Reynolds continued his stream of consciousness. "So somewhere in there, according to what has been said that when I called 911, probably on the third ring of my alarm clock, I probably started waking up, and uh, and uh, I probably laid there a little bit til I got awake and then I noticed Ronda wasn't in bed, and I got up and went out and looked in the living room 'cause, you know, a time or two when she couldn't sleep, she'd gone to the couch out there and she wasn't there, so I walked back in the bathroom, uh, and that's when I found her."

His words tumbled out hurriedly, each on top of the next. His recall seemed unable to keep up. He wasn't sure what time he discovered Ronda's body, but he thought it was a "pretty short time" after his alarm went off the third time.

"Right after I found her, I called 911 immediately," Reynolds said. "She wasn't breathing, she wasn't moving, and so I just went and called 911."

"Okay. During this process, did you do anything else? Check any of the kids, or check the other bathroom, or use the bathroom yourself? Did you examine her at all at that point? Or see anything that caused concern for you?"

"Well . . . I picked up the pillow to look at her and I saw that she had shot herself, and, you know, she wasn't moving. I didn't know anything I could do but call 911."

"What guns were in the house at the time of this incident?" Austin asked.

"Well, I have a set of hunting rifles, um, and um, target practice rifles. Like I had a single-shot Remington twenty-two. I had a Winchester thirty-thirty. I had, um, a twenty-gauge. I don't remember the make of that, um, a single-shot shotgun. I had a Springfield .30-06. Um . . . I think I had a twenty-two automatic that was my father's, and an eight-millimeter Lebel French World War I rifle that was his. I think that's all and then the pistol."

"The one that she used?"

"Yeah."

Reynolds knew it was a .32, but he wasn't sure of the manufacturer. He didn't think he had ever fired it.

"How did you come into possession of that firearm?"

"Well, when my father was getting old, um, and feeling bad, he started saying things to me like he didn't want to live like this anymore and stuff, so I just got it away from him because I didn't want him doing something with it, and so—"

Ron Reynolds was sure that Ronda had known about all the guns in the house, but he didn't think she had any guns of her own any longer. He said he had found the holster of his father's .32 lying on the right side of the toilet the evening before Ronda died. "I picked it up, and went back to where she was working on the waterbed, and I said, 'Where's my father's pistol?' and she said, 'I gave it to Dave Bell.' So at that point, I took the holster and put it back in the drawer under the bed where it had always been."

He hadn't mentioned this earlier, but he said he hadn't been worried about the missing handgun because he believed Dave Bell had it. Reynolds said he had forgotten about finding the holster during earlier interviews. He had also been confused about whether he had checked Ronda's pulse once or twice. He had told some investigators that he'd sought signs of life *before* he called 911, but now he was sure he hadn't checked for a pulse until the 911 dispatcher asked him to do so.

Reynolds said that both the bathroom door and the closet door off that were closed—although the latter might have been opened just a bit. He said he had had no trouble getting into the closet where Ronda lay. Her head had been at the back of the closet—close to the wall shared with Josh's room; her feet were toward the door.

He emphasized that both he and Josh were very sound sleepers, so it wasn't surprising that neither heard the fatal shot.

Reynolds was adamant that Ronda had no financial interest in his house. Asked how she might have charged $25,000 on his credit cards, he believed she had sent money to her mother and grandmother. He also said Barb Thompson had stolen a horse trailer from Mark Liburdi.

(In truth, the trailer belonged to Ronda, and she'd given it to her mother. Mark Liburdi, angry at the negotiations about their assets, had taken a tact squad from the Washington State Patrol to Spokane to retrieve that horse trailer. After Ronda's death, the WSP impounded the trailer because it was in Ronda's name. Legally, it probably belonged to her widower: Ron Reynolds—not Mark Liburdi. It sat in impound for years. Whether Ron ever took possession of it isn't known.)

* * *

ASKED IF RONDA used drugs or drank, Ron shook his head. "She was taking some herbal things, and I think she took something to help her sleep sometimes. Cheryl Gilbert mentioned that Ronda was taking that St. John's Wort, and I can remember seeing bottles of herbal medicines like that. But the prescription I found from Dr. Conover was for Zoloft—which she never had filled."

"Did you ever take a death investigation class—specifically that talks about death, uh homicide, anything like that?" Glade Austin asked, changing the subject.

"No," Reynolds said flatly.

"Okay. The officers at the original scene felt that they didn't see a lot of emotional response from you that morning. Can you comment on that in any way?"

"I was in shock that morning," Ron answered. "A lot of times in my life when loved ones have died, I don't always break down right away, but at some point when I'm by myself, I do that."

"That morning, one of the first things you did—well, let me back up. After you made the 911 call, when did you wake your children up—and have them do . . . what happened there as far as getting them out of the house?"

"Well, the lady on the 911 line was helping me 'cause I was having a hard time. She asked me, 'Are there children in the house?' and I said, 'Yes.' You know, I hadn't thought about that at that point. And so I called their mom and made arrangements for the boys to—Jon was old enough to drive, and he drove the boys up to their mom's house."

Ron Reynolds agreed that several people had showed up at his house. He'd called his superintendent and told him what happened, and Tom Lahmann came, and then Bill Waag, the middle school principal. "I called my mom and she came, and her significant other (Tom Reed). Cheryl Gilbert came, her father—who's a minister. I think at some point in the day, my sister and brother-in-law came. I don't remember everyone."

"Judy and Larry Semanko?"

"Yes—they spent several hours there."

"Now Detective Berry said that you stated to him, 'Is there any evidence that can be linked to me?' What did you mean by that?"

"I recall that. It probably had something to do with the fact that it was like two days after Ronda's death, and I was, you know, in bed in a depression and I get a call from him asking me to come in. I went through the questioning with him, and then he wanted me to take a lie detector test. It was probably in connection with that."

Ronda's widower readily admitted he had paid the premium on her insurance policy even though he knew she was already dead. He insisted he expected nothing more than the $50,000 payoff even though he had told Barb Thompson that he believed Ronda's insurance totaled

$300,000, and he'd been angry about that. Austin didn't push him.

Sergeant Austin asked Ron what he had been wearing at the time he woke up and discovered Ronda's body. He had forgotten many details, but he remembered his clothing that morning in mid-December three years earlier.

"I was wearing some flannel pants and a pullover long-sleeved shirt."

"Okay. And do you know what eventually happened to those?"

"I turned them over to my attorney . . . When the investigation was going on, I told my attorneys that nobody had looked at my clothing, nobody had asked me any questions about that, so they advised me, you know, to turn them over to them."

"Give them to your lawyers—or the detectives?"

"My attorneys."

"Had those clothes been washed between the morning of her death and the time you gave them to your attorneys on January twenty-second?"

"Well, I'm just not sure. They could have been."

(Perhaps they had been washed the morning Ronda died. That would account for Larry Semanko, Ron's brother-in-law, smelling fresh laundry when he walked in the house on Twin Peaks Drive.)

Yes, Reynolds admitted, his ex-wife Katie Huttula and he had had an affair going back to late summer—although he stipulated they had had intercourse on only one occasion. After Ronda died, Katie had moved back in to help with their boys. "She stayed at the house right after Ronda's death, but some time passed before she moved in, and then, you know, by May she was out of the house."

"I guess Ronda told more than one person," Glade Austin began, "that you stated that you loved her and your ex-wife, but because of the boys you needed to get back with your ex-wife."

"I don't think I ever said that. If Ronda would not have broken trust with me, I never would have even thought of going back to my ex-wife."

"Okay. I'm not sure you've aswered the last question— because it enters into what people say—is whether or not your ex-wife, Katie, stayed that night or was it after the night of Ronda's death or was it several days later? Or do you recall when she first stayed there?"

"She might have been there the night of her [Ronda's] death, but she didn't stay with me. You know, she might have been with the boys."

That was an odd thing to say. The house where Ronda died wasn't that big; how could Katie Huttula have been hidden from Ron so successfully that he didn't even know whether she was there or not?

Glade Austin had framed his questions to get certain responses, and most of them had been easy for Ron Reynolds. The detective sergeant was convinced Ronda had been a suicide, and his reports were full of derogatory statements about her, as if he'd been deliberately searching Washington State Patrol records to prove she was a neurotic woman and a bad cop.

Had Glade Austin detected the possible reverberations that might ensue if Katie Huttula had been at the house on Twin Peaks Drive during the hours when no one really knew what happened?

If he did, he didn't pursue it.

Austin's decision not to ask more questions about exactly who was at Ron and Ronda's house the night of

December 15 to the early morning hours of December 16 seems, in retrospect, to have been unwise.

But like most of the Lewis County detectives, Glade Austin believed that Ronda had killed herself—and that there was no reason to look at anyone else who might have fired the death gun.

Chapter Twenty-one

As New Year 2002 dawned, Jerry Berry had been resigned from the Lewis County Sheriff's Office for less than a month, but he had not lost his belief that Ronda Reynolds was a homicide victim. He planned to continue his probe as a private investigator. As for Barb Thompson, she would never stop seeking the truth. She was far more determined than the Lewis County investigators had foreseen. She sold off some of her horses to pay for the travel, phone calls, attorneys, and other expenses she faced in her personal investigation.

It had all seemed hopeless, when the Lewis County Sheriff's Office announced in the first week of January 2002 that they had reclassified Ronda's death once again. Surprised, Berry continued to work on his own.

Terry Wilson, the coroner, reverted to his "Undetermined" manner of death findings. Most gratifying of all, the Lewis County detectives were reopening the case. It had been a little more than three years since Ronda died, and now, at last, it looked as though there was a good chance that Barb Thompson's and Jerry Berry's belief that she had been murdered might be validated.

Still burned by Vernon Geberth's negative view of their handling of the case, Sheriff McCroskey and his top detectives asked for another review. This time, Chief Criminal Deputy Joe Doench formally asked to have members of the Washington State Attorney General's Homicide Investigation Tracking System (HITS) unit take a look at Ronda's death. HITS is a software application designed to store crime-related information that police and sheriff's departments around Washington and Oregon contribute voluntarily.

Not unlike the nationwide Violent Crime Apprehension Program (ViCAP), HITS has become a central nexus and repository for detailed information on violent crimes. There is no question that HITS, begun in 1987 after the Northwest experienced such savage serial killers as the "Green River Killer," later identified as Gary Ridgway, and "Ted," who turned out to be Ted Bundy, is an important tool in the criminal justice system. Its investigators almost always are selected from retired homicide detectives in Washington and Oregon.

In any calendar year, HITS responds to about eight hundred requests for assistance and information. Their official mission is to "collect, analyze, link, and then provide law enforcement with information that will link and facilitate the resolution of violent crimes and speed the apprehension and prosecution of violent criminals."

Doench's request for help was forwarded to HITS on November 28, 2001, although the announcement that Ronda's death investigation was being reopened wasn't made for several weeks. During that time, Sergeant Glade Austin had, of course, reinterviewed Ron Reynolds—to little avail. Her widower still insisted that Ronda had committed suicide. And he and Katie Huttula were among the few laypersons who did so insist.

On April 25, 2002, Attorney General Christine Gregoire (now in her second term as Washington's governor) sent the HITS findings to Sheriff John McCroskey. It was signed by the team who had reviewed the Lewis County investigation: Chief Criminal Investigator John H. Turner, Senior Investigator/Analyst George Fox, and Senior Investigator/Analyst Richard Steiner.

They had looked at evidence in Ronda's death consisting of three four-inch binders, written reports, transcribed interviews, polygraph records, and numerous photographs and newspaper articles—all provided to them by the Lewis County Sheriff's Office. They did no independent investigating on their own.

"We did not consider emotion, politics, or outside pressure in reaching our findings. Evidence was first independently evaluated by each investigator and then reviewed by the team collectively. Numerous team meetings were held to focus on each aspect of the investigation review.

"First, let us begin by saying there is not a death investigation known that couldn't be better critiqued at a later time with more favorable options noted. However, basic techniques should be consistent in all investigations of this type must be investigated as a potential homicide until proven otherwise."

It looked, initially, as if the HITS investigators agreed with Jerry Berry's and Barb Thompson's belief that county detectives had fumbled the ball and focused too quickly on suicide, and never considered homicide.

"The following is a list of issues that we feel should have been considered and are presented here at your request."

The list of mistakes made by the first responders followed but they were couched in terms that said they should be mentioned only because they might useful in future training exercises. The report pointed out that the Lewis County sheriff's men who entered the Reynolds house on the icy morning of December 16, 1998, should have:

1. Secured the entire house as a crime scene, rather than just a room, and allowed no access to the crime scene by either civilian or law enforcement personnel—regardless of rank—who were not directly involved in the immediate investigation.
2. Obtained a gunshot residue test on Ron Reynolds's hands and person.
3. Obtained verbal or written statements of medical aid personnel.
4. Interviewed the Reynoldses' children in a timely manner after they left the house.
5. Kept a log of the crime scene photos to assist in locating them.
6. Noted personal items left in the crime scene that occurred in photos.
7. Added the dates and times to some photos shown prior to the incident.
8. Documented the lighting conditions and room temperature.
9. Numbered and indexed the final report.
10. Diagrammed the crime scene with measurements that would have allowed them to re-create it accurately later.
11. Clarified conflicting issues in officers' reports.

12. Documented and filed some of the investigative materials in a timely manner.
13. Retained a complete case file, eliminating the apparent loss of missing photos, negatives, and evidence.

Yet, the HITS investigators didn't feel that any of the thirteen missteps—or all of them—raised any questions about their decision or altered their findings.

"A careful review of the evidence presented, excluding secondhand information and opinion, was completed. The full spectrum of evidence was considered, including the deceased's personal history, the events leading up to her death, the position of the body and postmortem changes, inconsistencies in some of the witnesses' statements, and motive or lack of motive were also considered."

And then the team from the Attorney General's Office stated their official finding:

This evidence is consistent with Ms. Reynolds becoming despondent and positioning herself in the closet after previously obtaining Mr. Reynolds' handgun. The position of the hands and blanket and the location of the weapon all indicate that Ms. Reynolds covered herself with the electric blanket and grasped it with her left hand. Ms. Reynolds held the weapon in her right hand and fired one round with the trajectory of the bullet through the pillow, entering her head by the right ear and traversing the brain to where it was recovered, to the right of center, is consistent with being self-inflicted. This injury would cause immediate death. The weapon then dropped to the right forehead, where it remained, leaving a notable impression, until either

Mr. Reynolds or first responders dislodged it from that location.

The weapon then dropped straight down, coming to rest between both hands, at a location between the chin and forehead. The first finger (trigger finger) of the right hand remained in an extended firing position.

It is our unanimous finding that the unfortunate death of Ronda Reynolds was the result of an intentional, self-inflicted single gunshot wound to her head and should be classified as a suicide.

It was a stunning conclusion, and it hit Barb Thompson hard. How could the HITS detectives eliminate emotion from their evaluation of Ronda's death? How could they dismiss all of the red flags, the autopsy findings, the motives, and the mass of circumstantial and physical evidence that shouted that Ronda hadn't committed suicide?

But they had. It seemed that the dichotomy between the sworn police investigators and the retired detectives who agreed with them and Barb Thompson and her volunteer team was growing wider and wider. To Barb, it was almost as if it was more important to the Lewis County Sheriff's Office and the HITS team to win than to find the truth.

Had they backed themselves into such a tight corner that there was no graceful way to admit any misjudgment?

Or could Barb have been blinded by what she wanted— and needed—to believe about her lost daughter?

Chapter Twenty-two

In the past, I had written a number of articles about actual murders that occurred—and had been solved—in Lewis County. Glade Austin was instrumental in bringing in many of those convictions, and those killers were in prison.

I knew that one day I would write Ronda's story, although I sometimes doubted that there would ever be an ending to it. As the years passed, it seemed less and less likely that anyone would ever be arrested for killing her.

Even so, I decided that her story had to be told—questions and all. It didn't seem fair that she should just be forgotten as the years passed.

* * *

I wasn't the only one who worried about the unfinished story. Sergeant Austin felt compelled to write a supplemental report summing up his feelings and decisions about

Ronda Reynolds's death. Austin seemed just as convinced that Ronda committed suicide as Jerry Berry was positive she had been murdered. Austin's report follows.

Glade Austin, 1/30/02

On January 10, 02, I was advised that *The Chronicle* was coming out with an article in the paper that day. On January 11, I contacted Mr. Ballew. He indicated he had read the article, and didn't feel too badly about how it had come out. I indicated to him that I had several releases I was preparing and would try to get them out to him that day, so he could get them to his client.

An additional article came out in *The Chronicle*, in regards to the superintendent of the Toledo School District supporting Ron Reynolds.

I took sick leave and some vacation time and will be going on disability for medical problems starting 3/08/02. However, I have been reviewing this case at home periodically to prepare a final report. I have addressed with Chief Criminal Deputy Joe Doench the areas of work that I feel still need to be done so he can assign an investigator to finish. Almost all the information I will discuss here is in my original reports. This will be an attempt to pull it together to some degree and explain my reasons why I believe this case to be a suicide.

On the morning of the death of Ronda Reynolds, Ron Reynolds gave a statement to Gary Holt, which throughout this investigation, although it been expanded upon, has remained consistent. He has told the same story over and over again, with the only difference being that he has been given the opportunity to provide additional detail.

He states that he was talking to his wife on the phone, that she was suicidal, and that he was trying to talk her out of it. This turns out to be an eighty-four minute phone call, which is on his cell phone record and on the house phone record. We know from talking to Cheryl Gilbert and David Bell that Ronda was despondent and depressed, so this eighty-four minute conversation seems consistent with the discussions that Mr. Reynolds states he had.

In a later interview, he states that he stopped for a burger in Toledo, and went to a Toledo school play—which seems inconsistent with his eighty-four minute call and his concern. However, in his original statement, he states he urged her to contact a friend because he was in Olympia, and indicates that she did have a friend come over . . . She told him not to come home, that she was feeling better, and that he felt that probably David Bell had arrived, which we later find out is true.

He indicates in his statement that he checked for a pulse on his wife's neck, that he could not feel one, and called 911. In the first interview I had with him, I asked him if he had checked his wife's pulse twice and he stated, "No—just once." From reviewing the 911 tape, it's clear the dispatcher asked him if he had checked the pulse. He stated, "No, should I go check?"

He indicates that he got home and when he went into the master bedroom and into the bathroom, he saw the holster to his father's .32 caliber handgun lying next to the toilet, and he questioned her about where the gun was, and she indicated that she had given it to her friend David Bell. We know from David Bell's statement that this was partially true. She did try to give him the gun, but he had unloaded it and either gave it back to her or put it in the drawer. I think this statement is of particular importance. One or more of the kids had walked by and stated that David Bell had handed Ronda the gun, but also have said that they did not tell their father of this until after the incident . . . It would seem that she took the gun from its holster and hid it somewhere in the house—most likely within the bathroom or the walk-in closet, as the holster was found—or observed by Mr. Reynolds next to the toilet in master bathroom. It is in this time frame that Mr. Reynolds sees the message on the mirror and states he told Ronda to "clean it up," which she apparently did not do.

Asked if she drank any alcohol, he indicates he saw the bottle and saw that she was having a drink, but did not know how much she had had and said there wasn't much left in the bottle. If she had, in fact, had a drink earlier in the evening, the amount that she drank could easily have been metabolized and out of her system by the time of her death at approximately five o'clock in the morning.

Asked about the phone book laying [*sic*] open, he said that she was going to fly over to Spokane to visit her mother, and that she was taking one of her dogs with her. This later is confirmed by Discover card records and Alaska Airlines records that she ordered a ticket to Spokane at 10:36 P.M. and she ordered a dog carrier to go with her.

In Cheryl Gilbert's first statement, she indicates that Ronda was completely devastated about the pending breakup of her marriage. She was also present on the 15th at [Ronda's] house . . . In their conversation, Ronda said she was going to take a muscle relaxer because she pulled her back that day while packing and working. In Cheryl Gilbert's second statement to Detective Berry, she said that Ronda was extremely upset, that she felt like she was in the dark, and that she was just so down. Because of her [Ronda's] mood, she might do something drastic and, without even mentioning the word "suicide," Ronda looked at her and said "No. I would never do that." So it would appear that they were both thinking the same thing.

I interviewed Cheryl Gilbert several times and she said she never considered Ron a suspect in Ronda's death—that if she hadn't killed herself, she thought Jonathan would have had something to do with it. This was based on a story that Ronda told her, and many others, about Jonathan coming into the bathroom when she was bathing or showering. . . . Later, in separate interviews, Jonathan and Mr. Reynolds denied that these incidents ever occurred and showed no indication to me that they weren't being truthful.

In my interview with Jonathan, he said he had not been in the master bedroom at all on the evening of the 15th or the morning of the 16th, prior to Ronda's death.

Even knowing that the story Ronda told may not have occurred, for Jonathan to be a suspect at all in this death would mean that he would have had to open the door to the master bedroom, go past his father who was in bed, open the door to the bathroom—possibly—and the closet, fire the shot, come back out through those doors, close them, pass his father again, and go back to his own bedroom. This does not seem reasonable, especially in the light that Mr. Reynolds passed a polygraph, and if he had any knowledge of such a scenario, he would not have passed the polygraph, nor have I found any motive for Jonathan to have committed such an act—in particular, since he knew Ronda was leaving the household.

Ronda had Cheryl Gilbert coming to pick her up the next morning to take her to the Portland airport, which later turns out to be inconsistent with what she told David Bell and the ticket that she purchased to travel out of SeaTac to Spokane. With the number of phone calls she made that night, it seems like she could have called Cheryl and advised her of any change of plans.

Ron Reynolds indicates that his wife talked him into making love the night of the 15th and that that did occur and he did ejaculate. The autopsy report confirms that sperm were found in the slides and swabs. I inquired of David Bell about any possibility that he and Ronda had had sexual relations during the time they were together on the 15th and he emphatically stated that nothing like that occurred.

. . . David Bell was interviewed the morning of the 16th at the scene, and later by me. He discussed the incident where Ronda gave him the gun, and that he unloaded it and put it back in a drawer. He stated this incident was very odd. . . . I asked him why he had unloaded the gun, indicating it's not normal—especially for police officers—to unload other peoples' guns. He stated it was a habit of his and also because the kids were in the house, that he just automatically unloaded it.

After loading his truck up with her belongings, dropping the keys off at Cheryl Gilbert's, and shopping for gas, Ronda indicated that she wanted to go to his house and stay until she got her feet on the ground. He didn't want to do that because he had kids at home who

hadn't met her. He didn't want to bring her home late at
night under those conditions, and he also had a number
of cats and she had a number of dogs. He offered to take
her elsewhere but she elected to go home.

Austin talked with Krista Liburdi, Ronda's ex-husband
Mark's new wife, who said Ronda had phoned her about
the division of profits from the sale of the little ranch where
Ronda and Mark once lived. Krista said Ronda always had
the last word, but in the final forty-eight hours of her life,
she had agreed to let Mark decide how to split the money.

Glade Austin went to the Washington State Patrol and
noted all of Ronda's alleged reprimands, on-the-job injuries, and financial obligations there. Ronda had gone to
an attorney—Susan Sampson—asking that any allegations
against her be investigated.

Annette Sandberg—who later became chief of the
Washington State Patrol—worked in internal affairs at the
time, and took on the probe. But somehow the entire investigation had been purged from the Patrol's files.

(Sandberg eventually determined that the allegations
against Ronda were "unfounded and unsupported.")

Sergeant Austin continued in his quest to show that
Ronda Reynolds had been depressed and dishonest. Although he wasn't at all disturbed that Ron Reynolds had
reaped $50,000 from her insurance—even though he paid
the premium after Ronda died—Glade Austin picked away
at Ronda's honesty. He noted that someone had used ten
different versions of her name to obtain credit: her maiden
name, Liburdi's surname, and Ron Reynolds's name, with
nine different Social Security numbers. Sometimes the person applying had listed Ronda's middle initial as "E." and
sometimes as "F."

In addition Ronda E. Reynolds had entered into a diversion program with ten different conditions she had to adhere to. She was to complete 120 hours of community service, and pay program fees every quarter of $550 at $150 down and $50 a month. This had been paid in full—in the amount of $1,375.

Glade Austin did not consider that several people might have tried to get credit cards in names close to Ronda's. There was Katie Huttula, who had a continuing drug problem and had forged checks within days of Ronda's death. There was Cheryl Gilbert, who had used Ronda's bank account to write checks to pay her own bills—and Ronda was letting her pay it off by cleaning her house. There was even Ron Reynolds, for whom money seemed more important than almost anything.

Now that Ronda was dead, it was easy to blame her for any financial flaws.

"Thus, it appears." Austin wrote,

> there is a pattern of behavior that would indicate that on a lot of occasions, Ronda Reynolds was not a truthful person . . . It would be consistent with the statements Ron Reynolds has made in regards to the monies that Ronda Reynolds had absconded with during the marriage, without his knowledge, and in fact had apparently forged his signature on a number of credit applications, where she ran up thousands of dollars of bills, which were later dropped and taken off of Mr. Reynolds' account, when he was able to show that the signatures on the forms were not his . . .

If not, whose signatures were they?

One got the feeling that if Sergeant Glade Austin would

have painted Ronda with an even darker brush if he could. He had ignored the arguments against her taking her own life, and he even took issue with the number of Barb Thompson's horses. He insisted she had only one. At the time, she had dozens.

At the time, Ronda and Freeman owned the ranch in Spokane. Barb had long since put it in their names, although she currently lived there and was the one who bred the prize quarter horses, attended the mares' labors, and raised the colts, training them and other horses brought to her. She wanted to be sure that her two children would get the ranch property, divided equally, if she should die suddenly.

Austin clearly viewed Ron Reynolds as a kindly school principal and Ronda Reynolds as an "absconder" and a liar. There were no shades of gray in his opinions.

He went on to misquote Ronda's attorney, completely changing the meaning in the statements she made after she learned Ronda was dead.

> Ms. Sampson had indicated something to the effect that she was surprised Ronda Reynolds hadn't committed suicide before she actually did.

Asked to comment on this, Susan Sampson was appalled. "What I said in terms of 'surprise,' " she said, "was that I'd heard a former female trooper named Ronda had died. When I checked, it was Ronda Reynolds, and I wasn't surprised that it was the woman I represented—because how many Rondas could there be in the Washington State Patrol? It had nothing at all to do at all with my thinking I expected her to commit suicide. Because I never did."

CHAPTER TWENTY-THREE

THE SPRING OF 2002 was a low point for Barb Thompson. She felt like a pawn on a giant chessboard, a pawn that was losing ground. Ronda had been dead for more than three years and they were further from finding out what had happened than they had ever been.

Barb had loyal supporters; Sharyn Decker, who wrote a very long article exploring the case for *The Chronicle*, believed that Ronda had not killed herself. All of Ronda's closest friends continued to refuse to accept the possibility that she had taken her own life. Jerry Berry wasn't about to give up, but Barb was afraid that people would forget. She knew that they had their own lives and their own problems.

She also knew she needed an attorney and some forensic investigators who could check out aspects of the case and evidence. But she couldn't afford anything like that. Jerry Berry had never charged her a penny; he was as consumed with finding the truth as she was. So Barb developed a knack for connecting with the media. It was her only way of keeping the story alive.

After the publication of Decker's reprise of the case in *The Chronicle,* Barb got a call out of the blue from a man who gave his name as Marty Hayes. Hayes told her he was running for coroner of Lewis County in the fall or 2002. Coroner Terry Wilson had held the post for decades and voters couldn't seem to visualize anyone else. There had been rumors about Wilson's disregard for the dignity of the dead—but they weren't widespread.

Barb had attempted to speak with Wilson many times, but he always refused. The only person on the coroner's staff she had ever spoken to was Wilson's deputy, Carmen Brunton.

Now his opponent, Marty Hayes, was asking her if he might obtain a copy of the investigation into her daughter's death.

"I was short with him—suspicious. I guess I didn't trust anyone after all this time with no results. Well, anyone but Jerry," Barb said. "I told him it would cost about one hundred and fifty dollars to copy the file and buy postage to send it to him. If he wanted to send me a check for that, I would get a copy of what I'd been able to compile for him. I thought if he was elected coroner, he should know about Ronda's case. But how could I have been so snippy? I didn't realize how much Marty was willing to do to help me."

Jerry Berry convinced Barb that bringing Hayes into the probe could be a positive thing.

Marty Hayes was in his mid-forties, a burly, smiling giant of a man. He had a long history of interest in law enforcement since he was twenty-two. He'd worked as a commissioned officer, a reserve officer, and even a guard at a nuclear plant, in Idaho and Washington state. He seldom stayed with any particular agency for more than two or three years. Although he'd taken many hours of advanced classes in criminal justice and forensics and was an expert in firearms and ballistics, he was working toward a law degree at the Concord Law School in Los Angeles, an online university and the first in the country to offer a juris doctor program. (He has since earned his law degree and is preparing to take the bar exam.)

When he moved to Lewis County in 1995, Marty Hayes opened his own gun training school, the Firearms Academy of Seattle, where about 10 percent of his students are law enforcement officers. Hayes estimates he's trained five thousand cops and private citizens over the fifteen years since its inception. He teaches handgun safety, fundamentals of home defense, and tactical handguns. There isn't much he doesn't know about guns.

"I read about Ronda Reynolds's death, and I got to wondering about how it was being handled," Hayes recalled. "Maybe I could make a difference. I didn't mind sending Barb the check."

And Barb did send Marty Hayes the reports and the information that she had gathered on her own.

"He offered to do tests for me—ballistics, other things we needed, like how the recoil would have worked, the sound, loudness of a handgun, and if a pillow really could muffle that sound. And he would work pro bono. That meant I would have two experts working on Ronda's case, for free! I felt as though my luck was changing again. And that we had a chance."

To avoid any conflict-of-interests claims, Hayes would

have to wait until after the 2002 elections before he began conducting tests that might explain Ronda Reynolds's death. In the meantime, he studied the reports, photos, and documents Barb Thompson had sent him.

Initially he found few answers to his questions, only more questions.

*   *   *

CORONER TERRY WILSON would be a hard man for anyone to beat. He was locked into his position as coroner of Lewis County, popular with many of the old guard there, and they pooh-poohed the stories that circulated around Wilson. It was true he never went to the death sites of those who died in his county; he assigned deputy coroners to that often-disturbing facet of his job. Nor did he attend autopsies. He signed the documents that specified cause and manner of death based on his deputies' opinions and those of the mobile forensic pathologists who crisscrossed the state. He was highly visible at charity auctions and social events in Lewis County. When asked for quotes, he invariably turned reporters away.

Tracy Vedder, an investigative reporter for KOMO-TV in Seattle, later presented a shocking half-hour documentary about Wilson. But on the surface, he was a family man with two talented daughters and a very tall son who was a basketball star.

Terry Wilson was the head man in the coroner's office, and the buck should have landed with him—but he never responded to what he called "rumors." Vedder dug deep into some of his past cases and was shocked at what she found.

In one instance, a teenage boy was killed as he walked on railroad tracks in Lewis County. It was a disastrous accident and the victim's body was left—literally in pieces—afterward.

But the coroner's office removed only the largest segments of the boy's body and left many behind. To spare the family, friends went to the tracks and collected the bloodied parts that were still on the railroad tracks.

A middle-aged man suffered a heart attack and an ambulance was sent to transport him to the closest hospital's ER. Unfortunately, he died halfway there. The coroner's office directed the ambulance to return the deceased's body to his home and to leave it there. With the coroner's orders, they placed the body outside the house.

Sometime later, the dead man's son and daughter drove up, only to find their father's body lying on a stretcher next to the driveway. They were, of course, horrified and in shock. They wondered why someone hadn't had the decency to at least carry their deceased father inside and put him in his bed instead of leaving him outside, half clad and all alone.

A highly skilled electronic technician passed away suddenly of a coronary occlusion at home. He had all the myriad tools and sophisticated equipment his career demanded in the house. His body was removed to the morgue, but his relatives discovered that every bit of his electronic equipment was gone—stolen; his home was literally stripped when his family arrived. No one ever said that the coroner's deputies had failed to lock the door behind them—or if they were suspects in the theft. No arrest ensued.

It seemed to be hard to die with dignity in Lewis County. But Terry Wilson sailed through the November 2002 elections, gathering far more votes than any of those who had filed against him—including Marty Hayes. Only then did Hayes feel free to concentrate on helping Barb Thompson continue investigating her daughter's violent death.

Along with Barb and Jerry Berry, Hayes met with Deputy Bob Bishop on December 29, 2002. Bishop and Berry agreed that they were the only two commissioned officers in the Lewis County Sheriff's Office who believed that Ronda had been murdered.

Although the HITS team said they had never talked to Bishop—or anyone else involved—Bishop shook his head, puzzled. He assured Hayes that he had indeed talked with them about his personal conclusions.

Bishop said that Ronda's right hand was underneath the blanket, and her left hand grasped it tightly. How could they have come to their conclusion, with no photos showing where her right hand was? They believed she had shot herself, ergo her right hand would have had to be on top of the blanket. It was a backward kind of reasoning.

"Where did you see her hands—in relation to the blanket?" Barb asked Bishop.

"She was lying on her side, covered with a blanket. I could only see a small part of one hand—her left. Her right hand was covered by the blanket. I didn't see the gun."

Bishop recalled that the covers had been tucked in neatly on what he learned was Ronda's side of the bed, and the pillow was missing. "It didn't look like the picture you have there," he said. "Ron's side of the bed was more messed up in the photo."

It was Bishop who had noticed the vapor and humidity in the main bathroom of the house—as if someone had taken a shower very recently. And he was sure the strongest smell of incense had come from Jonathan's room.

Bishop said that if Ronda's case should ever be re-opened, he would be willing to testify about what he saw, and about his interaction with the HITS detectives.

Chapter Twenty-four

THE MAN BARB CALLED SKEETER was gone from her life, and she didn't blame him. She was still obsessed with finding Ronda's killer, and every other part of her life took a backseat. Skeeter came to believe that he was only a background person in her life, a dogsitter and an overseer to her horse ranch. Although she hated to admit it, Barb knew it was true. She missed Skeeter, but she knew she couldn't quit until she found the answers Ronda deserved. To this day, she remains close to his daughter Cheri-Lynn.

Barb took care of Gramma Virginia, whose health was fading, and she rejoiced when Freeman graduated with degrees in civil engineering and mathematics from Gonzaga University. They weren't getting enough of her time, either, but Barb knew they understood how much she loved them and that she would be back in their lives one day—hopefully sooner rather than later.

Freeman soon found a good job as a civil engineer in

Seattle. He was living in Bellevue, a suburb about fifteen miles to the east of the city, across the Floating Bridge. On June 23, 2003, Freeman was coming home at 11 P.M. from a church function, riding a motorcycle he had just bought. It had been raining and the roads were slick with a combination of oil and rainwater. According to police reports, he'd been going only about twenty-five miles an hour, but as he leaned into a slight curve in the road, the rear wheel went out from under the bike.

He went down, sliding on his back into a curb next to the sidewalk. He was wearing the strongest protective helmet money could by, and yet it cracked on impact.

Freeman's motorcycle was a brand-new model that had a hidden compartment where he carried his ID. But the police didn't know that, and he was, for the moment, "Oscar Doe" as he was loaded into a rescue helicopter and transported to Harborview Hospital.

The young man who was still unidentified was admitted in "very critical" condition.

The Seattle police patrolmen who had responded to the accident had time to search the ruined motorcycle more thoroughly and went through his clothing. They found a Bellevue address and were able to contact Freeman's roommates.

It was 3:30 A.M. when one of the officers reached Barb Thompson. They told her that Freeman had been in an accident, but that they couldn't tell her anything more than he was in "very, very, critical condition," and she needed to call the ER at Harborview Hospital as soon as possible.

It seemed that fate or bad luck or something else was conspiring to rob her of both her children. She didn't think she could bear it if she lost Freeman, too.

Her hand trembled as she punched in the phone number for Harborview. The physician working on Freeman told her that he was in a coma, caused by a traumatic brain injury. His brain had swollen and it was possible he would need surgery to drill holes in his skull that would keep the brain from crushing itself against the calvarium. He also had three broken vertebrae and several broken ribs.

It was touch-and-go whether her son would survive, or what brain damage he might suffer.

Barbara made a few phone calls, and one of her friends immediately offered to make arrangements to find someone to take care of Gramma Virginia. The horses she had in training would be transferred to other trainers, and she was assured that her own horses would be cared for, their stalls cleaned. Her home would also be cared for.

"Friends came out of the woodwork so early that morning," Barb remembers. "They took care of everything. One of my neighbors gathered a thousand dollars in cash and another brought over their brand-new car with less than seven hundred miles on it! It was all gassed up and ready to go."

Barb arrived at Harborview Hospital less than four hours after the Seattle police phoned her.

She found Freeman was in a deep coma as she sank into a chair beside his bed. She became aware of the whooshing and beeping sounds of the machines that were monitoring his heartbeat, pulse, blood pressure, the amount of brain swelling, and the pressure from his unyielding skull.

She prayed harder than she had ever prayed before, and Barb had prayed a lot during the prior four and a half years. She wanted her son to live, but she could not ask God for his life if he should come back handicapped by the awful injuries he had suffered. "I asked God to give Freeman back to me whole—or to take him. I knew my son wouldn't want to live a compromised life, and it wasn't fair for me to ask for him to live like that—just because I couldn't let go."

For sixty-nine hours, Freeman lay in his coma. Finally he opened his eyes. Barb could tell he didn't recognize her. Nor could he move his arms and legs or talk.

"Still, during those long hours of coma, every monitor had indicated that all systems were within 'safe limits.' Barely so sometimes, but the doctors were hopeful."

Freeman stayed in Harborview for thirty-four days, and once again Dave Bell was there for Barb. "He was my support, my shoulder—my rock," she says. "When I thought I couldn't go on waiting and hoping, Dave was there."

Members of Freeman's church brought Barb at least two meals a day, every day. All of them took turns preparing food for her, and coming in to sit with her, or to give her some free time away from her watch over her son.

"I was never alone. They took such good care of me."

Freeman himself made a miraculous recovery. His determination and willpower exceeded anything most people could summon. He came home in a wheelchair, but he followed up on physical therapy in Spokane. His mother walked beside him as he regained the health and coordination she had thought he might lose.

And he came all the way back. He returned to work as a civil engineer, bought his own home, and audited classes at Gonzaga University to sharpen his skills.

When his mother needs him, Freeman is there.

*　　*　　*

ALTHOUGH BARB HAD TAKEN a "sabbatical" from her quest to find Ronda's killer during Freeman's recuperation, she was far from finished. Her files filled with names of people who had known and interacted with Ronda, Ron, his sons, and his ex-wife Katie, and she became knowledgeable about the workings of the law. Both Jerry Berry and Marty Hayes were solid members of her investigative team, and she was definitely a thorn in the side of the original sheriff's investigators, who had expected she would drop away after testing them years earlier.

They had had no idea how obstinate and dedicated mothers could be.

One thing Barb had learned in the now five and a half years since Ronda died was that the old saying that "it's always darkest just before the dawn" was true. Every time she thought she couldn't keep fighting, something happened to tell her she had to. Another dawn came.

Barb had set up a website (www.JusticeforRonda.com) honoring Ronda, asking for information. In it there was a brief explanation of the still-open case and photographs of Ronda going back to when she was a pixie-faced toddler and continuing to a picture of Ronda in her Washington state trooper's uniform, proudly receiving her insignia from the governor. The website helped Barb feel hopeful, especially when she received a flood of mail from those who supported her cause. There were scores of posters who believed her and remembered Ronda as a lovely, happy young woman.

And then Barb saw that someone had posted a message sent at 2:38 A.M. on Friday, June 25, 2004. The sender was one of the last people she expected to hear from: Katie Huttula.

It is produced below exactly as it was posted on the Justice for Ronda website, including Katie's misspelling of Ronda's name as "Rhonda":

dear Barb, I only tonight was made aware of this page. I have had no idea how your work on Rhonda's case has advanced. I want to go on record as saying, I personally do not believe that Rhonda killed herself. I believe she was murdered. I do not know who, how or why but I believe her killer(s) should be found and prosecuted to the full extent of the law; whomever that person[s] may be.

I have no other information than that which I have told both you Barb and the authorities.

I loved Rhonda. I know that me being in Toledo after her tragic death was not appropriate. I in no way was trying to produce more deep hurt, to her mother, by giving you the poem. It was my only way of expressing how I felt. Rhonda's death was tragic . . . I am alive. I am basically alone.

That is my cross to bare [sic.] *My mental illness and past addiction with resulting crimes of the past are also part of that cross.*

My fourty [sic] *five year sister killed herself on Thanksgiving this year.*

My wonderful parents are still alive and I am very very close to them. I know from a daughter's standpoint how important a mother is. I do not know how I will go on if their death(s) occur before mine.

I wanted to responed [sic] *personally to your note.*

Sincerely,
Catherine

What did Katie mean in her strange post? She "knew" Ronda had been murdered, and she hinted that more than one person had been involved in killing her, but she disavowed any knowledge of who the guilty person or persons might be. She certainly sounded depressed—far more than Ronda ever had.

Was Katie Huttula's website post a cry for help, asking for sympathy, or did she really know something about Ronda's death and was sending hints to follow up?

Or maybe this was just another cog in a giant wheel that no one could turn smoothly?

When Barb Thompson tried to follow up, she couldn't locate Katie Huttula.

A rare photo of Barb Thompson laughing. Used to wearing boots on her horse ranch, she'd worn high heels to a hearing before Judge Hicks in Olympia, but Royce Ferguson hadn't told her how far the walk was. She was happy because Hicks set a hearing date in November 2009, but her feet were killing her. Walking home, she took off her heels and put on the socks. Ferguson grabbed his camera.
Royce Ferguson Collection.

David Reynolds (left) was one of Katie and Ron's sons who lived with Ron and Ronda. Neither he nor his next older brother, Jonathan, liked their stepmother very much.

Micah Reynolds is the second oldest of Ron and Katie Reynolds's five sons. He didn't live in the house in Toledo, but sometimes visited.

Ron Reynold's son Jonathan, lower right, was seventeen, the oldest of Katie and Ron's boys who lived with them. He and Ronda didn't get along, and he was very angry when she used a "takedown" move on him, forcing him on his face. She was small, but she had WSP training and experience.

Blair Connelly was a single mom with two sons when she met Ron at a school football game. She thought he was great—at first— but complained later that she was more a maid and housekeeper than a girlfriend. Blair Connelly.

Blair and Ron during the first—and happiest—days of their relationship. Ron still had Ronda's china cabinet (left). Katie Huttula had moved out four months before, and Ronda had only been dead for nine months when the couple started dating.Blair Connelly.

Ron Reynolds and friends celebrate his fiftieth birthday at a barbeque in his honor. He is much heavier than he was in his school years. Blair Connelly.

Ron at the Elma High School 40 Year Reunion in August 2009. He was married to his fourth wife, who accompanied him. His first wife, Donna, attended the event with her second, longtime husband; his second wife, Katie, was missing; and Ronda, his third wife, had died under mysterious circumstances. Fellow classmates recalled that he was jovial and at ease during the festivities. Darryl Prowse.

November 2, 2009: Judge Richard Hicks raises his right arm to swear in the jury who will decide if Coroner Terry Wilson "has been derelict in his duty in determining the manner of Ronda Reynolds's death. KOMO-TV, ABC Seattle.

Coroner Terry Wilson (rear) of Lewis County, Washington, and his deputy, Carmen Brunton. Carmen went to the scene of Ronda's death; Wilson did not. Over eleven years, Ronda's manner of death was officially changed four times. KOMO-TV, ABC Seattle.

Left to right: Deputy Coroner Carmen Brunton, defense attorney John Justice, and Coroner Terry Wilson. The big question for the jury and the gallery was: "Will Terry Wilson testify?" But Wilson wasn't in court for most of the November hearing. Carmen sat in for him, and his wife, Donna, was always there, too. KOMO-TV, ABC Seattle.

Ron bought this new home on Twin Peaks Drive in Toledo. Ronda brought all her furniture, and gave Ron $15,000 she borrowed from her mom to help with the down payment. Ron's three younger sons lived with them. Ronda was found dead here. Barb Thompson Collection.

There were so many "players" in the courtroom drama in Chehalis that Royce Ferguson wisely used charts to introduce them to the jurors. They all listened avidly as he made his opening remarks. KOMO-TV, ABC Seattle.

Barb Thompson was the first witness in the hearing to determine if Terry Wilson was derelict in his duty. She wore Ronda's pink and gray suit to give her courage. Although she had longed to tell her daughter's story to a jury, testifying was very difficult for her. KOMO-TV, ABC Seattle.

Sergeant David Bell of the Des Moines, Washington, Police Department testifies. Years before, he and Ronda came close to marrying. They remained good friends for many years. He still loved her and was one of the last people to see her alive. Being on the witness stand was obviously anguishing for him. KOMO-TV, ABC Seattle.

Jerry Berry, who risked his career in law enforcement to find out who killed Ronda, on the witness stand. He told jurors about the nearly two dozen red flags that popped up in his mind as he worked the case as a Lewis County sheriff's homicide detective. KOMO-TV, ABC Seattle.

I am talking with Barb Thompson at the railing as a day in court ends. (I'm having a bad hair day because I was caught in a squall that whipped around the Law and Justice Center.) Carmen Brunton, the Lewis County coroner's deputy, is in the background. KOMO-TV, ABC Seattle.

Tracy Vedder (back to camera) and Paul Walker of KITI Radio in Lewis County interview Barb Thompson as other reporters wait nearby in the hallway just outside Judge Hicks's courtroom. The November 2009 hearing made headline news not only in Lewis and Thurston counties—but also in Seattle and Portland. KOMO-TV, ABC Seattle.

Marty Hayes, a firearms expert who volunteered to help Barb, testified about the death weapon, the sound of a gun blast, and the pillowcase found over Ronda's head. Here he points a handgun at the ceiling as he begins to describe angle of fire and Ronda's wound, and states he doesn't believe Ronda shot herself. KOMO-TV, ABC Seattle.

Marty Hayes had to show slides of Ronda, deceased, to explain her wound and how the gun would have to have been held. Barb thought she could handle it, but seeing her dead daughter in blown-up photos on the court screen was too much for her and she'd left sobbing. Here she returns, carrying a box of Kleenex, in control of her emotions again. KOMO-TV, ABC Seattle.

Attorney Royce Ferguson demonstrates a possible position if Ronda had shot herself—but she was right-handed and the gun appeared to have been fired by her left hand. Her other hand was under her body. It just didn't fit the facts. KOMO-TV, ABC Seattle.

Firearms expert Marty Hayes shows a slightly different angle where a suicidal person might point a gun. But the bullet that killed Ronda didn't even cross the brain's midline. Another angle that didn't fit the facts. Why had the gun been in her left hand? KOMO-TV, ABC Seattle.

Dr. Jeffrey Reynolds, a forensic pathologist, points to where the bullet entered Ronda's head and brain. He testified he had never seen a bullet path like Ronda's in a suicide— even though he had performed thousands of autopsies. KOMO-TV, ABC Seattle.

Dr. Jeffrey Reynolds refers to a file to prove his point. This is the huge white notebook that Barb Thompson put together with information on Ronda's death and the investigation that followed. She believed it was inadequate and misguided. The notebook was entered into evidence at the hearing in Judge Hicks's courtroom. KOMO-TV, ABC Seattle.

Now a private investigator, like all witnesses Jerry Berry was allowed to sit in the courtroom after he testified. He listened to John Justice, Terry Wilson's attorney, with skepticism. KOMO-TV, ABC Seattle.

On an evening during the hearing, Barb Thompson meets with her crew and an expert on forensic interviews, Gary Aschenbach. Eating at the Kit Carsons Restaurant in Chehalis are, left to right, Gary Aschenbach, Royce Ferguson, Marty Hayes, Jerry Berry, Barb. Barb Thompson Collection.

Judge Richard Hicks looks very serious as he reads instructions to the jury before they retire to deliberate. KOMO-TV, ABC Seattle.

Barb, crying, being hugged by her "adopted" daughter, Lieutenant Kim Edmondson of the Kootenai County, Idaho, Sheriff's Office after the jury agreed unanimously in their judgment. KOMO-TV, ABC Seattle.

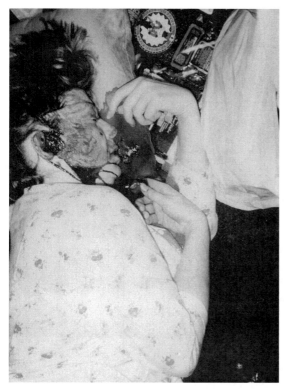

Although a detective prematurely removed the death gun, this is Ronda Reynolds as she was found in the closet off the master bathroom. Her body is in full rigor mortis, which would have taken several hours. She was right-handed, and that hand is under her breast. Her left hand position—as demonstrated by investigators in other photos—is awkwardly positioned and almost impossible to achieve—PLUS she would not have had the strength to pull the trigger, which would have taken a minimum of three pounds. Lewis County Sheriff's Office crime scene photo.

One of Barb's world-class American quarter horses, the Palomino she named "Slide Me a Dollar" stirs up the dust in her corral in Spokane. When she is with her horses, she feels close to Ronda, too. Barb Thompson Collection.

After Barb lost Ronda, she felt blessed that she still had her son, Freeman.
He was almost killed in a motorcycle accident, but, working together, Barb
and Freeman saw that he came all the way back. He is an accomplished engineer,
and he is always there when she needs help. Barb Thompson Collection.

Gramma Virginia Ramsey
loved Ronda dearly. She
passed away on February 4,
2010. Barb admits there
are times she feels almost
envious. She knows her
mother and her daughter
are together now, and that
they are happy. Although
she herself has years to
go, she looks forward to
joining them "on the other
side." In the meantime, she
works tirelessly to bring
out the whole truth about
Ronda's strange death.

CHAPTER TWENTY-FIVE

BARB THOMPSON HAD TRIED numerous times to meet with Coroner Terry Wilson over the eight years since Ronda died, but he had always refused to speak with her. Finally, on March 24, 2006, he agreed to a meeting in his office in Chehalis. Accompanied by Larry Semanko, the retired Lewis County deputy and former deputy coroner who was also the husband of Ron Reynold's sister Judy, Barb at last faced the man who was responsible for declaring the manner of her daughter's death.

Carmen Brunton, the current deputy coroner and the staff member who went to the scene of Ronda's shooting, also attended this meeting.

"Why did you put my daughter's time of death at five A.M.?" Barb asked Wilson.

"That was determined by her husband's statement that he was with her until five A.M.," Wilson answered.

"Did you consider anything else?"

Terry Wilson said he had also studied Dr. Selove's autopsy report and Ron Reynolds's statement. That was all.

She asked the coroner about the section on the death certificate for "Interval between onset and death."

"You wrote 'minutes,' " Barb asked. "Why was that?"

He had no recall of why he'd done that.

She asked Wilson to review a report submitted by neurosurgeon Dr. John Demakas that suggested that it would have taken between thirty and sixty minutes for Ronda's heart to pump out the amount of blood found on and around her body.

"After reading this," she began, "would you change the interval from 'minutes' to 'thirty to sixty minutes'?"

He shook his head. "That could mean two minutes or could mean sixty minutes. I see no reason to change it."

Barb asked for another change. Given the patterns of dual lividity on Ronda's body—which would take hours—would Wilson consider changing time of death to range of 1:30 A.M. to 3 A.M.? Or even from 1:30 A.M. to 5 A.M.?

No, he would not. "If I did that, it would be saying that Ron Reynolds murdered her. I can't do that."

That answer shook Barb. Why should Ron be exempt from tightly focused attention? Should a coroner hold back information to protect "a person of interest"?

"No, it wouldn't mean that," she argued with the coroner. "It would only mean that Ron was lying about the last time he saw Ronda alive."

Barb felt she was making no headway at all. She asked Wilson if he would still say Ronda was a suicide after he read the information she had brought for him to read.

Terry Wilson said he would go through it, but it would probably take several weeks.

Six weeks later, Deputy Coroner Carmen Brunton called

Barb and told her that while Wilson had reviewed her evidence, he'd found no reason to change his documentation.

"How—and why—is he still making the determination of suicide?" Barb asked, her voice tight with extreme frustration.

"He didn't say," Carmen said, and hung up.

*   *   *

BY EARLY SUMMER 2006, Barb Thompson, Jerry Berry, and Marty Hayes had reached an impasse. They needed an attorney—a criminal defense attorney—who knew his craft. But such lawyers were expensive, and Barb had few funds available. Neither Jerry nor Marty had charged her for their hundreds of hours of work trying to vindicate Ronda and save her from being inaccurately listed as a suicide.

Marty had an idea. He knew an attorney who might just be willing to take on the challenge, even knowing there would be little cash incentive.

"I'll call him," Hayes told Barb. "All he can do is say no. His name is Royce Ferguson, and he's good. I'll tell him that you sent a letter to Terry Wilson in May where you threatened him with a judicial review."

Ferguson met with Hayes and the two men went out for pizza. Barb, Jerry, and Marty needed to have a judicial review—if they could pull it off—to spark any further action in Ronda's case, now eight years old. If they succeeded, it would be a landmark case, which is why Marty Hayes suspected Royce Ferguson might want to take it on.

Ferguson listened as Hayes outlined the bare bones of the case. By the time they had finished their pizza, Ferguson had agreed to meet with Barb. He hadn't committed to anything at that point, but he was willing to hear her out.

Royce Ferguson's one-man office was in Everett, Washington, about 120 miles north of Lewis County. It had none of the ostentation that many attorneys affect: the leather chairs, thick rugs, huge desks, paintings, and heavy drapes. Nor did he automatically start a timer as they began to talk. Barb had met lawyers like that and quickly sensed that the hourly fees they stipulated were paying for all the pomp and glitter. She knew she couldn't afford them.

His secretary and paralegal, Cece, was gracious and efficient as she welcomed Barb, who felt completely comfortable and optimistic for the first time in a long time. Royce looked to be in his fifties, a compactly built man with a burr haircut out of the past.

Although Royce Ferguson had handled a number of high-profile cases, he didn't talk about them. Until the writing of this book, Barb was unaware of the myriad unusual cases in which Ferguson had acted for the defense. Some were deadly serious, and others were almost whimsical.

Ferguson was a man for all seasons whose interests varied from fishing to cooking to history to music to writing and updating textbooks on Washington state law criminal practice and procedure. His two volumes are cited as authority by both the Washington State Court of Appeals and the Washington State Supreme Court. But it was the law that fascinated him the most.

"Each lawyer has a different set of dreams and goals," Ferguson wrote on his blog, "Mouthpiece Notes": "Mine include wanting to help the little guy, take on some cases which other lawyers may fear as too hard or impossible, solve some tricky legal questions in a novel way, and then be recognized for a tough job well done. So, I guess, I wanted to be a hero (hopefully) and help 'make some new law' by having a case reported in the law books as a 'case of first impression.'

"The promise of fees has never been the determining factor. Fitting cases usually involve modest or no fees at all. I recall a quote attributed to Abraham Lincoln—'Do a good job practicing law and the fees will take care of themselves.' Or something like that. It's true."

Royce Ferguson grew up admiring Lincoln, Atticus Finch from *To Kill a Mockingbird,* Don Quixote, Clint Eastwood's Detective Harry Callahan, and an assortment of heroic cowboys who once galloped across black-and-white television sets.

It was only natural that he would soon be jousting at windmills himself and representing an assortment of both good and bad guys.

In perhaps the most disastrous serial arsonist case in the Northwest in decades, Ferguson defended Paul Keller, twenty-seven, an advertising salesman in his father's firm, on charges of setting seventy-seven fires that terrified Washington state residents in four counties during a six-month spree in the summer and fall of 1992.

Financial loss from the charred buildings, churches, homes, businesses, and retirement homes was estimated at $14 million.

But worst of all, three elderly women died in the inferno that destroyed the Four Freedoms House retirement home on September 22, 1993. Bertha Nelson, ninety-three, Mary Dorris, seventy-seven, and Adeline Stockness, seventy, perished and several other residents were injured. Damages totaled half a million dollars.

Keller was a troubled man whose own father turned him in.

Royce Ferguson didn't argue that Keller was innocent, but did ask that he get mental health treatment for problems that had begun when he was a child. He was so hyperactive as a boy that his father would drive him miles from home and leave him there, hoping that he would work off some of his energy walking back.

Paul Keller received a ninety-nine-year sentence, and, of course, remains in prison. But there is not enough money in Washington's prison budgets to provide psychiatric help that might reveal who or what Paul was railing against as he set fire after fire after fire.

I wrote about another of Ferguson's high-profile clients in *Ann Rule's True Crime Files: Vol. I.*

One of the most infamous killers in Washington state's history was Charles Campbell, who was in his early twenties in 1974 when he raped Renae Wicklund while holding a knife to her baby daughter, Shannah. He went to prison but obtained an early release in 1982.

On April 14, 1982, Charles Campbell returned to the Wicklunds' home in Clearview, and killed Renae and Shannah, as well as Barbara Hendrickson, a fifty-one-year-old woman who lived across the street. He was arrested almost at once and charged with three counts of murder on April 19. Campbell was an attorney's nightmare. He was an ungrateful client who did nothing to cooperate with any of the lawyers who represented him.

Royce was appointed by the Court to represent Campbell, along with Ken Lee, who was the lead attorney on the case. The two of them worked on his case for about a year, but it became so frustrating that Lee asked to be fired. Although Royce could work with the very difficult Campbell, he looked at Lee's request as a chance for him to leave the thankless case. New attorneys were appointed.

It's probable that none of them wanted to see Charles Campbell walk free; he was too dangerous—but they tried to save him from the gallows. It was impossible. He spit on the governor who came to his cell opening, hit his own small son on the head when he came to visit, and was cruel to a female corrections worker, whom he had seduced and impregnated.

Over the years, Campbell wrote or called Royce—collect, of course—from prison, asking for copies of legal cases or decisions. Royce obliged, figuring that even a despicable convicted killer deserved a little help in his quest to stay alive.

Twelve years later, Royce Ferguson represented a journalist who wanted to videotape Campbell's execution by hanging in 1994. The case was dismissed on grounds that the state constitution specified "there was no right to access the visual images of a hanging."

As Campbell ran out of appeals in late May 1994, he wrote to Royce again. The end was near for him. Royce wrote back, choosing his words and phrases very carefully.

"I was looking for the right words to tell a condemned man there was nothing more I could send him, and nothing more that I would do. You don't want to say goodbye," he explained later, "because then the guy might give up what little hope he has, but it was a way, for me, to end it. Kind of a no-hard-feelings letter, without saying, 'Hey, you're a dead man.' "

For Royce Ferguson, dealing with Charles Campbell was a front-row seat from which to study a classic psychopath. "I was able to get some insight into a man awaiting death for the three murders he'd committed."

Charles Campbell died on the gallows, so terrified that

he could not walk there and had to be carried by corrections officers.

Criminal defense attorneys are often maligned, but Ferguson almost always looked for the small specks of humanity in potential clients or those he was suing on behalf of someone else. He tried to find the reasons that made them do what they did.

He didn't find many that explained psychopathy. However, there was a case where a man named David Schubert was the prime suspect in the presumed murder of his wife, Juliana.

On June 30, 1989, Juliana Schubert, thirty, was seen alive for the last time. Her employer at the Everett Steel Company said goodbye to her on that Friday. On Monday, July 3, David Schubert, forty-seven, called to say that his wife would not be working that day. Two days later, he called her employer again and said Juliana was in Colorado with a "friend" and would not be returning to work at all. Later, he went to her office and picked up her personal belongings and returned her post office box key. Schubert asked about her check, but her boss refused to give it to him. But the missing woman's husband did collect a refund from the employment agency that got her the job, citing a "sixty-day clause."

The couple and their two sons had lived on some sixteen acres in Arlington, Washington, but they just didn't get along. Juliana had talked with her friends about seeking to have her marriage dissolved, and said she hoped to get an apartment for her sons—then seven and five—and herself.

One witness said that about a month before Juliana went missing, David Schubert had said, "I will kill Juliana to get peace of mind."

Over the weeks following Juliana's disappearance, Schubert gave conflicting accounts of where she was. Besides Colorado, he said she was vacationing in Chicago, in New York "back east," and was in Arizona with another man.

On July 24, almost four weeks after she vanished, David Schubert finally told her mother, Karil Nelson, that she was missing, and that she had taken neither her car nor her clothes—but he thought she might have taken her purse or five hundred dollars. Her mother immediately called the police in Everett, only to find that David had not even filed a missing-persons report.

This was particularly strange since Schubert had served as a reserve police officer. He was also an insurance agent. He testified later that he and Juliana were having marital problems and were in the process of a "do it yourself" divorce.

He had sought advice on that, however, from their family attorney, when he learned they had to have a parenting plan for their two young sons. Juliana had allegedly reacted badly to his choice of attorneys—since the lawyer also represented her mother. He said she threw the car keys at him, saying "It's your car, it's your house . . . I hate it! I hate it! I hate it!"

And then he said she left, deserting her little boys, her whole life. David Schubert said he figured she would come back when she cooled down.

But she never did. Her sons grew up believing she had left them on purpose.

David Schubert sometimes said, "Only stupid people get caught for murder."

Police suspected that Schubert had murdered Juliana, and they went so far as to arrest him on charges of second-degree murder. But after the lead detective on the case, Rick Blake, fell ill with leukemia and died, the charges were dismissed.

When Juliana had been gone for seven years, David Schubert filed to have her declared legally dead. The court obliged on September 23, 1996. The next day the widower filed a petition for an order to probate Juliana's will and appoint him personal representative.

But Karil Nelson went to Royce Ferguson. This couldn't be right. She believed that Schubert had killed her daughter. Royce alleged that since the "widower is the slayer of Juliana M. Schubert, he is otherwise disqualified to serve, administer, and inherit."

Karil Nelson was appointed as special personal representative of Juliana's estate, and she filed a wrongful-death action against her former son-in-law, seeking to have him legally declared the "slayer" of her daughter.

Juliana's murder began a series of events that brought tragedy after tragedy. The boys had never been allowed to know their grandmother, and totally believed what their father told them over the years.

David Schubert was subsequently charged once again with the second-degree murder of his wife, and went on trial thirteen years after Juliana vanished. Although her body was never found, he was convicted in 2002 and sentenced to thirteen and a half years in prison.

He is now seventy years old. His only hope of early release would be Juliana walking out of the mists of time to prove that she is not dead after all.

Royce Ferguson represented Juliana's mother, Karil Nelson, pro bono.

* * *

Barbara Thompson knew virtually nothing about Royce Ferguson's other cases, nor did she realize that he was probably one of the few attorneys who would take a chance on her—even if she had little money, and even though years had passed since Ronda's death. She remembers the first time she met him at his Everett office.

"We began to discuss Ronda's case," Barb recalls, "and, at first, I could tell he wasn't really buying what I was saying. But he kept listening. He was very polite and intent, and as I talked on, he started asking questions. He asked me to show him evidence backing up what I was saying. I was able to illustrate my points in the case file I had put together, and I could see he was growing more and more interested."

Their conversation went on for two hours. As they neared the end of their meeting, Ferguson realized that Barb had come prepared. She wasn't there to complain or cry or say that life isn't fair. She had the facts, statements, and evidence to validate everything she was telling him.

"He decided to take the case," Barb remembers, still in awe that thanks to Marty Hayes, she had "found the best person possible to join us in our struggle to get a judicial review. He made no promises, and asked only to have a small fee up front and money to cover court costs deposited in his trust account. We shook hands and never looked back."

*   *   *

In the years ahead, Barb found that Royce was honest, sincere, and "so very dedicated" to his profession. "Anyone who says attorneys are heartless, money-hungry crooks, with no conscience hasn't met Royce Ferguson! He is an example of what all attorneys should be and he has fought as hard as I have since he came on board. In spite of everything that lay ahead, I don't think Royce has ever regretted taking Ronda's case."

Once or twice every month, Royce Ferguson plays trumpet and keyboard with his fellow musicians in the North End Jazz Quintet. Their usual venues are the Wayward Coffee shop in the Greenwood district in North Seattle, and the Jewel Box Cafe. It's one of his many ways of easing the stress of filing briefs and motions and the trials that ensue.

*   *   *

BASED ON HIS HISTORY OF CASES, and his avocations, Royce Ferguson could be the model for a television series, but he's probably too modest for that.

The team of Barb Thompson, Jerry Berry, Marty Hayes, and Royce Ferguson were dedicated, hardworking, and innovative, and they soon formed a tight bond. They met often, laughed when they felt like crying, and vowed to find justice for Ronda.

But they faced some hard times ahead.

*   *   *

GEORGE FOX, the retired detective from California who was on the HITS team that had reviewed the case and came back concurring with the Lewis County sheriff's team's opinion that Ronda had killed herself, was particularly scathing when he described the men who were helping Barb Thompson, as he wrote to the incoming Lewis County sheriff, Steve Mansfield, in June 2006.

"I found it very troublesome that individuals with no—

or limited experience—prey on a grieving mother for their own personal financial or political gain."

Not surprisingly, this did not sit well with Marty Hayes. Hayes had worked almost a thousand hours for Barb, all pro bono—as had Jerry Berry and Royce Ferguson. He'd charted the decibel level of a ringing alarm clock against the sound of gunfire and tested the pillow placed over Ronda's head and face for gunshot residue. With a nearly identical handgun, he checked to see where the recoil direction of the gun should have been. Certain photographs—alleged to have been taken the morning after Ronda died—were missing; they were either lost, stolen, or had been thrown away for no good reason.

Hayes knew guns—and that was obvious. He didn't have as much hands-on experience in homicide investigation as many of the detectives involved in the seemingly endless search for Ronda Reynolds's true manner of death, but he knew what guns will do, how loud they are, and how people used them. Since the gun used to kill Ronda Reynolds had been moved prematurely by Detective Dave Neiser, it was very important to have someone with that kind of knowledge in reconstructing the shooting.

Hayes and George Fox spent a lot of time trying to prove the other was misguided, incompetent, conceited, deluded, and overly ambitious.

Small and large turf wars are far from uncommon in high-profile investigations. The important thing is that they should not be allowed to interfere with finding the solution to the mystery.

Fox said that Vernon Geberth, the New York homicide expert, had acknowledged later that he had changed his mind about the fallacy of Ronda's "suicide," and now be-

lieved she had killed herself. Since Geberth is an old friend, I
called him and asked him about that—was he really coming
around to thinking Ronda had killed herself?

"No!" he said. "I've never said anything like that to
Fox. If I had further thoughts, I would have written them
down. I don't casually comment that I've changed my mind!
I still believe Ronda Reynolds was a victim of homicide!"

In the end, I came to believe Marty Hayes. Yes, he
wanted to be the Lewis County coroner. There wasn't anything wrong with that, and there were many reasons why it
was time for a change in that elected office.

When—and if—a judicial hearing would take place,
Marty would be a powerful witness in demonstrating how
Ronda died.

Hayes began a series of tests. First, he had to find a
revolver similar to the death gun. He located a Rossi .32-
caliber long revolver.

He wanted to see if it would have been possible for
Ronda to wrap a pillow around that gun and then shoot
herself. The first two times he attempted to fire the gun, the
pillow's case caught between the firing pin (which is connected to the hammer on a Rossi revolver) and the cartridge.

Holding the gun *clear of the pillow* allowed the firing
pin enough leeway. But tests done this way produced a dual
pattern on the pillow case—which did not coincide with the
actual pillow detectives removed from Ronda's head.

"It would have been extremely difficult, if not impossible," Hayes wrote, "for her to have positioned herself in
the manner in which she was discovered, wrapped the gun
in a pillow, fired it, and have the gun come to rest on her
forehead or temple."

There had been a distinct imprint of the revolver in the
skin of Ronda's forehead, and that was difficult to explain.

Especially since it was underneath the pillow, with the gun-shot hole on the outside of the pillow.

Unless someone had placed it there.

Marty Hayes continued to experiment with various diagnostic devices in an effort to either prove or disprove whether the first deductions by the sheriff's office were correct.

CHAPTER TWENTY-SIX

WHILE MARTY HAYES, Jerry Berry, and Royce Ferguson were working with Barb Thompson because they believed that Ronda deserved to have the truth known, there were others who were parasites—vultures—looking to make money or to take some kind of perverse pleasure out of her grief.

Dear Barb

    It's time for some hard truth. If you're easily offended, you should stop reading now and hit your delete tab. If not, you may want to read on. However, please be advised that you've been fairly warned and you're probably not going to like what you're about to hear.

    What was it that I was going to learn from you in our meeting that I don't already know?

    I know your daughter was murdered.

    I know who did it.

I know it was covered up.

I know why it was covered up.

I know who murdered her.

I know how he did it.

I know why he did it.

I know who helped him.

I know how to solve the case.

What else do I need to know?

I don't need to build a closet or break into John McCroskey's evidence room to solve the case.

I don't need to watch you cry or hear your tale of heartbreak to solve this case.

I don't need to hear you talk about "protecting the identity of anonymous witnesses" to solve this case.

I don't need someone who has never worn a badge to tell me how to solve this case.

Professionals trade their time, their education, their efforts, their experience for things of value . . . preferably money.

If you really wanted to solve this case, Barb—If you really wanted "Justice for Ronda" you'd find the money and you'd compensate me for doing my job.

The hard awful truth of the matter is that you don't really want me to do my job.

You don't really want this case solved.

All you really want is to continue on with your "drama" and keep finding new people to feel sorry for you.

I won't do that for you. I have too many dead friends to grieve for myself.

Men that died in the line of duty protecting others.

I've got enough grief of my own to last a lifetime.

$10,000 is an absurdly low fee for a murder case. Other investigators laughed at the price I quoted you.

However, I am a man of my word. Any time you "choose" to come up with the money, I'll solve this case. However, I won't play into your drama anymore.

Life is about choices, Barb. Ronda chose to marry Ron. Ronda chose to divorce Ron. Ron chose to murder Ronda. Ron got away with murder because you made a "choice" to let that happen.

No amount of crying or hand-wringing is going to bring Ronda back or put Ron in prison for his crime.

Make a choice, Barb. Get professional therapy for your grief or pay someone a fair wage to solve this crime.

Move on with your life or continue feeling sorry for yourself. The choice is yours.

Professor "Mean"* didn't know all the answers, as smug as he came across. He taught criminal justice in a 2-year college in Clark County. He knew a few things he'd picked up from listening to one of his students years before, and he had kept his ear to the ground for gossip. Mostly, he was looking for a quick $10,000. Sadly, high-profile unsolved cases attract con artists—anywhere from fake psychics to would-be preachers to so-called friends of the victim. And desperate families often *do* pay them, hoping they know the answers to the questions that haunt them.

Barb Thompson was not so easily intimidated, and cut off all contact with this man.

* * *

WHEN IT BECAME CLEAR that Coroner Terry Wilson was not going to change the "suicide" determination on Ronda's death certificate, Barb Thompson was ready to move ahead on a threat she'd made to Wilson. With Royce Ferguson's advice, she decided to sue him civilly for dereliction of duty and to ask for a judicial review.

They didn't want a judge in Lewis County; they hoped for a judge from another county—who would have no preconceived opinions about the way Ronda Reynolds died.

Thurston County was just north of Lewis County, Grays Harbor County to the west, and Cowlitz County to the south. Easterly, there were miles and miles of forest before Chelan County began.

Before that took place, however, Coroner Terry Wilson's attorneys filed a motion to dismiss the review, saying that the statute of limitations had run out after two years had passed. Wilson's motion was granted by Superior Court Judge Richard Hicks of Thurston County on May 4, 2007.

Royce appealed this decision to the Court of Appeals.

While Barb, Marty Hayes, Jerry Berry, and Royce Ferguson waited for the Court of Appeals' decision throughout the rest of 2007, another strong supporter came on board. Tracy Vedder, an investigative reporter from KOMO-TV, the ABC affiliate in Seattle, began to follow the long struggle of a single mom from Eastern Washington.

Vedder traveled to Barb's horse ranch and interviewed her, filming her "other life" when she wasn't pounding on courthouse doors over on "the coast."

The KOMO reporter looked over the paucity of evidence that suggested Ronda had killed herself and became an expert on this case of what might very well be long-delayed justice. She talked to those who had known Ronda in life, and their recollections of the cheerful, stubborn former state trooper didn't mesh in Vedder's mind with the picture that Ron Reynolds painted of her.

Tracy set about writing a documentary that would inform viewers in Washington state of what was happening in the quiet county that they drove through obliviously, where they stopped for an hour or so to shop at the outlet malls and dine at the Country Cousin.

Like many of us who had followed this case, Tracy was unable to let go of it.

*　　*　　*

ON JANUARY 29, 2008, the Court of Appeals overturned Judge Hicks's dismissal of the case. The court found that Wilson himself had stalled the statute of limitations because he had refused to meet with Barb Thompson as required by law. Consequently, the time period had been "tolled"—or put on indefinite hold.

Barb Thompson had waited so long. She could wait out any legal process—just as long as she was keeping her silent promise to Ronda that she would fight for her.

On September 19, 2008, Judge Hicks ruled that a judicial review would take place after all, and instructed the opposing attorneys to submit briefs on how they would want the judicial review to go forward, and also to submit records of the case for each party.

Barb Thompson's team was gaining ground, although sometimes it seemed as though it was only inches when they wanted miles. As one of the worst winters Washington had seen approached, Barb had to drive across two mountain passes on many six-hundred-mile round-trips so she could attend all the legal proceedings that she devoutly hoped would lead to—at the very least—a change on Ronda's death certificate that would, once and for all, eliminate "suicide." Gramma Virginia's health was failing and Barb worried about leaving her. She also had many prize horses and other animals to take care of. This meant she had to make arrangements for someone to come in and do all the chores she usually did. Many times when Barb was on the "other side of the mountains," she got phone calls saying her mother had been rushed to the hospital. She was pulled in so many directions.

But Ronda's Gramma always urged Barb to keep fighting, and somehow they managed. Barb felt that her mother was hanging on to life until she saw Ronda vindicated. And that probably had an element of truth.

On December 5, 2008, there was yet another hearing on Coroner Terry Wilson's motion to dismiss, this time on constitutional grounds. Judge Hicks denied it.

Barb and her three "musketeers" were so elated with this decision that they set out enthusiastically to walk from the courthouse to their hotel. This was the biggest legal battle they had won! But Barb was wearing high heels when she was used to cowboy boots, and the distance stretched longer and longer. Finally, she handed her shoes to Royce Ferguson and put on a thick pair of "lumberjack" socks. She drew a lot of stares as she strolled along in stocking feet, but she didn't care.

Royce grabbed his camera and caught that carefree moment.

It had been ten years—less eleven days—since Ronda had told her mother that Ron Reynolds was leaving her and returning to his ex-wife Katie. Ten years—minus a week—since Ronda was shot to death. Windows all along the street where they walked were decorated for Christmas, just as they were in 1998. Every Christmas since then had been bittersweet because Ronda wasn't there to celebrate with her family, or with David Bell, who hadn't remarried or dated anyone seriously in the decade Ronda had been gone. It was sometimes so hard for Barb to think of what might have been, but she usually could keep those thoughts to herself.

And yet, somehow this was the first Christmas since then that she could feel a sense of hope. Maybe the new year would bring about what they had hoped for for so long.

On January 9, 2009, there was a hearing on a new motion from Coroner Wilson's attorneys asking for an appellate court review on Judge Hicks's denial on December 5.

Hicks denied this motion, too.

On May 19, 2009, there was a short hearing to consider yet another motion from Terry Wilson's legal team. They wanted the coroner to be dismissed from the action. Judge Richard Hicks also denied this motion. He said he would not dismiss Wilson from the actions brought by Royce Ferguson, but it was up to Wilson if he wanted to attend the hearing seeking to have "suicide" removed from Ronda's death certificate. He could stay away if he chose to.

At the same time Judge Hicks responded to a request from Ron Reynolds and quashed a subpoena requiring Reynolds to give a deposition in the case. Reynolds's position was that he would become a suspect in Ronda's death if the verdict in the upcoming hearing found that Ronda's death had been "homicide."

Ron Reynolds was still the elementary school principal, and he had many people who supported him, and more current and former students who recalled him as a kind man who smiled and talked with them when they met on the streets of Toledo. There were also those, though, who treated him like a pariah and refused to sit next to him at school sports events.

But he had become something of a recluse—at least as far as the media was concerned. Any attempt to talk with

Reynolds was intercepted by Ray Dudenbostel, his family's attorney in Elma, who continued to represent him. Dudenbostel usually replied to requests for interviews with Ron by saying his client had suffered enough loss when Ronda died, and didn't want to relive that time in his life.

*   *   *

THE MAY 2009 HEARING was the first time Barb Thompson and I had a chance to talk for hours in person, although we had corresponded for years by phone, mail, and email, and met briefly at book signings. If I had expected to meet a grieving, morose woman, I was certainly surprised. I liked her immediately and we must have talked for five hours or more.

We bonded further as I walked out of my house with her, saying goodbye as she prepared to leave for the long drive back to Spokane. Just at that moment, my rambunctious Bernese Mountain Dog, Yogi, knocked me down my steps, through a railing, and I landed on my head on a brick wall. Barb picked me up, wiped the blood off my face, and ran to get ice to stop the swelling in my right eye. She insisted on staying with me until another friend arrived.

I ended up with the biggest black eye I've ever seen, which lasted for weeks, but also knew that Barb Thompson and I would be friends for the rest of our lives.

CHAPTER TWENTY-SEVEN

RON REYNOLDS AVOIDED ME and every other media person who sought to talk with him, but he didn't shun social events. His former classmates from the Class of 1969 at Elma High School were startled when he and his fourth wife appeared at the class's fortieth reunion in August 2009. With all the rumors that had circulated about Ron when Ronda died, they didn't expect him to show up. But he was there, very convivial, if soft-spoken, seemingly glad to see the people he'd gone to school with, all of them in their late fifties now.

Ron looked very different from the way they remembered him. He had once been thin—but forty years later, he appeared to have put on about a hundred pounds. Of course, he wasn't the only one who had changed. Almost everyone was heavier, many of the men were bald, and the girls had become women with gray hair or the slightly false color that even the most expensive dyes leave. But if they hadn't read Ron's name tag, he would have been almost impossible to recognize.

He didn't seem at all concerned about the pretrial hearing that was set for only a month away, or the hearing itself scheduled for November 3. And no one mentioned it.

At least no one mentioned it to Ron. They gathered in private groups and talked about it. And after the reunion, his fellow students compared notes on what they knew about Ron, his four wives, and his five sons. The gossip bubbled just below the surface, but never quite turned into outright accusations.

With the progress Barb Thompson had made over eleven years, it would be only a matter of time now for people to come forward.

The Elma Class of '69 counted the weeks until the judicial hearing would take place in November.

Initially, Judge Richard Hicks had planned to listen to the hearing testimony and make the decision on his own. But he changed his mind and asked that a twelve-person jury be selected, over which he would have the final say.

The addition of a jury made this legal platform seem far more like a trial than a hearing.

One wondered how much clout this jury would have, given that they would be selected from the citizens of Lewis County. In initial trips there, I had found that everyone I talked to seemed to know about the Ronda Reynolds case. Some had firm opinions—on one side or the other. Picking a jury might be difficult, but a large jury pool appeared at the Lewis County Law and Justice Center on Monday, November 2, 2009.

It might take all day to select jurors.

*   *   *

THE FIRST WEEK OF NOVEMBER 2009 was bitterly cold in Chehalis, and the rain-filled wind whipped around the corners of the Law and Justice Center as those lucky enough to find a parking spot ducked their heads and leaned into the gusts.

John McCroskey was no longer the sheriff—although he remained a sure source for quotes on Ronda Reynolds's case for the media. By 2009, Steve Mansfield was the sheriff, and he had inherited the troubled Ronda Reynolds probe.

On November 2, the fourth-floor courtroom assigned to Judge Hicks was filled with potential jurors, and there was precious little space on the six rows of long oak benches for anyone else. Coroners from other counties had arrived early and sat in the last row, curious to hear the evidence for and against Coroner Wilson. About half of the media corps had to wait in the hallway.

At 10:48 A.M., Judge Hicks strode in and took his place on the bench. He looked like a judge from central casting with his thick head of graying hair, mustache, and beard. Reading glasses hung from strands around his neck. He was a tall man with wide shoulders.

There was no question at all that Hicks was in total control of this courtroom.

John Justice, an Olympia attorney hired by the Lewis County District Attorney's Office, would represent Terry Wilson. He looked very young, undoubtedly younger than he really was. He had a crew cut and was dressed impeccably. Both Wilson and Carmen Brunton were seated at the defense table. Marty Hayes and Royce Ferguson flanked Barb Thompson at their table. The jury members who were selected sat off to their left in an alcove section of the courtroom, where several areas of the gallery could not see them.

Most of the potential jurors had heard of Ronda Reynolds's death, but they stated they had not formed firm opinions one way or the other. One tall man who appeared to be in his fifties kept warning the judge and the opposing lawyers that he would not be a juror anyone wanted. He was argumentative—almost cocky—as he described his occupation; he was employed by city government. One got the impression that he knew a secret and was enjoying his jousting during voir dire.

Finally dismissed, he looked across the courtroom at Terry Wilson and called out "Good luck, Terry!" as he walked from the room.

True, he probably would not have made a good, impartial juror.

The jury was selected by 2:30 that first afternoon. In the end, there were eight women and four men in the jury box, who looked to be in their early twenties to their seventies. Judge Hicks declared a ten-minute recess.

The courtroom had no windows, although it was well lit. The carpet was gray with multicolored speckles. I have attended over a hundred trials, and during delays and tedious arguments on obscure legal points, I tend to count carpet speckles or ceiling tiles. But most of the time, I take notes so furiously that my hand cramps up.

The hearing finally began at 2:40 that first day. Judge Hicks introduced John Justice and Royce Ferguson, and reminded jurors to listen carefully, "Memory beats notes," he said. "You don't have to take notes—that may interfere with listening."

He explained that this was a civil hearing. After a witness testified, the jurors (and the judge) could ask questions. In a criminal trial, jurors must agree on a verdict reached beyond a reasonable doubt. In a civil trial, they need only agree that the preponderance of the evidence says the defendant is guilty or innocent.

He warned the jurors not to talk to one another about the case until both sides of the case had been presented and the time came for them to deliberate.

"When it's over, and you've come back with your verdict," Judge Hicks said, "you can talk about anything you want."

"Mr. Ferguson." Judge Hicks indicated with a nod to Barb Thompson's attorney that he could begin.

Terry Wilson sat stolidly in his chair at the defense table, apparently unconcerned that Ferguson's back and his charts were turned away from him. Carmen Brunton rarely shifted in her chair or changed expression. Sitting behind her husband, Donna Wilson was the image of "the woman behind her man." Tall, blond, and brightly dressed, she was a friendly, gracious woman. It was obvious this was an ordeal for her, but she was trying to appear okay with the hearing.

Donna Wilson would be in the courtroom every day, although her husband wouldn't appear again until the final day of the hearing.

Surprisingly, there were many vacant seats in the gallery now that so many jurors had been dismissed. Perhaps townspeople hadn't expected the hearing to start until the next day.

And then it began. Ronda's family was about to spend their twelfth Christmas without her, but first they had to get through the hearing and then Thanksgiving. The holiday season was still a painful time for them to face. Even in early November, the store windows in Chehalis were already decorated for Christmas.

Sitting in Judge Hicks's courtroom, Barb Thompson knew that she was far luckier than many parents who rail against the way their children's deaths were investigated.

Still, she dreaded what was to come.

*   *   *

ROYCE FERGUSON rose in response to Judge Hicks's signal. He turned to the charts he had prepared so that the jurors could quickly become familiar with the players in this tragedy.

Television cameras from KOMO-TV were allowed in the courtroom, and so were newspaper photographers. A few interested laypersons had also brought their digital cameras.

Ferguson described Ronda—how she was born in 1965 and grew up to become the youngest female Washington State Patrol cadet. He covered Ron and Ronda's premature May-October wedding. Neither of them had been free to marry for very long. Many couples would have waited until the ashes of their former marriages had cooled, but Ron and Ronda rushed into a wedding ceremony on January 2, 1998. Everything had seemed right then; even the similarity of their names seemed to validate that.

Ron and Ronda.

Ronda had been so happy at her wedding on the second day of a new year. Her life with Ron stretched into the future, full of second chances. She was only thirty-two; she hoped to bear Ron's children as well as help him look after his sons.

But Ferguson explained that Ronda lived for only eleven months after her wedding.

She knew as the next holiday season approached that her new marriage was over. Ferguson told the jurors that Ronda planned to fly to Spokane on December 16 to spend Christmas with her mother, grandmother, and brother. Her marriage had wound down to the end at Ron Reynolds's request, and she needed to be with those who loved her.

"She was going to come back from Spokane and find an apartment."

But, of course, Ronda never left the house on Twin Peaks Drive on that long mid-December night.

This was not a murder trial. This hearing wasn't to indict anyone for Ronda's shooting, although Ferguson acknowledged that the three persons of interest were Ron Reynolds, Katie Huttula, and their son, Jonathan (who was the prime suspect in the killing of Ronda's pet dogs, and was rumored to have shot cats).

None of them was required to be in the courtroom or to testify.

No, the legal question before them was to decide whether Terry Wilson had been derelict in his duties as coroner. Why had he had made *four different* judgments on the manner of Ronda's death on succeeding death certificates over the prior decade?

"Terry Wilson didn't go to the scene where Ronda died," Ferguson explained, "nor did he attend her autopsy. In both instances, Carmen Brunton did."

All detectives know—or should know—that they must first consider that a death is a homicide. Then suicide. Then accidental. And finally either "natural" or "undetermined." Except for Jerry Berry and Bob Bishop, all of the sheriff's staff who looked into Ronda's death skipped over "homicide" as a possible option.

Royce Ferguson listed the death certificate explanations, pointing out that the first one had been "corrected" three times.

1. Undetermined
2. Suicide

3. Undetermined
4. Suicide

"No wonder Jerry Berry came to wonder if the crime scene was a staged suicide. No way is this a real suicide!" Royce said. "There are none of Ronda's fingerprints on any of the six bullets."

Nor were there anyone else's.

Barb Thompson wasn't seeking money. The Lewis County Sheriff's Office's investigation wasn't at issue. Ron Reynolds wasn't technically involved. This was all about how Coroner Terry Wilson had handled Ronda's death investigation on December 16, 1998—and in the years that came after.

All Barb Thompson wanted in this hearing was to have "suicide" removed from Ronda's death certificate. She had learned to modify her goals after so many years of disappointment.

* * *

FERGUSON TOLD THE JURY of the red flags that had popped up, making both Detective Jerry Berry and Deputy Bob Bishop question what had really happened on the very first day. Why was Ron Reynolds's wedding ring off his finger, leaving a pale strip of skin? Why was the main bathroom in the Reynolds's house all steamed up as it would be if someone had recently taken a shower? And, yes, Ron Reynolds's wedding ring was there in the soap dish of his master bathroom.

The bottle of Black Velvet in the master bedroom—allegedly removed from its usual place in the kitchen—was on Ronda's nightstand. There was a can of Pepsi and two glasses sitting on the floor near the waterbed. The whiskey had, Reynolds said, been a quarter full. When deputies arrived, it was empty—but who had drained the bottle? Ronda didn't drink hard liquor. Ron said he hadn't drunk any of it on December 15–16.

Royce Ferguson read the list of witnesses he intended to call: Barbara Thompson, David Bell (Ronda's longtime friend), Robert Bishop (the second Lewis County officer on the scene), Jerry Berry, Marty Hayes, and Dr. Jeffrey Reynolds, a forensic pathologist unrelated to Ron.

He informed the jurors of Jerry Berry's twenty-one questions that he needed answers for. "These were important questions," Barb's lawyer pointed out, "but he was shut down. He butted heads with the brass, and finally, he's off the case. He's working in a hostile environment [in the Lewis County Sheriff's Office] and he resigned."

The jurors' inscrutable expressions changed just a little when he told them that Katie Huttula, Ron's ex-wife, had walked out from the master bedroom only about a day after Ronda's body had been removed.

"Ronda's own mother can testify to that—Barb Thompson saw Katie there, in a bathrobe."

Coroner Terry Wilson had, Ferguson, said "relied on the sheriff's office to decide the manner of Ronda Reynolds's death. Jerry Berry never sued the sheriff's office. He took his retirement and kept going until he got another job."

Ferguson said that Marty Hayes would testify. He explained that Hayes was a ballistics expert. "He came into Ronda's case one hundred percent sure that Ronda Reynolds had been murdered."

Sergeant David Bell would tell the jurors about his long

friendship with Ronda, Ferguson said. Bell was the last person to see Ronda alive—other than the Reynolds family—on that deadly Tuesday night.

Not surprisingly, the surname of the last witness scheduled came as something of a shock to the gallery. Dr. Jeff Reynolds, the chief medical examiner for nine Washington counties, would give his opinion on the method of Ronda's death. He was not related to any of Ron Reynolds's family, but it seemed bizarre that one of the prime witnesses for Barb Thompson's side of this hearing had the same name as one of the prime suspects.

Royce Ferguson was winding up his opening statement.

"No way," Ferguson said in a loud voice, "is this a real suicide!" He promised to show the jury evidence and testimony to prove that.

*   *   *

THAT MADE SENSE, but there were those in the gallery who murmured to each other in the hall later—wondering why further investigation hadn't been able to come up with a category for the manner of Ronda's death. Why had Wilson's office waffled over that for eleven years? They stopped their whispered comments as the jurors walked by, headed for a break in the jury room.

Attorney Justice skipped rapidly to criticism of Ronda. He brought up the credit cards that Ronda was reputed to have used with phony names. Perhaps she had turned to thoughts of self-destruction when that came to light? But had she been suicidal? The coroner's attorney brought up the prescription that Ronda had had filled for Zoloft seven months before she died. Detectives had found the bottle in the master bathroom; Justice didn't mention that more than half of the capsules were still in the container. He may not have known that Ron Reynolds was the one who first mentioned Zoloft to the detectives.

Justice told jurors that Ronda had no financial interest in the house she'd shared with Ron Reynolds. He said there had been no monetary input from her. He told them that Ronda had a trace of gunshot residue on her hand— he did not tell them that none of the others known to be in the house the night she died had been tested for gunshot residue.

He quoted Cheryl Gilbert, Ronda's clingy friend, whom she'd allegedly told she wished she could go to sleep and never wake up. Didn't that suggest she was suicidal?

Those few people who knew about Ron Reynolds's rumored affair with his ex-wife Katie could correlate the date on the mood-elevating drug's container to the time Ronda first suspected he wasn't being faithful.

"There is no physical evidence tying anyone to Ronda Reynolds's death," Justice stated.

That was essentially true. In intrafamily situations, the physical evidence that detectives often depend on— fingerprints, bodily fluids, hairs, fibers, etc.—are already there when a crime is committed. So it is much harder to incriminate suspects who live in the same house with the victim or who visit often. All that physical evidence is virtually useless. Had someone who lived outside the Reynolds's home left that telltale physical evidence, it would have been important.

But not in this case. Investigators hadn't found any unknown prints or hairs or fibers. And the unfired bullets in the death gun had been wiped clean, as well as the gun itself.

No one could argue with Justice as he ended his remarks: "This is one of the most unusual cases you'll ever hear—and the most difficult."

Indeed, it was—and it would continue to be so.

*   *   *

BARB THOMPSON was the first witness. She wore one of Ronda's suits. It was pink and gray, and it fit her perfectly. Even though they hurt her feet and gave her blisters, she wore matching high-heeled pumps. Barb was far more comfortable in cowboy boots, but she and Ronda had always traded clothes.

Barb's hair had gone white over the eleven years and it went startlingly well with her bright blue eyes. She had been a beautiful young woman and she was now a striking middle-aged woman. But she was so nervous she practically vibrated; the week ahead would be vitally important to her. Wearing Ronda's suit made her a little less nervous.

She took the stand at 3:55 P.M. on that first Monday afternoon. Royce Ferguson asked her about her own profession, and she explained that she bred and sold registered American quarter horses—Palominos and Paints—and that she also trained and showed them. Ronda had been, she testified, just as enthusiastic about horses—and all animals—as she was.

"Ronda won numerous horse riding awards," she said.

Barb's eyes were dry at first as she recalled how much Ronda had packed into her sadly short life. After high school graduation at eighteen, Ronda went to community college and then signed on with the Washington State Patrol at the age of twenty.

"That was her dream since she was a girl," Barb said. "Her motto was 'No fear.' She spent eight years on road patrol after that."

Barb hadn't worried about Ronda when she was a trooper; she knew her daughter was capable and smart, and if either one of them ever felt uneasy, they reminded each other that "No fear" was what they both lived by.

When her marriage to Mark Liburdi ended, Barb told the jurors that Ronda and Mark put the ranch in McCleary up for sale. Ronda was due to get about $5,000 when the sale closed.

"Did you know Ron Reynolds before Ronda married him?" Royce asked.

Barb explained to the jurors that she hadn't met Ron Reynolds before Ronda married him. They lived three hundred miles apart, and Ron and Ronda's decision to marry happened so quickly.

"They moved from McCleary to Toledo when Ron got a job there—and I lent Ronda fifteen thousand dollars to put into their new house," Barb added.

Ronda had been a little concerned about Ron's three sons, who lived with them, describing them as "troubled boys with issues." But Ronda had helped raise Mark's three children and their early frostiness toward her melted; she felt she could do it again with Ron's boys.

It hadn't been as easy.

Barb testified that she had been worried about her daughter's safety after Ronda told her that Jonathan, seventeen, had threatened to kill her in early 1998, after she had been his stepmother for only a few months.

Ronda hadn't been as worried as Barb, but she had been angry when Jonathan snuck into the master bathroom and peeked at her when she was naked, taking a shower.

The third time it happened, she had to physically "take him down."

Ronda told her mother that Jonathan was embarrassed and infuriated to find himself weaker than a woman, but Ronda had hand-to-hand-combat training.

"After that incident, he appeared to hate her more than ever and wasn't going to change his feelings."

Ronda had always worked, Barb testified. After resigning from the state patrol, and before her divorce, she had undergone the Walmart chain's store security training in Aberdeen, Washington, in Grays Harbor County and then in Centralia.

Barb testified that she would take horses over to McCleary and she and Ronda often rode through the woods and on the beach.

Barring the horse trailer incident, Ronda and Mark Libirdis' divorce had been as amicable as such an event could be. Each had gone on to other relationships once they were free.

As Royce Ferguson questioned Barb Thompson about the trouble in her daughter's second marriage, she answered that Ron had admitted his affair with Katie Huttula, and that it was he who wanted the divorce. But it had hardly come as a surprise. Ronda was aware of Katie's interference in her marriage for months before that.

"Did you speak with your daughter on December fifteenth?"

"Yes—three times. In the early morning, later that day, and then late at night."

At the time of their last call, Barb said Ronda was planning to fly to Spokane the next morning. She already had her life planned out. Since Katie had been convicted on drug charges, Ronda said she wanted to wait for a clean six-month HIV test before she would agree to go ahead with a divorce. She intended to finish out her probationary period in store security at Macy's, and then ask for a transfer to another area. Barb and Gramma Virginia had hoped that meant she was soon coming home to Spokane.

For good.

But, of course, Barb had met two Alaskan flights at the Spokane airport to pick up Ronda for her Christmas visit. And Ronda wasn't on either one.

And so Barb Thompson's nightmare began.

Royce Ferguson led his witness through the ups and downs of eleven years. The case of Ronda's death had been closed, reopened, closed again, while Barb gathered information. It was only through the grace of God, she felt, that Jerry Berry, Marty Hayes, and Royce himself had jumped on board to help her in her almost impossible quest.

Ferguson had explained to Barb that the best hope was to file for a judicial review of the case.

"Then let's get one," Barb Thompson had said.

With his questions to Barb, Ferguson acknowledged to the jurors that that was what he aimed to do. Barb explained that she filed for the judicial review in 2006, only to be turned down. Two years later the Washington State Court of Appeals reversed the earlier decision and unanimously granted the judicial review to be held here in November 2009.

It was a tremendous victory for her and her team. And it was also a landmark case. That was why, he explained, coroners from other counties were monitoring this hearing. They would give their findings to a special meeting of the Washington Association of Coroners and Medical Examiners. Cowlitz County Coroner Tim Davidson was in court; he was vice president of the association.

* * *

VIEWING THE JURORS, it was obvious that some of them were probably Barb's age, with children about Ronda's age. Would they identify with Barb? There were a few young women who would probably identify with Ronda. But trying to guess what jurors are thinking is a fruitless task; once jurors are sworn in—in any trial, anywhere—they almost immediately master a noncommittal facial expression.

There might even be some of them like the dismissed juror who had cheerfully wished Terry Wilson good luck.

One thing was clear: the jury was listening intently to what Barb Thompson was saying on the witness stand. I'd never seen a jury so universally attentive. This was really the first time she had gotten a chance to tell the story of her lost daughter to a jury. Her face was easy to read; she was stressed almost to the breaking point—but she managed to finish her testimony.

It had been a very long day. John Justice had cross-examined Barb Thompson, but that had done nothing to endear him to the jury, and she bristled at his questions.

David Bell was the next witness. Still working for the Des Moines Police Department, he was fifty-three now—his hair and mustache snow white, and grief had etched lines on his face. Bell probably wished he was anyplace but in this courtroom. But he had promised Barb Thompson that he would always be there for her. And he had total recall of the last time he had seen Ronda Reynolds. Indeed, he might be the last person—save her killer—who saw Ronda alive.

Bell had never married over the years. He'd raised his sons and risen to sergeant in his department. Des Moines police had had a number of homicides since Ronda's death, including the cold-blooded shooting of one of their own.

Bell had lived through it all, and as he testified, there was the sense that he had asked the same questions of himself hundreds—thousands—of times. Why had he left Ronda alone in Toledo? Why didn't he at least take her to a motel, where she could lock the door and be safe? Had she been giving him some message that he hadn't picked up on?

Did he still blame himself for making wrong decisions the last night of Ronda's life? And yet there was no way he could have known about the danger there.

He told the jurors how he had driven to Toledo at Ronda's request on December 15, a distance of about eighty-five miles. He had arrived about 7:30 P.M. to help her move out of the home she had shared with Ron Reynolds. "I was there to help her get out of there."

Ronda had tried to get him to take a handgun—which he recalled was a PPK Walther. But he refused when he learned it was Ron's, one of his late father's guns.

"I asked her 'Why?' and I was met with a shrug."

Bell testified that he had ejected six rounds of ammunition from the gun. "I automatically do that when I know there are children in the house."

Moving Ronda's things was slow. She was most worried about her dogs and they loaded dog crates and her VCR into her car.

"Was anyone else in the house at that time?" Royce Ferguson asked.

"The boys—Ron's sons."

Ferguson wondered if the two teenagers and the grade school student had seen the gun exchange between Bell and Ronda.

"They could have."

If they had seen Ronda give him the gun, it was likely one or more of them had seen him scatter the bullets—either on the bed or the floor—and then place the weapon in the drawer under their father's side of the waterbed.

Bell said he and Ronda had gone for a drive, just to talk on neutral ground—without Ron's sons listening in. Ronda was trying to decide what she should do. She had thought about staying with her friend, Cheryl Gilbert, but she changed her mind. She asked Dave Bell to take her there; no one was home, and Ronda unlocked the door, tossed the keys in, and relocked it.

They stopped at Mary's Corner to get gas. "Ronda borrowed my cell phone and called Ron's mother. Then she called Ron. It was about ten or ten-thirty then. She also called her friend Dan at Macy's to change her shifts [while she was in Spokane]."

"She wasn't resigning?" Ferguson asked.

"No. She had no plans to quit her job." Bell added that Ronda intended to come back to Lewis County in time to work during the last-minute Christmas rush. She just wasn't sure where she would be staying.

Ronda and Ron's mother, Laura, liked each other and Ronda wanted to tell the older woman personally that she and Ron were breaking up. Dave Bell didn't hear much of her conversations on his cell phone because he was pumping gas and then paying for it.

Still, Bell recalled that Ronda had vacillated over where she would stay that night. It would be only a matter of hours until he picked her up to catch her flight to Spokane. She didn't want to stay with Cheryl Gilbert, or her old friend and work partner, Dan Pearson. When she called him that night of December 15, Pearson had told her that she was welcome to stay with him and his wife.

She and Bell had already agreed that this wasn't the time for her to meet his sons, or for her dogs to meet his cats—so his home was out. Over the years, both of them had put Bell's sons first, and they didn't want to upset them now.

"I know I don't want to stay in a motel," Ronda said.

Ronda finally wondered if she should stay at the Toledo house—for just one more night. Virtually everything she owned was in that house—her furniture, paintings, family photos and treasures, and, of course her three dogs. If she left without some sort of an agreement with Ron, it could be considered legal desertion.

She no longer believed he would share the equity in the house with her as he'd promised. She would be left with nothing.

When they pulled into the driveway of Ronda's home, Ron's car was there. Bell didn't know what to expect, but there was no angry confrontation; it was all remarkably civil. Ron didn't seem angry or jealous that his wife had been driving around with another man, or that David Bell was helping her move out.

"It was all very matter-of-fact," Bell told Royce Ferguson. "Reynolds and his sons stayed in another part of the house."

"No sign of danger for Ronda?

"No. No!" Bell said emphatically. "I would have dragged her out of there kicking and screaming if there was."

David Bell had to leave at that point to drive back to Des Moines and finish his shift. "Sometime after midnight, I called Ronda to check on her. She said she had gotten a little sleep and she felt better. She planned to fly out of Portland to Spokane in the morning. I explained to her that that would be hard for me—to drive her almost a hundred miles south to Portland, and then I'd have to drive all the way

back to Des Moines. I asked her if she could change her reservations and fly out of SeaTac instead. That's only ten minutes from my police station.

"She said she would," Bell testified, "and she asked me
to give her a wake-up call in the morning if I hadn't heard
from her by the time I was in Lewis County."

But there was no call from Ronda to Dave Bell the next
morning. As he cruised into Lewis County, he said he had
called Ronda, expecting to hear her sleepy voice. But an unfamiliar male voice answered.

"It was a Lewis County detective or deputy who handed
the phone to Ron. He told me Ronda was dead. I couldn't
grasp that," Bell remembered. "I was shocked. I didn't know
what could have happened, so I just kept on driving to her
house."

Dave Bell found Ronda's widower "very calm."

Because he was a police officer, Bell was allowed to
walk beyond the "Crime Scene: Do Not Enter" tape. He
remained in shock. He should be driving Ronda to the airport—getting her safely on board a jet on her way to her
family. But she lay dead inside—apparently of a gunshot
wound to the head.

Bell testified that he was eventually interviewed by
Sergeant Glade Austin once, and by Detective Jerry Berry
twice, both of whom wanted him to remember every detail
he could about his last hours with Ronda.

But on that day, December 16, 1998, one question
asked of him stood out in his memory more than any other.
It came from Carmen Brunton.

"She looked me right in the eye and asked 'Did he
kill her?' "

He knew she was talking about Ron Reynolds, but

Dave Bell scarcely knew the man. He didn't know the answer to that on December 16, but he intended to find out everything he could about Ronda's shocking death.

"You have stayed close to Barbara Thompson?" Ferguson asked.

"For the last ten years."

It was time for John Justice to begin his cross-examination.

"How long was it between Ronda Reynolds's marriages?" Justice began.

"I'm not sure—maybe one and a half to two months," Bell answered. "We didn't have much contact since about December 1997—she was going to marry Ron in January. I know she was very disappointed when her second marriage didn't work out."

"Did you know much about her finances?"

"To a limited extent. Ronda had little access to money. Even if she wanted to go to the ATM, Ron had to go with her. She told me that she had fifteen thousand dollars invested in their home."

Judge Hicks occasionally asked questions of the witnesses. Now he asked Bell why he threw the bullets on the floor or the bed instead of in a drawer, but he couldn't answer why he'd done that. Bell remembered putting the empty gun itself back in its holster and placing it in a drawer under the waterbed, a squeaky drawer that was hard to open.

"What happened to the items you put in the truck?" Hicks asked as follow-up.

"We returned them to the house."

Like all the people who had known Ronda well—except, perhaps for Cheryl Gilbert—Dave Bell could not imagine that she would have considered suicide. She was pulled in many directions the last night of her life and she'd gone back and forth about what would be the wisest thing for her to do. She'd wanted so much to get to her family but she was afraid something bad might happen to her three dogs.

But kill herself? Absolutely not. She would have worked things out. It was obvious she didn't love Reynolds any longer. Still, she was ready to cut her losses and start over. She had plans and David Bell was positive they never included killing herself.

In time, they might well have been together. But a single bullet ended that hope.

CHAPTER TWENTY-EIGHT

BARB THOMPSON WAS SUFFERING not only emotional pain as Ronda's life and violent death were presented to the jurors; she was also suffering physical pain. She had a completely torn rotator cuff in one shoulder and it was agonizing, but she didn't tell anyone. She had vowed to see the hearing through before she had the surgery she needed so badly. Barb carried heavy court records and the huge white binder she had put together on Ronda's case, but she made sure no one caught her wincing as she lifted them. She had driven herself once more across the mountains, and that hurt, too.

She was used to hurting—she'd been stomped on by cattle and horses, and she had never quit before. She wasn't about to now.

Barb worried constantly about her mother. In her late eighties, Virginia had a bad heart and a handful of other ailments. She was failing rapidly. Several times a day, Barb called the caregiver to check on Virginia. And every day or so, there were emergency calls from home. Virginia had been taken to the hospital, or she wasn't able to eat. Barb had long since begun sleeping in a recliner next to her mother's bed, and it was wrenching for her to be so far away. Every time her cell phone rang, she was afraid the caregiver or Freeman would tell her mother had died.

Still, she knew what Ronda's beloved Gramma wanted her to do: stay at this hard-fought-for hearing that might open the doors to the truth about Ronda's death.

*   *   *

ROBERT BISHOP was the next witness Royce Ferguson called. He was the second deputy on the scene of Ronda Reynolds's death, following Deputy Gary Holt's arrival only three minutes later.

Bob Bishop had spent thirteen years in law enforcement, although he was no longer a cop. He was a tall, beefy, dark-haired man in his early thirties with a calm voice. He stated that he was currently a production manager for a local manufacturer. When asked why he had resigned from being a Lewis County deputy sheriff, he said it was for "personal reasons."

While Holt had tended to believe Ron Reynolds's conclusion that his wife had killed herself, Bishop wasn't so sure. The three Reynolds boys had already left the house when he got there; Holt had given them permission to drive to their mother's house. No one knew what they might have seen or heard during the night and predawn hours.

Holt was interviewing Ron in the kitchen, and the widower was explaining that he and Ronda had both been in bed at 4:30 A.M. They were awake and he'd been trying to keep her from harming herself. Overwhelmed with exhaustion, he hadn't been able to keep his eyes open. When he woke at six, she was gone.

He had searched all over the house for Ronda, checking the kitchen because he thought she might be feeding her dogs. Finally he located her body in the "closed closet."

"I didn't hear the shot," Ron Reynolds told Holt—a statement he would repeat scores of times over the years. "That's because the doors to the closet and the bathroom were both shut."

Bishop testified that he'd studied Ronda's body. "She was on her left side, with her right hand under a blanket. I didn't see the pillow—and I didn't note where her left hand was."

But something was "hinky," at least in Bishop's opinion. Ron Reynolds had appeared to be "calm, intelligent, and without any emotion."

Why didn't he hear the shot? Bishop testified that he saw the white strip on the widower's third finger, left hand, and it was he who found Ron's wedding ring in a soap dish in the master bathroom. He also had had the sense that someone had taken a shower in the bathroom within the previous hour.

"Did you form an opinion on what happened to Ronda Reynolds?" Royce Ferguson asked him.

"I didn't believe this was a suicide."

*   *   *

AT 11:43 A.M. on the second day of the hearing, Jerry Berry was called to the witness stand by Royce Ferguson. In a sport jacket and slacks, starched shirt and tie, and cowboy boots, he looked like a country lawman dressed up for court—which was what he was. All he needed to complete the look was a ten-gallon hat.

Berry has a good face, a kind face, and it was easy to see why Barb Thompson had trusted him from the first time she met him.

Jerry Berry testified about his years in law enforcement. He held nothing back; he had experienced a meteoric rise in the sheriff's office after he switched careers in midlife. By 1995 he was a homicide detective, and he participated in twenty-three death investigations between then and 2001. But he fell from his place as the fair-haired boy in the department when he didn't agree with his superiors and fellow detectives, and plunged into being constantly criticized just as rapidly.

"After I recommended Vernon Geberth to our chief criminal investigator—Joe Doench—everything fell apart," Berry told the jurors. "Joe was very upset when Geberth pointed out errors in the investigation of Ronda Reynolds's death. He said Geberth made the department look like Keystone Kops."

"What happened after that?" Ferguson asked.

"I was forbidden to work on the case—and if anyone in our department mentioned it to me, I was supposed to report it to Doench immediately. I was demoted to road deputy. I was ordered to undergo counseling," Berry answered. "This all happened on the same day."

He had abided by all the reassignments and conditions Joe Doench had specified, but things just got worse for him.

"Finally, I just came in and quit."

Jerry Berry had resigned from the sheriff's office, but he hadn't quit the case. He was clearly a stubborn—perhaps even obsessed—man who had never let go of what he considered a miscarriage of justice, even though it cost him his career.

Berry testified that he arrived at the Reynoldses' house at 8:30 A.M. on December 16 after Detective Neiser called him and asked for a second opinion. Even Joe Doench said there were "things" that didn't look right to him. "He told me the husband seemed 'too composed,' and that there were other things too—but he didn't tell me what they were."

"Dave Neiser led me to the body, and told me he had removed the gun for safety's sake. It was already a suicide in his mind—not a death investigation," Berry said. "It should have been treated as a crime scene unless—and until—proved otherwise."

Berry was distressed because the gun had been removed. "They had taken some photos—but I never got to take my own photos of where the gun ended up after the single shot."

"Who did what at the scene?" Royce Ferguson asked.

"Within the first hour, Neiser did interviews in the living room, and I processed the scene," Berry responded. "The impression of the gun on her—Ronda's—forehead was pronounced. There were red flags accumulating into clusters—so many discrepancies . . ."

"What kind of 'discrepancies'?"

"The lipstick message on the bathroom mirror—all her makeup had been packed. Neiser said the gun had been 'near' her left hand, but that hand was grasping the blanket. She could not have held a gun in it."

"Anything else?" Ferguson pressed.

"Ron Reynolds said he kept his wife in bed with him until about four thirty A.M.—but only the left side of the bed was slept in—not the right. The Black Velvet was there—

empty—but she turned out to have no alcohol in her system. The closet was only about five or six by five. The clothing hanging there and the boxes made it smaller. The door opened inward. It wasn't possible to close the door with her feet and legs there."

"What was the distance from the body to the left side of the bed?"

"Ten to twelve feet, maximum."

"But Ron Reynolds didn't hear the gun fire?"

"He said he didn't—didn't hear anything until his alarm rang later."

"Anything else? Did you talk with Terry Wilson about these 'red flags' you saw?"

"He would never talk to me about that."

Berry testified that Carmen Brunton, who had come to the death site that first morning, believed that the note on the mirror had been written by a left-handed person.

"Anything else?"

"The writing was at my eye level," Berry continued. "And I'm five eleven. People tend to write on a blackboard or a wall at their eye level. Ronda was much shorter than I am."

Even Brunton, who had come to the death site that first morning, had thought the "goodbye note" had been written by a left-handed person. Ron was left-handed and Ronda had been right-handed—although Ron couldn't remember which hand she'd favored. But, of course, Brunton had no special expertise in graphology.

"Where are your photos of the crime scene?" Ferguson asked.

"I can't tell you. I took lots of pictures but they've disappeared. I thought they would be with the case file in the sheriff's office . . . but they aren't. I don't have them."

Jerry Berry testified that some time later Barb Thompson had asked the sheriff's office for everything in the case file she had a right to have under the Public Information Act. "She finally got some of them, but when I looked at what were supposed to be the crime scene photos, I said, 'My God, Barb—these aren't the crime scene photos. These were taken a years later.'"

Berry described the uphill battle he'd fought. Oddly, at first, it hadn't been so negative. "We took a straw vote, and most of our investigators thought Ronda's death was a homicide. Even Joe Doench said he was leaning that way."

But that changed all too soon. "I remember that Dave Neiser taunted me, saying, 'Leave it to Jerry Berry to make this into a murder.'"

By then, it was clear that that derogatory opinion of Neiser was shared by others in the Lewis County Sheriff's Office.

At least unofficially.

But Barb was determined. Of course, by that time she had found out all the telephone numbers for Jerry—his office, home, cell phone, and she tracked him down.

He recalled Barb's statement to him that she could have accepted even the suicide verdict if she just had proof. "I would know that was Ronda's choice," she told Berry. "But there is no proof. I don't know what happened to her."

Soon he was as involved in finding Ronda's killer as her mother was.

"Did Barbara Thompson pay you for your work on the case?" Ferguson asked.

"Not a penny. I never asked for anything, either."

Jerry Berry testified that he still had twenty-one red flags and questions to go with them. "But Ron Reynolds got an attorney and he wouldn't talk to detectives any longer. That door was closed."

It might not have made a difference anyway. Berry testified that Ron Reynolds had not been consistent in the statements he gave to anyone over the eleven years since Ronda died. "He changed his statements to fit the truth," Berry said.

Both Dr. Selove and Dr. Donald Reay, the medical examiner of King County, which includes Seattle, had said that her paralysis would have been instant. "How then could she get her hand(s) under the blanket?" Berry asked.

What did her broken fingernail mean to the case? Ronda was a woman who always kept her nails in perfect shape. David Bell hadn't noted a torn nail on the last evening of her life, and yet, in the morning, it was evident. Why hadn't she filed it and fixed it before her flight?

Maybe she couldn't.

One by one, Royce Ferguson led Jerry Berry through the almost two dozen items he had flagged as suspicious as he'd investigated Ronda's death.

The jurors leaned forward in their seats as Berry ticked them off.

Surely they were listening—but what were they thinking?

"Did you talk to Ron Reynolds's three younger sons who were supposedly there at the house on Twin Peaks Drive on the night of December fifteenth–sixteenth?"

"I wanted to question them—as hostile witnesses—but Sergeant Austin told me to let Reynolds's attorney do that."

Ron's attorneys had tried to persuade the Lewis County investigators to close the case. That was no surprise, but Berry was discouraged when he found the department was indeed considering doing that.

It appeared that Jerry Berry had been blocked from following several good leads, and his frustration showed on his face as he testified. He wondered why Reynolds—who was said to be such a light sleeper that Ronda's dogs couldn't sleep in the bedroom—hadn't heard the shot. Why hadn't the Reynolds boys heard the gun fire?

"The GSR [gunshot residue test] showed that Ronda had just a little trace of gun debris on her hand. Sergeant Austin had stopped issuing GSR kits because they're not of much value," Berry said. "And why would a suicide wipe her prints off the bullets before she loaded the gun? Why was the gun itself without fingerprints? Ronda had handled the gun earlier in the evening, and David Bell had held both the gun and the bullets."

Their prints should have been on the gun and bullets. But they weren't.

Someone, for whatever reason, had wiped them clean.

Jerry Berry had been on the witness stand since 11:30 A.M., with an hour recess for lunch, and it was now 3:32. Outside the windowless courtroom, the icy wind tore at the Law and Justice Center building and there were snowflakes mixed in with the rain.

John Justice asked few questions on cross-examination. That had been his technique from the beginning. Terry Wilson didn't have to prove anything; the word was, he might not even testify in his own behalf. After the first day, he hadn't been in the courtroom.

Justice homed in on an eighty-four-minute phone conversation Ron and Ronda had allegedly had the late afternoon before she died. That would have been while Ron was driving home from his doctor's appointment in Olympia. No one knew for sure what they had discussed, though Ron said she'd been upset and suicidal—but was a lot calmer as he drove into Toledo. And so he had stopped for a hamburger and gone to the school Christmas musical instead of going home to check on her.

"Did Ronda threaten suicide during that long call?" Justice asked.

"I have no way of knowing, Berry answered."

If Justice was trying to show how caring and connected Ron Reynolds was on December 15, it seemed a faint argument. The picture of Reynolds chewing on a hamburger and enjoying Christmas music when—and if—his wife talked about killing herself made him appear shallow.

Asked if an expert on graphology had studied the writing on the Reynolds's bathroom mirror, Berry said, "Yes," and agreed that the authority had surmised that it was probably Ronda's writing.

Justice did not, however, call the expert to testify.

Justice asked Berry if the investigators on the first day had found a bottle of Zoloft, prescribed for Ronda, in the master bathroom.

"Yes," Berry agreed. "We found Zoloft. I can't remember who it was for. As I recall, it was written in May 1998—seven months before Ronda died. There were many capsules left in the container."

"As for the time of Ronda Reynolds's death and the rigor in her body, didn't Dr. Reay, the medical examiner of King County, comment on that?"

"He did."

Jerry Berry testified that Dr. Reay said that it would be very unusual for someone whose joints were that frozen with rigor mortis to have died only an hour or so before. "But he said it wouldn't be *impossible* for the time and the rigor to match . . ."

"No more questions."

* * *

IT WAS 4 P.M. ON TUESDAY, and the gallery expected Judge Hicks would break until the next morning. But he didn't.

The oak benches felt as hard as steel, and many of us were eager to leave—probably to stop at the Kit Carson Restaurant on the way to our homes or motels. The prime rib, chicken, and pot roast there tasted like home cooking and the portions were generous. The coconut cream pies were cut in fourths.

The happy-hour martinis were doubles.

And the puddles in the parking lot would be deeper than usual and edged with snow.

But Judge Hicks didn't show any sign of adjourning early. Marty Hayes followed Jerry Berry to the witness stand.

Beyond their obsession with finding the truth, the two men could hardly be more different. While Berry was quiet and soft-spoken, Hayes was bombastic, a large bearded man with a loud voice. He exuded self-confidence, and he frequently stepped down from the witness chair to demonstrate something. He often approached the rail in front of the jurors to speak directly to them.

It was clear that they were fascinated with his testimony. (After the hearing, several members of the jury picked Hayes as one of their "favorite" witnesses.)

There was a verbal scuffle in the courtroom as the defense attorney objected to Hayes's testifying as an expert in homicide investigation—or as a firearms expert.

Judge Hicks agreed that Hayes probably didn't have enough experience with murder cases to qualify as an expert, but ruled that after almost twenty years of teaching at his own company—the Firearms Academy of Seattle—he had the background, experience, and expertise to testify on firearms and ballistics.

Guns were not as alien to this small-town jury as they might be to city dwellers, so they grasped Hayes's demonstrations quickly.

Using a gun as similar to the death weapon as he could find, Hayes testified that he had studied the recoil dynamics of a Rossi handgun, using a sandbag to represent a victim's head. He then fired eighteen shots into the dummy head as he repositioned the hand grip on the gun three times. The location of Ronda's single head wound could not be matched to either of her hands' positions.

Another test Hayes conducted, with his wife Gila's assistance, was to measure the decibel level of a gunshot fired ten to fifteen feet away from the bed where Ron Reynolds said he'd been asleep. His alarm clock had allegedly wakened him, but he hadn't heard the shot that killed his wife.

This had been a huge point of contention for everyone consumed by the death of Ronda Reynolds.

Marty Hayes accomplished this test by measuring the decibels of objects such as a ringing phone, alarm clock, and gunfire as they would sound fifteen feet away. Normal conversation is 58 to 72 decibels, an alarm clock is 62 decibels, and a television set at high volume is 65 decibels.

How much noise would a gun make?

Hayes answered that. "A gun shot is from 120 to 130 decibels," he testified. "Keep in mind," he continued, "70 is twice as loud as 60, 80 is twice as loud as 70, and 100 decibels is twice as loud as 90."

At the gun range, Hayes had first twice tested the sound level of a gun pressed firmly to the dummy's head against a weapon pressed loosely. He listed the decibels for each.

Gun Pressed Firmly	Gun Pressed Loosely
114	129
92	127

Then Hayes closed the bathroom door of the range's office and put the decibel meter about fifteen feet away from the door:

Pressed Firmly	Pressed Loosely
97	101

His conclusion was that gunshots that were louder than high volume on a television set, an alarm clock's urgent ring, or a loud conversation should have wakened someone sleeping less than fifteen feet away. True, the sound was lower when the bathroom door was shut, but tests had shown that that wasn't possible because Ronda was too tall to fit.

Marty Hayes testified: "All of the above analysis indicates to me that Ronda Reynolds could not have fired the Rossi .32 S&W long revolver with her right hand—down through the pillow—and [have] the gun come to rest on her temple. On the other hand, the photos of the scene and this analysis are consistent with the gun having been placed on her temple/forehead by a second or third person, who positioned her hand to brace the pistol so it would not fall. The pillow could have been placed on her head to cover the side of her head and the gun."

Hayes held the now-unloaded gun he had used for his tests up to his right temple, demonstrating different angles of fire. Even though the gallery and the jury knew there were no bullets in the chamber, it was still unsettling to watch.

He suspected that the gift box of cheeses and sausage had probably been used to prop up her right arm and hand.

Why did the pillow with bullet holes in it fail to match up with Ronda's head wound? Perhaps that had been an afterthought—something meant to explain why no one else in the house had heard the shot?

Or, possibly her killer or killers could not bear to look at her.

* * *

It was Wednesday, the third day of the hearing, and Marty Hayes returned to the witness stand. He said he had tried to re-create the position of the pillow that covered Ronda's face.

"When I held the pillow close to the gun, it didn't work because the pin and hammer were trapped in the pillow's fabric and would not fire. I had to hold the pillow a little ways away from the gun."

The pillow might have been used to muffle sound, but the burn marks in it didn't match the gun position. Marty Hayes tried shooting the weapon to see how much difference it might make to muffle the sound with and without the pillow.

During this test, Gila Hayes had again called out the decibels on the meter fifteen feet away.

Without the Pillow	With the Pillow
112	91
113	83
94	86

Once more, Hayes used noise to educate the jury. Hayes walked in front of the jury box, his voice rising as he moved. He was shouting as loud as he possibly could—producing an extremely high-volume sound in the courtroom. His voice rattled the room, and the decibel meter registered it. And still he wasn't making as much noise as a single gunshot would.

It was a most effective demonstration; the walls themselves seemed to shudder sympathetically.

Why hadn't Ron Reynolds—or someone else in the house—heard the shot?

*   *   *

HAYES HAD WARNED Barb Thompson that he might need to include some body pictures in his testimony so that the jurors could actually view what the witnesses so far had seen. She knew it was coming as the screen was being set up.

After eleven years, Barb Thompson had learned to deal with most of the emotions that rose in her throat and made her eyes brim with tears. She had read, evaluated, and memorized gruesome details about her daughter's death. She had even learned to laugh again, although sometimes she joked because she didn't want to cry. But there were still some things she couldn't handle.

Barb had seen the crime scene and morgue photographs of Ronda's body. She knew that Marty might enter them as evidence. They had been shocking to her, and would be to anyone who wasn't a cop, doctor, or a forensic pathologist. But she had come to a point where she could look at them, and she even put them up on her "Justice for Ronda" website.

If anyone in the cyber world could help with advice or assistance, Barb wanted them to see all the details of her daughter's case.

And yet, when the time came to show the jurors the enlargements of the bloody photos, Barb realized she couldn't stay in the courtroom. So many people would be staring at her dead, vulnerable child—from jurors to strangers in the gallery, to the judge, to Donna Wilson and Carmen Brunton. (Terry Wilson, of course, wasn't there.) She hadn't realized how much more heart-wrenching it would be to see the photos blown up this large.

With tears coursing down her face, Barb whispered to Royce Ferguson and then bolted from her seat and ran to the courtroom doors. She hadn't expected the emotional force that suddenly assailed her; all she knew was that she could not bear to be there while Ronda's last photos were shown.

Ronda's facial features were obscured by a curtain of blood. The entrance wound was just in front of her right ear, but the blood made it difficult to see the exact location. Her pink rosebud pajamas were stained with her blood, too. In the morgue shots, Ronda was nude, and the red fluid was washed from her face, pajamas, and her hair. It was easy to see the delineation between the initial lividity that stained her fair skin when her heart ceased to beat and the secondary, lighter pink that occurred after she was placed on her back for removal to await autopsy.

A half hour later, when the photos had all flashed on the screen and it was white and clear of images, Barb came back into the courtroom holding a box of tissues. She thought she would be able to handle seeing the crime scene photos, but she wasn't. She didn't trust her reactions now; something else might very well take her unaware as the hearing progressed. She hadn't wanted to cry, but she could not stop the tears.

Still, she vowed to herself, she would not break down again.

Chapter Twenty-nine

John Justice began cross-examining Marty Hayes at 1:45 on Thursday afternoon. He struck first at Hayes's lack of actual experience as a detective.

"Have you ever been involved in suicide or homicide cases?"

"No."

"Ever testified about it in court?"

"No."

"What would the impact be on a sleeping person of just one loud sound as opposed to a continuous sound like an alarm clock?" Justice asked. "Would one quick sound wake a person?"

Royce Ferguson objected, and both attorneys approached the bench. It would clearly be impossible for the witness to assess how various subjects would react to either short or drawn-out noise.

Cross-examination of Marty Hayes had ended, but the court had some queries.

Judge Hicks asked his questions for Hayes: "Could Ronda Reynolds have wrapped the gun with the blanket? Could that explain no fingerprints on the gun?"

Hayes shook his head. "No."

"The gun would have recoiled down—not up on the forehead," Hayes added. "Recoil follows the path of least resistance. Ronda's aiming position wasn't right."

The track of the bullet was odd, too. It had entered just above and slightly forward of her right ear, but stopped short of midline; instead it went down and back toward the occiput.

It was only mid-afternoon on Thursday, but Judge Hicks called for the courtroom to be dark on Friday and said they would begin again at nine on Monday morning.

Barb Thompson headed home over the mountains, trying to get as much driving in before it was pitch black outside. The days were growing shorter. She knew her mother would be waiting eagerly to see her and hear more details of the first four days of the hearing. Royce Ferguson had only one more witness to call: Dr. Jeffrey M. Reynolds.

However, Dr. Reynolds was on a trip outside the United States, and Barb and her team were holding their breaths until he was actually in Chehalis and prepared to testify.

They need not have been concerned; Reynolds was waiting outside Judge Hicks's courtroom on Monday morning. He looked very tired from his long journey and wasn't dressed as most expert witnesses are. Instead he wore a casual leather jacket, probably what he'd worn on the plane. When he took that off, he had on a blue-striped dress shirt and tie.

With his striking white hair growing to his collar,

Reynolds resembled the stereotype of an English literature professor more than a forensic pathologist. But he certainly had an impressive background in his special area of medicine. Although he had a master's degree in mechanical engineering from the Massachusetts Institute of Technology, his three years' service as a medic in the U.S. Army Special Forces (Green Berets) led him to go to medical school at the University of Miami. His residency was in pathology at the Oregon Health Sciences University in Portland, Oregon.

Beginning in 1989, Dr. Reynolds had been the circuit-riding medical examiner for eight counties in Washington and Idaho. He had performed two thousand autopsies. Early in her search for answers, Barbara Thompson had called him and asked him to review Ronda's case. He agreed to look at the thick white binder with the myriad information Barb had gathered.

"If you had been told Ronda Reynolds's death was a suicide," Royce Ferguson began, "would you have concurred?"

The witness rubbed his forehead and shook his head slightly. "It was a very unusual death," he answered. "Women rarely shoot themselves in the head."

But he had another reason to doubt the conclusions of the coroner and sheriff's investigators. "A temporal—self-inflicted wound—almost always goes out the other side of the head. This was very odd. The bullet didn't cross the midline of the brain; instead, it went down."

"That was unusual?" Ferguson probed.

"It would be almost impossible [for her] to fire from that angle."

Dr. Reynolds held the empty gun up to his own head just as Marty Hayes had. His wrist bent improbably as he tried to aim down through his head instead of aiming straight across the brain, transecting it. His hand bent almost back to his wrist.

"The angle of the wound track is wrong," Reynolds said firmly, agreeing with Hayes.

The forensic pathologist continued to point out aspects of Ronda's shooting that did not ring true. "It took three and a half pounds of pressure to pull that trigger. With her right hand in that cramped position, I don't think she could have done that. And there was a *deep* impression at the entrance wound."

"Would the person be dead—instantly?"

"The brain is shocked by the bullet and the gas and superheated air that follows. It shuts down immediately," Dr. Reynolds answered. "The subject can't move, although the heart still beats—ten to fifteen minutes possibly— making blood soak into the carpet beneath her body."

The witness explained lividity carefully to the jury. "The blood settles and clots in the 'first lividity.' Then, in this case, there was a second lividity pattern when her body was moved hours after her death. So you had 'dual pattern lividity.' "

"Ron Reynolds has said he saw his wife alive at four-thirty to five A.M., and he called 911 at six-twenty A.M.," Ferguson began. "Could she have fixed lividity in one hour and twenty minutes?"

"She had to have been dead for at least three hours for that first lividity to become fixed."

"Did the [electric] blanket over her make any difference in the degree of rigor mortis present?"

"No difference. The rigor begins when the muscles no longer have oxygen. The jaw muscles are often first, beginning at two hours."

"Did Ronda Reynolds have gunshot residue on her hand?"

"No way!" Jeffrey Reynolds said emphatically. "She didn't have GSR on her hand as if she'd fired a gun—unless the lab was wrong."

"Nothing?"

"Nothing in evidence shows that Ronda's forefinger was the trigger finger," he added.

"Then your opinion is that this was not a self-inflicted gunshot wound?" Ferguson asked.

"No. In suicides, I have *never* seen a bullet's path that didn't cross the midline."

"What would you estimate was the time of Ronda Reynolds's death?"

"Four to six hours before she was found. Probably six hours."

That meant Ronda had probably died sometime between twelve-thirty and two-thirty A.M.

* * *

JOHN JUSTICE then cross-examined Dr. Reynolds. The doctor was a devastating witness against Terry Wilson's case, but Justice pursued his time-of-death conclusions.

"If there was fixed lividity at seven A.M., what is the minimum time that has elapsed since death?"

"Three or four hours."

That was another repetition of the strongest evidence against Terry Wilson's case, and again it gave the lie to Ron Reynolds's statements. With prodding from Justice, according to Dr. Jeffrey Reynolds, Ronda had to have died much earlier than Ron said she did—passing away at 2 or 3 A.M., and not after 6.

Neither side was very forceful when speaking of whether or not there was gunshot residue on Ronda's finger or hand. Lab tests had not detected antimony—which suggested there was no residue.

Except for final arguments, Barbara Thompson's challenge to Coroner Terry Wilson appeared to be over. Everyone in the gallery, the media, and the jurors anxiously waited to hear Wilson's testimony and the position Justice would take to prove that the coroner had not been derelict in his duties.

The jurors had a few more questions before the lunch break on Monday, November 11. They asked to see the photograph of Ronda lying in the bathroom closet, to view the lividity of her legs. They were told they could see all the photos available when they adjourned to deliberate.

"Were her hands bruised—as if she had shot the gun?" another juror asked.

"No."

"Was the drug—Zoloft—or other drugs found in her blood?"

"No."

*   *   *

THERE WAS AN AIR of expectation when the court watchers and participants returned after lunch at 1:30 P.M. as they glanced around looking for Terry Wilson or Carmen Brunton, who would probably both be witnesses.

But Wilson wasn't there. Carmen was, and Donna Wilson and a friend were there on their usual bench behind the defense table.

But when Judge Hicks turned to John Justice and asked

him to call his first witness, Justice said he would call no witnesses.

A muted murmur swept the courtroom.

Perhaps it was the wisest move. Terry Wilson wasn't required to prove anything. It was up to Barb Thompson, Royce Ferguson, and their team and witnesses to prove their case. Wilson had already demonstrated that he didn't even have to be in court if he didn't want to. It seemed less likely that he would want to face cross-examination from Ferguson.

But surely Justice had intended to call Carmen. She had been involved in Ronda's case within hours of her death.

No, Justice had no witnesses to call.

The trial was truncated, cut off in its middle. After eleven years, people in Lewis County and many from farther away wanted to know what the coroner had to say, and they had fully expected he would take the witness stand. This hearing was supposed to be an opening door that would lead to Ronda's killer—if, indeed, there was a killer.

Without hearing from either Terry Wilson or Carmen Brunton, how would it end now?

Judge Hicks wasted no time in beginning his instructions for the jurors. After closing arguments, they would retire to deliberate. It had all gone so fast, a river racing by. It was possible that there might be a verdict by evening—or even tomorrow.

The bailiff passed out copies of the Court's rules to the jury. And Judge Hicks explained that it would be their responsibility to decide whether Terry Wilson had been "arbitrary and capricious" in his evaluation of Ronda Reynolds's death—and if he was accurate or inaccurate in his decisions.

He explained to the jury that they should make their

choices based on facts supported by evidence that had come out during the trial.

"Your personal opinion shouldn't come in, nor should any testimony that may have been stricken from the record. Consider *all* the evidence and each witness's testimony. Disregard my opinions—if any. Remember that the lawyers' statements are not evidence.

"Don't let your own emotions overwhelm you. There are two kinds of evidence," Judge Hicks said. "Direct evidence is something a witness has directly perceived; circumstantial evidence is what can be inferred. They both have the same weight in your decisions."

The judge said that an expert witness—such as Dr. Jeffrey Reynolds—may give his or her personal and educated opinions.

"The coroner must decide both the *cause* and *manner* of death."

The cause of death is the method used—strangulation, drowning, gunshot, bludgeoning etc. The manner of death could be undetermined, homicide, suicide, intentional intervention of a second or third person, or accidental, among others.

The jurors would have "Exhibit 2"—their copies of the white notebook Barb Thompson had compiled; it had been entered into evidence. However, the judge warned that some of the information there was only opinions of laypersons.

"Coroner Terry Wilson had this notebook—and determined that Ronda Reynolds's manner of death was suicide. Mrs. Thompson has to prove that wrong—or that Wilson *was* 'capricious and arbitrary.' "

"You must decide if something is probably more true

than not true," Hicks said, "or more likely than not that Coroner Wilson was arbitrary and capricious.

"Don't surrender your honest opinion to other jurors. Memory is more accurate than notes—I told you that when we began. Elect a presiding juror.

"Ten jurors must agree on each question on the form. Each is separate. When all of them are answered, the presiding juror will notify the bailiff that you have a verdict."

No one in the courtroom had realized how close we were to seeing Ronda's case go to the jury.

But first they would listen to final arguments. Although they are rhetoric and opinion and not necessarily facts, these last remarks have been known to sway a jury.

Chapter Thirty

ROYCE FERGUSON began his final argument. "What would Ronda's testimony have been if she was here? Or Ron Reynolds's? He invoked the Fifth Amendment. Terry Wilson is here, but we don't have his opinion."

He asked how the jurors could agree since no else had. And his answer for them was simple. "Common sense."

They needed only to use common sense to evaluate if certain suspects had been there at the crime scene, and to trust their own memories as they considered manner, demeanor, contrary facts, behavior, or testimony of witnesses. They needed to consider "What's in it for them?"—referring to various persons of interest in this case.

"Could the blanket have been used to wipe off the gun?" he asked, and then answered his own question. "Yes—there was a blanket fiber caught in the gun."

Jerry Berry had seen blood on some of the bullets, Ferguson said, and placed the gun in a glue tank for an hour to preserve any prints there. Then the WSP lab had tested them. Neither Berry nor the state lab criminalists had found any prints on the bullets or the death weapon.

"Terry Wilson didn't go to the scene, talk to the sheriff's staff, or to Barbara Thompson—until 2008," Ferguson submitted. "Evidence was screwed up. Maybe they just got tired of listening to Barb? Ron was the one who first said, 'She must have muffled it with a pillow or something,' and that word—*muffled*—starts to contaminate the real evidence. The first deputies on the scene focused on a suicide—a gunshot through a pillow.

"Ron Reynolds said that Ronda died sometime between five A.M. and six-twenty, but the double-lividity patterns show that she died before five A.M.—actually sometime between twelve-thirty A.M. and five."

But Terry Wilson had refused to say the latter, and his explanation had been: "I can't say that because that would mean that Ron was guilty."

Odd. Why had Ron received some kind of benediction that kept him safe from prying by the authorities? Yes, he'd hired an attorney, but most persons of interest do. That didn't mean he was impervious to hard questions.

Ferguson suggested that the Lewis County Sheriff's Office wouldn't admit that they didn't have the money or resources to investigate further than they had—so they had decided to call Ronda's death a suicide.

Reminding the jurors often that they had only to apply their own common sense to the evidence, witness statements, and possible motive, Royce Ferguson continued. He said Ron was the sole financial problem Ronda had. She had worked hard, and Ron believed she had life insurance in the amount of $300,000. That would have taken care of all Ron Reynolds's financial obligations—and then some. In truth, of course, Ronda had only $50,000 in life insurance—and her widower had paid the premium on that after she was dead. "He collected that a year later."

And Ron Reynolds had tried to collect the $7,500 Ronda would get when the sale on the Liburdi house closed. (Ronda had meant for that to go to her mother to pay her back for the loan that helped buy the Twin Peaks Drive house.)

Royce spoke of how Ron Reynolds had told deputies he found the gun holster next to the toilet the night of December 15. He said he had asked Ronda about his father's gun. According to him, Ronda said she had given it to David Bell. Ron said he put the holster in the waterbed drawer.

"But the detectives never found that holster. And Mr. Reynolds then said that he put it in the drawer after they left. Two years later, he told Glade Austin he'd been confused."

Some investigators had reported the gun was in Ronda's left hand, others said it was between her hands, and Bob Bishop saw it resting on her forehead. Jerry Berry had seen its imprint there. No one could be sure exactly where it was, because Dave Neiser had removed it, even before clear photographs could be taken.

Judge Hicks called for a break, but few observers left the courtroom. At 3:20, Royce continued his arguments.

"Ron Reynolds gave three different answers about the Black Velvet bottle in the master bedroom when he was asked if Ronda was drinking from it: 'Yes—I noticed she was having a drink'; 'She could have had a drink'; and 'I don't know. The bottle was in the bedroom—I didn't see her drink.'

"He told Glade Austin that he woke up briefly at five-thirty A.M. and he *felt* that Ronda was there in bed beside him."

The attorney asked the jury how long Ron waited before calling 911. Could he have waited until she bled to death? Why was his wedding ring off, left in the family bathroom, where the steam from a shower hadn't yet dissipated? Why had Ron pushed the snooze button on his alarm clock twice, which extended his sleeping time for thirty-six minutes?

There were twenty-one red flags—and Royce Ferguson went over every one. Nothing matched up or fit properly with physical evidence or some of the statements given.

"Jerry Berry begged his superior officers not to close the case. He begged them to simply suspend it. The HITS team didn't even have a copy of Berry's twenty-one questions."

Who would have the most experience and expertise in determining manner of death? Dr. Jeffrey Reynolds, a medical doctor, board-certified in forensic pathology, and who had performed thousands of autopsies—or Terry Wilson, who was a physician's assistant, who hadn't gone to Ronda's death scene or her autopsy?

"Dr. Reynolds told you that it was 'highly improbable' that Ronda had committed suicide. I suggest to you," Ferguson said in finishing, "that the preponderance of the evidence says that Ronda Reynolds was murdered, and that's what I want you to come back with."

*   *   *

JOHN JUSTICE began his final arguments at 3:42 P.M. He had little ammunition. He couldn't go over what his witnesses had said—because neither Terry Wilson nor Carmen Brunton had testified. Justice had presented no expert witnesses to refute Dr. Jeffrey Reynolds's testimony. Indeed, he had called no witnesses at all to the stand.

Justice argued that "nowhere does it say that there are no fingerprints on the gun," referring to one report.

In a sense, Ron Reynolds was on trial, too, although this hearing was about how Wilson had handled Ronda's case. Yes, it was true that Ron had demonstrated little emotion on the morning of Ronda's death, but Justice pointed out that people react to shock and grief in different ways. Some are overemotional and some are stoic, and there are many degrees of observable grief between those extremes.

Justice had one strong area. He referred to the HITS report where homicide detectives with years of experience came to the conclusion that Ronda Reynolds had died by her own hand. Just as the Lewis County Sheriff's Office did. Just as Terry Wilson had.

John Justice spoke for less than thirty minutes. He was between a rock and a hard place. Attacking a mourning and determined mother wouldn't win any points with the jurors. He surely didn't want to bring up why Coroner Wilson hadn't attended Ronda Reynolds's autopsy or why he made it a habit of avoiding death scenes.

*   *   *

AND SUDDENLY the hearing was over. The jurors had their instructions as they retired to deliberate. The day was almost over; in November, it was dark outside. Would they choose their presiding juror and begin to discuss the case right away? Would they ask to have dinner first? Would they want to wait until they'd had a good night's sleep before they began deliberation?

There was no word in the first hour. Or the second.

Nor would there be during the night. What would happen in the morning?

CHAPTER THIRTY-ONE

THE USUAL SPECTATORS and media were in Judge Hicks's courtroom early on Tuesday morning, not wanting to miss the jury's return. And they waited, fully aware that it might be days before there was a verdict.

Royce Ferguson filed a motion asking that the jury be polled if Coroner Wilson should be found to be in the wrong. He wanted to know what they thought. If suicide wasn't accurate, could the jurors be asked if they felt the manner of Ronda's death had been homicide or some other answer.

Judge Hicks denied Ferguson's motion. "This is not an inquest. If it were, some testimony or evidence wouldn't have been admitted—and vice versa."

Court broke for lunch. Most of us in the gallery didn't leave. We smelled a verdict in the air—and we were right. The jury sent word at 1:15 P.M. They had reached their verdict.

At 1:32 P.M., the jurors filed in.

The court clerk asked if the jurors had indeed come to a decision on Case Number 062010441, and the presiding juror announced that they had. Since this was a civil procedure, only ten of the jurors needed to agree.

There were three questions that had to be answered satisfactorily:

One: Did Terry Wilson do a good job and make an accurate decision on Ronda Reynolds's manner of death?

The jury's answer was "No."

Two: Was the suicide determination inaccurate?

The jury's answer was "Yes."

Three: Was the coroner's office handling of Ronda Reynolds's case "arbitrary and capricious"?

The jury's answer was "Yes."

The jurors then were questioned individually to be sure of their votes.

Barb Thompson, still not sure that she had won after so many frustrating obstacles, watched and listened as every single juror agreed that Wilson had been derelict in his duty and allowed the wrong manner of Ronda's death—the most painful for those who loved her—to stand.

The courtroom was very quiet. Terry Wilson, who had come to court that day, chewed gum steadily and didn't change expression. But his face flushed much more than it had the first day he was present. Then he got up to leave.

Tracy Vedder from KOMO-TV and a team from KIRO-TV had to move fast as Terry Wilson and his entourage exited the courtroom. Tracy, who had worked for years now to help Barb Thompson in her seemingly hopeless quest, held out a microphone and asked, "Are you going to change the death certificate now?"

"I'll do what my lawyers tell me to do," Wilson answered brusquely as he disappeared into a waiting elevator.

Barb was crying—this time with joy. She didn't care if anyone saw her with tears rolling down her face. The first thing she did was grab her cell phone and call Gramma Virginia to tell her about the verdicts. Far away across Washington state, Barb's mother was sobbing, too.

As soon as Barb said goodbye to her mother, she called her son, Freeman, with the amazing news.

Kim Edmundson, a sheriff's lieutenant from Idaho, and one of the many young women whom Barb had "adopted" over the years, had come to the coast with her. She knew how hard it was for Barb to drive with her torn rotator cuff, and she was also afraid for Barb to drive if the hearing had ended in another loss.

The two of them hugged while strobe lights flashed and cell phone and digital cameras captured their happiness.

Royce Ferguson, Marty Hayes, and Jerry Berry, who had all been dead serious throughout the hearing, joined arms and grinned widely. I'm not positive but I think they did a quick jig, too.

To have "suicide" be ruled inaccurate was a tremendous boost for Barb.

*   *   *

TERRY WILSON HAD TEN DAYS to appeal the jury's verdicts, but no one expected him to do that.

Judge Hicks had denied Ferguson's motion to poll the jurors to determine if they believed Ronda was a murder victim. So although there were a number of "likely suspects," more than in most homicide cases, officials and lawmen in Lewis County weren't rushing out to find the killer—or killers.

With every year that had passed, memories of possible witnesses to a murder had surely grown dimmer. People had moved away or perhaps convinced themselves not to get involved if they did know something about the case. Or they had died.

But Ronda was still dead—robbed of the precious years of a young woman's life. She would be forty-four now, probably married to someone who loved her, and possibly the mother of young children.

CHAPTER THIRTY-TWO

TWO WEEKS AFTER the hearing ended, Barb Thompson and I returned to Lewis County. We had become good friends over the years—first through emails and letters, and then as we sat a foot or two apart at the hearing in Chehalis. We both stayed at the Best Western Inn during the hearing—almost everyone involved who lived outside Lewis County did.

But Barb was always up and gone early in the morning, while I showed up in the Law and Justice Center just before Judge Hicks walked in. Evenings, Barb conferred with her team, and then dropped into bed, exhausted. On a few occasions, we had a screwdriver together after court and relaxed a little. But in Barb's case, it was only a little. The hearing demanded every ounce of strength she had.

From the beginning, back in 1998, when I first heard the news about the former female state trooper who died mysteriously, I doubted that Ronda Reynolds committed suicide. Everything I'd learned about physical evidence in thirty years of writing about murder warred with that.

I freely admit that I went to Chehalis in the cold November of 2009 with prejudice: in my head and heart, I believed Ronda had been murdered.

Still, I had no idea who her killer might be. I knew the forensic science and facts of the case but was unfamiliar with the personalities of those who passed through Ronda's life.

Now, Barb Thompson and I set out on a journey that we devoutly hoped might result in information that would narrow down suspects. As we headed west, the weather seemed to promise good news ahead; the sun shone as brightly as the gray clouds were dim in Lewis and Grays Harbor counties only two weeks earlier. We had both had a chance to catch up on sleep, and, strange as it might sound, this trip seemed almost like a short vacation. She and I each tended to be workaholics, never taking any *real* vacations.

Before the hearing began in the first week of November, Judge Richard Hicks had told the jurors that they could not talk to anyone about what they heard in court. Now that it was over, they could discuss their thoughts with anyone they wanted. A half dozen of them had supper with Barb and me, all women—although a male juror had wanted to come and was prevented by a storm in the foothills.

They were as eager to talk with us as we were to talk to them. Out of respect for their privacy, I choose not to give their surnames.

One of the jurors said she had been a little stunned to see that the diagram of the house on Twin Peaks Drive showed a floor plan almost identical to her own. "The master bedroom, the bathroom, and the closet were just like mine, so I had no trouble following the scene description."

All of the jurors we spoke with said they had no trouble reaching a verdict in a relatively short time.

They had been puzzled when Terry Wilson didn't testify. One juror summed it up: "If you're not guilty," she said firmly, "you defend yourself."

Wilson's decision not to take the stand was clearly the wrong one. As was his attending so little of the trial.

"He disrespected the judge—and the jury, too," one said.

"Who were the best witnesses, in your opinion?" I asked.

They picked Marty Hayes as one of their first choices. His demonstrations and dramatic flair had caught their attention. Most of the jurors hadn't been to a trial before, and some of them expected the hearing to be similar to how television shows depicted trials. Hayes was a natural.

David Bell's obvious grief as he took the stand had touched them deeply, and so did Jerry Berry's refusal to give up on solving Ronda's death, and his analytical mind.

One member of the jury had hoped that something leading to Ronda's killer would have emerged at this hearing. "They wasted all this money for a hearing and nothing really came out of it."

Barb didn't feel that way. She had just won a major battle and if it took another eleven years, she would find the person who had destroyed her daughter. Still, it felt good to know that twelve complete strangers had come to the same conclusion she had.

The jury foreman was named Angel. Barb considered them all angels.

*   *   *

THE NEXT MORNING, we drove down country roads and located places where Ronda had once been happy. In McCleary, Barb directed me to the ranch where Ronda and Mark Liburdi had lived. It was a welcoming spread with a rambler built toward the back, horse stalls, and a wide pasture where their horses could run. There was a brook in back of the house, a tumble of blackberries, and tall evergreen trees.

I could almost feel Ronda's relief and joy when she came home to this place after a long night on patrol.

There was a dirt road on the left of the pasture, leading back to a chained-off area.

"That's Mark's," Barb said. "It was his secret place. You can't see it—but there's a really small cabin back in there. I think he still owns it."

We crossed over into Grays Harbor County and came to Glenda and Steve Larson's ranch. Glenda, who had been Ronda's matron of honor at her wedding to Ron Reynolds, opened her kitchen door with a huge smile, delighted to see Barb. Glenda poured coffee and told us about her friendship with Ronda and the comfort they both felt in the Larsons' barn in a hard rainstorm, and about the many good times the two women shared.

Glenda called her husband, Steve—a Grays Harbor County sheriff's deputy currently on patrol on the day shift—to tell him we were visiting. He came right home and regaled us with the story of the boys on the bridge who dropped rocks on Ronda's windshield—and how the two of them tracked down "the criminals."

One of the things I had learned since the hearing began was how many people had loved Ronda—and how many loved Barb, too. Almost everywhere we went that day, we were welcome.

Well, there was one stop where that wasn't true.

We were headed toward Aberdeen, Washington, which seemed to be the most likely place to find Katie Huttula. Barb had visited Katie months before with reporter Tracy Vedder. She hadn't been particularly forthcoming then, but she had let them into her mobile home and talked with them. Katie had always seemed to be fond of Barb. Five years earlier, it was Katie who had written to Barb, telling her that she knew that Ronda hadn't killed herself. Barb wanted so much to finally ask Katie what she meant by that—and perhaps this was the day.

As we neared Aberdeen, Barb and I were both eager to talk with Ron's second wife. Maybe she would feel more at ease to talk now that the hearing was over.

Neither Katie nor Ron Reynolds had been seen anywhere near the Law and Justice Center, and no one was surprised. Ron was given time off by the school district and was reportedly staying at home, and Katie's whereabouts were unknown.

We rolled into Aberdeen, a once-booming logging and fishing town that had been hit hard by the recession. Many store windows were blank except for CLOSED signs, and there were blocks even in the center of the city that were a little shabby. It looked as if the town had almost given up after so many years of rising unemployment.

After driving about ten blocks, Barb turned left. She was fairly certain she could find the mobile home park, although she couldn't recall the exact address.

"Katie's father is such a nice man," Barb told me. "He's retired from his drugstore now, and he's done his best to help Katie. He lost his son Carl to Vietnam and Katie's younger sister Mary to suicide, and I heard he took a terrible fall recently and may have fractured his skull."

And still Blake Huttula had purchased the mobile home we were looking for, hoping that Katie would do better if she had safe place to live.

"I know Mary killed herself in a trailer," Barb continued. "But I don't know if it's the same trailer Katie has been living in. Mary died six years ago."

Barb told me to watch for a mobile home park on the left side of the street and a block ahead it came into view. It was a neat, well-groomed park with mature plantings and trees, now bare of leaves. There looked to be about three or four rows of trailer lots, each with a handkerchief-sized lawn.

"She lives at Nine Meander Way," Barb said. "And it's pretty close to the front of the park."

Katie Huttula's blue and white mobile home was the first one on the left as we drove through the gates of the park. It was a good-size, modern mobile with a living room in the front, then a kitchen, bath, and two bedrooms.

And there was a FOR SALE sign in the front window.

Although we saw no signs of life around Katie's mobile, we knocked on the door. And waited. We knocked again and, shading our eyes from the sun with our hands, we peeked in the door's window. There was very little furniture and no personal items visible. The mobile home screamed "abandoned," and there was such a lonely sense about it. It was obvious that nobody lived here anymore.

We could sense that eyes were watching us—but not from Katie's trailer. Curtains pulled back a little in a neighboring trailer dropped instantly as we turned around. Figuring that people who lived so close to one another were aware of their neighbors' comings and goings, we asked a man walking by if he knew where Catherine Huttula had moved. He shook his head; "Ask up at the office—fourth unit on the right."

A man who said he was the manager answered our knock. We explained we were looking for Katie.

"Oh, she moved."

"Do you know where?" Barb asked.

"Up on the hill—she's in one of those subsidized apartments up there on Salmon Street."

He smiled at us as he shut his door.

Naïvely, Barb and I headed back the way we had come, looking for a hilly section of town. We had a map, but we couldn't find Salmon Street on it. We drove up several hills, and even a few sloping streets that some might consider "hills," but we never located a Salmon Street or any homes or apartment complexes that looked as if they were subsidized housing.

We asked for directions at a Safeway store and a fast-food drive-through. Nobody was familiar with the address we'd been given. We ended up at railroad tracks with a view of the backside of buildings.

"Barb," I finally said, "I think he does know where Katie lives now, but he lied to us."

"I think you're right," Barb muttered as she turned the steering wheel and made a U-turn. "Let's just go back and see him."

We drove down Meander Way again, stopping at the manager's office. This time he wasn't there, but a sour-faced woman answered the door.

When we asked about Katie Huttula, she shrugged and said, "I don't have no idea where she went."

"Your husband—or the gentleman who was here earlier—said she lived in some Section Eight housing on

Salmon Street," I said, "but I guess we misunderstood his directions."

"I don't know nothing about that."

"Could you tell us where Salmon Street is?"

"Nope," she said, and shut the door in our faces.

So much for our ability as investigators—or even as likable strangers. Both Barb and I were convinced that the people overseeing the mobile home park knew where Katie was but for some reason didn't want to tell us.

Maybe they thought we were friends of hers and she'd left owing them rent, so they weren't going to do any favors for her. Possibly they thought we were bill collectors or even private detectives and they were protecting her. Perhaps they just enjoyed having a good laugh at our expense as they sent us off on a futile "wild goose chase."

At any rate, both Barb and I knew they weren't going to tell us anything remotely useful. It was getting dark, and we had a long way to drive, so we headed back to Chehalis.

Neither of us wanted to contact Katie Huttula's parents—they had been through enough pain and loss in their lives and they were elderly and ill. And there was the possibility that they didn't know where she was, either.

*   *   *

I MAKE IT A PRACTICE not to interview possible witnesses before a trial or a hearing, so there were many people I had yet to meet personally. Barb invited Blair Connery to have dinner with us at a Chinese restaurant in Chehalis, and to my surprise, she accepted. She was as outgoing and friendly as Barb described her, and was quite willing to talk about

the years she spent with Ron Reynolds. She was a little chagrined at herself for not recognizing the part she played in
his life. But when she grew tired of being an unpaid maid
and cook, she thought seriously about leaving Ron. Their
sons had different interests and different rules, and Blair
realized they would never mesh. Luckily, she became so involved in one of her sons' wedding that leaving Ron was
easy.

Blair appeared to have suffered no ill effects from what
had quickly become a one-way relationship. Her sense of
humor was intact. Because they lived in the same area, she
said she occasionally caught a glimpse of Ron across the
street or in a store, but it was hard for her to believe she had
once loved him.

Mostly she was relieved that Ron was no longer in her
life.

Barb and I stopped in Olympia one day as we retraced
Ronda's life. Dan Pearson, who had worked in store security with Ronda for years, invited us in and was eager to
tell me about how brave and funny she was as they worked
together to catch the "bad guys." As Dan talked, tears filled
his eyes and marked his cheeks. Ronda might have been
killed yesterday, rather than eleven years before; his memories of her were that clear. Although they had always had a
platonic friendship, it was obvious that Dan still grieved for
his lost partner.

I took pages of notes on my yellow legal pad as Dan
Pearson recalled a series of incidents with shoplifters in both
Walmart and the Bon Marché.

I met a number of Washington state troopers—both
male and female—who remembered Ronda as a superior
police officer. I got the same reaction from county deputies

who said Ronda was always there to back them up if there was trouble out on lonely country roads in the middle of the night.

When I gave a seminar on high-profile offenders at the annual convention of the International Association of Women Police, I talked to one of the Washington State Patrol sergeants. I told her I was researching a book about Ronda Reynolds's mysterious death, and her first reaction was "Oh, thank God! Ronda deserves to have someone tell her story."

Barb introduced me by phone to Judy and Larry Semanko—Ron's sister and brother-in-law—and I talked for hours with them. Since Larry had been a Lewis County deputy *and* a Lewis County coroner's deputy, he had the experience and knowledge to spot murky areas of the probe into Ronda's death. It was Larry Semanko who went to the house on Twin Peaks Drive the morning Ronda died and found Ron wrapping Christmas presents. Larry had also smelled fresh laundry, and wondered about that. Why would his brother-in-law be doing a load of laundry while his wife still lay dead in their bedroom?

Larry Semanko's "cop antenna" went up. He's been suspicious ever since, sensing that not everyone connected to Ronda's demise has told the truth.

*   *   *

WHEN I PUT A REQUEST on my website, asking to hear from anyone who had known Ronda, Ron, or Katie Huttula, I was deluged with calls, letters, and emails from people—now in their fifties—who had grown up with them and gone to Elma High School. They all recalled incidents in earlier years involving the three people whose meeting in the Jehovah's Witnesses congregation had broken two marriages apart and ended in disaster.

Of course, Ronda wasn't part of Katie and Ron's school life; she was much younger and grew up hundreds of miles away. With Barb's help, I located friends from her younger years, some going way back to elementary school.

One of their fellow graduates, a woman who worked in a government facility in McCleary, called me. She was one of the forces behind the August 2009 class reunion. Like so many classmates, she was surprised that Ron came to their fortieth anniversary, but said he seemed completely at ease. His first wife was there, and his fourth wife accompanied him to the reunion.

"Was Katie there?" I asked.

"No, we didn't really expect her to be. One of the gals in our class went to her mobile home early last summer. We were going to have this section of our reunion program with a lot of photographs of people we graduated with that was called 'Then and Now.' "

It was after that when a former schoolmate at Elma High School came to her door. When Katie answered, she seemed not to recognize her old friend, and she absolutely refused to have her picture taken.

"Actually," the woman who called me said, "she acted paranoid and ordered our photographer off her property! After that, we didn't make any more attempts to get her 'Now' picture."

I couldn't find Katie Huttula. I searched for her on the Internet, and found an email address for her. I wrote to her, asking her to meet with me—either in person or on the phone. Two days later, I received three emails that seemed to be written in some kind of code. I didn't recognize the screen name on these emails, nor could I make out what the writer was talking about.

I wrote back, asking if I was writing to "Katie." The reply said I had the wrong screen name and the person writing back said he—or she—had no knowledge of anyone named Katie.

I get a lot of email, and this could easily have been just a mistake.

Or not.

Although I knew where Ron Reynolds was, where he lived, where he worked, even his telephone number, that did me no good. I wrote to him by ordinary mail first and I got no direct reply from him—but his attorney Ray Dudenbostel did answer.

Dudenbostel said that since his client had been through such a tragic ordeal, he didn't want to go back to the day in December when he was suddenly widowed.

Ron Reynolds would remain as unapproachable as he had been for years, choosing not to give any interviews.

That door remained closed.

*   *   *

THERE WERE OTHERS who wouldn't talk to me. Vince Parkins, who was another classmate from Elma High and the man Katie Huttula once lived with, was seemingly impossible to locate. His brother did not deny the report that Vince had suffered arsenic poisoning while he lived with Katie, but would not officially confirm it. He gave me Vince's phone number, but when I called—several times—the rings went on endlessly.

Many secrets are transparent in small towns, but there are others that a stranger cannot unravel.

There were those in Toledo who didn't like Ronda. One woman told me that she had been to a women's group function that Ronda attended. "She wanted attention and she was too animated. She didn't seem the type who would make a good wife for a principal. I guess I just expected someone more dignified or maybe quieter."

But Ronda was her own person, and she never intended to fit the old-fashioned image of what an educator's wife should be. She'd been a cop for eight years and worked store security since. She had seen things that many of the women in Toledo could never imagine. She was vibrant and funny and ladies' teas weren't her favorite social occasions.

A few months after her marriage to Ron Reynolds, of course, Ronda had discovered that he was having an affair with his ex-wife. If she talked too loud or was a little too animated, it probably took everything she had to fake the way a bride should act. Besides, she didn't expect to be living in their new Toledo house for long. She loved the house, but as she decorated it, it didn't feel like hers.

CHAPTER THIRTY-THREE

CHRISTMAS 2009 CAME AND WENT. Barb had achieved a certain amount of relief and peace when twelve jurors agreed that Coroner Terry Wilson was wrong when he declared Ronda's death was by her own hand. Gramma Virginia was just as peaceful.

"I'd felt for the past few years that my mother was willing herself to stay alive until Ronda was vindicated," Barb Thompson said. "After the hearing, she seemed to hold on to life less tightly. She wanted to be here for me until we proved that Ronda didn't kill herself, but she was sick and tired and old. She wanted to be with Ronda. I halfway teased her that I was jealous that she would see Ronda before I did."

The paramedics knew Barb's address by heart and they were called to Virginia Ramsey's aid several times. Each time Barb wondered if she would survive—but she did. Barb had vowed she would keep her mother in her home, in her own bed, and that she would die at home. She still slept in a recliner next to her mother's bed every night.

Her mother barely ate anything; nothing tempted her.

"I know I'm going to lose her," Barb told me at one point. "She's ready to go and I can't hold on to her forever."

The torn rotator cuff in Barb's left shoulder grew steadily more painful. Still, she did her chores with her horses and around the property and didn't complain. She had a mare who was going to foal in the winter, and kept a close eye on her. If some things were just too difficult for her, Freeman would always show up to help.

*   *   *

TERRY WILSON had had ten days to file an appeal on the verdict that came down in his hearing. He asked for an extension—and got it. He'd already announced that he wouldn't run for his office in the next election. Barb knew his decision on whether or not to appeal was coming to the next deadline. But surely he would let sleeping dogs lie and move on.

No. At the last possible minute, Terry Wilson filed his appeal. It looked as though he would use every legal means possible to delay changing Ronda's death certificate—until his term as coroner was over.

Again, it was a nightmare.

Royce Ferguson told Barb not to worry; he would take care of it.

As always, she knew he would.

*   *   *

VIRGINIA RAMSEY seemed to fail more each day. She no longer cared to eat at all and even turned away from liquids. Working with her mother's doctors, Barb was able to keep her mother pain free. But on February 4, 2010, Virginia died.

For all intents and purposes, she had decided it was time for her to let go when the hearing jury came back with their unanimous decision that Terry Wilson had used tragically bad judgment in writing her precious granddaughter off as a suicide. Virginia lived only three more months after that verdict.

Although Barb had expected it, losing her mother was a huge blow. She had taken care of Gramma for so many years. Indeed, they had taken care of each other—and Ronda and Freeman, too. There were many times when neither of them could have made it alone, but together they survived. Virginia was always the first person Barb called with news about her fight to find Ronda's killer. Now Barb felt aching emptiness. Everyone was gone: her mother was gone, her sister was gone, her daughter was gone, her first husband was dead. She had no idea where Hal Thompson was; he hadn't called her for several years.

Skeeter had been dead for almost nine years, and Don Hennings had suffered a stroke in October 2007. He was very ill, but Barbara brought him to her house to care for. She had lost him, too, in July 2008.

She still had her son, Freeman, her brother, Bill, and scores of friends, but the world turned colder without Gramma.

Her shoulder pain had increased a great deal in the weeks before her mother's death. Now Barb was free to consider having the surgery to reattach the torn ligament. True to her concern for both people and animals, she arranged to have her operation as an outpatient.

One of her mares was pregnant, and Barb wanted to be home to help her when her time came.

*   *   *

As Royce Ferguson prepared to answer Terry Wilson's appeal, Jerry Berry and Marty Hayes continued their search for a killer. They had won the first round of a long, long, fight—but they were far from finished.

Media publicity had grown tremendously during the prior November hearing, and a number of tips rolled in. Berry followed each one as far as he could. He tried to erase his convictions about who Ronda's killer(s) was and start fresh, looking into new scenarios.

As expected, many reports from the public consisted of theories rather than substance, but Berry and Hayes had to weed them out. During the hearing, several people had come up to me in the hallway with their opinions on who Ronda's murderer was—including one woman who was convinced that the "Mexican Mafia" was responsible.

In January 2010, Barb Thompson received a phone call from a man named Sig Korsgaard*, who told her he had some information about the morning of December 16, 1998, when Ronda was killed. Sig's wife, Karen*, had apparently seen one of the Reynolds's sons early that morning. Barb passed the information on to Jerry Berry—who immediately set out to contact the couple with the number Barb had given him. He called Korsgaard and made an appointment to talk with him and his wife that same night at eight.

It was January 9, 2010, twelve years and one week since

Ronda married Ron Reynolds. Berry was encouraged to believe that the couple he was about to meet *could* have valuable information when he noted that they had lived very close to the house on Twin Peaks Drive.

Karen Korsgaard said she had left her house very early on December 16—sometime between 6 and 6:30 A.M. To get to the main highway, she had to pass the Reynoldses' house. She knew who lived there because her son, Tom Spencer, nicknamed "Bing," occasionally associated with Ron Reynolds's two older sons who lived there.

"As I passed their house," she said, "a car peeled out of their driveway—followed by another car. Both drivers were spinning their tires and throwing gravel up at my car. It pissed me off, frankly."

"Did you recognize those vehicles?" Berry asked.

She nodded. "One was the tan Taurus that Jonathan sometimes drove. The other was a small pickup truck, kind of dark-colored."

Karen Korsgaard had continued on to the intersection of Twin Peaks Drive and Drews Prairie Road. The two vehicles had beaten her there and were now parked at the intersection. It was still dark out; the shortest day of the year was only five days away. But Karen recognized one of the young males of the two who were outside their vehicles. "It was Jonathan Reynolds," she said firmly. "The other might have been one of Jonathan's older brothers. Anyway, it looked as if they were arguing."

"Do you know his name?"

"I'm not sure—but I know I could identify him if I saw a picture."

Karen Korsgaard said she continued on to work, mildly curious about what was going on between the two men.

"It was unusual enough that I called my husband when

I got to work and told him about it. Sig told me to call the sheriff's office and report it."

Karen did that, and the detective who answered said that he would pass that on to Jerry Berry. Of course, when the Korsgaards learned about Ronda's death later that day, what Karen had seen took on more importance.

But whoever that detective she talked to was did not relay the message. "I never saw that information," Berry said.

"No one came to talk to us, either," Sig said. "We called several times, but we finally gave up."

Korsgaard told Berry that someone—who didn't want to be named—had revealed that there had been a party at the Reynolds house the night before Ronda died. "My source told me that he hadn't even seen Ron Reynolds there—it was just the boys and some friends. Jonathan Reynolds told my source that 'Ronda's in her room, pouting.' "

If true, this was startling information. Ron had told detectives that he and Ronda went to bed about 10 P.M., and that he'd spent the night trying to talk her out of suicide until, exhausted, he'd fallen asleep in the early morning hours.

Was it possible that Ronda had been alone in her house except for some rowdy teenagers who were partying?

It might have been.

On January 31, Berry arrived for another scheduled interview at the Korsgaards' home. He showed Karen a "lay-down" of three photos of students who had graduated from a local high school in 1998. In a few seconds, Karen pointed to #3.

"That's Micah Reynolds," Berry said. "Have you seen him before?"

"Many times. He doesn't live there, but he visits often.

I know it was him fighting with Jonathan at the intersection the morning Ronda died."

Now the Korsgaards said that the person who had told them about the party was Karen's own son, Bing Spencer.

"He was going to call you last week," his stepfather said, "but he got arrested. He's in the Lewis County Jail."

Bing Spencer had told Karen that there were other youths at the 1998 pre-Christmas party on December 15–16. He was quite sure that Adam Skolnik* and, possibly, *his* brother, Ace, were.

Both were teenagers at the time of Ronda's murder but were now in their early thirties—as Bing Spencer was.

Jerry Berry searched the Department of Licensing to see if he could find what kind of car Micah Reynolds drove. One of the vehicles that turned up was a 1991 Dodge Dakota pickup.

Berry checked to see what colors the Dakota came in in 1991, and found one had been a "Dark Spectrum Blue," which closely matched the dark pickup Karen Korsgaard had seen.

Jerry Berry had developed tenuous bonds with the current Lewis County sheriff, Steve Mansfield, who had taken over from Bob McCroskey in 2005.

"He told me that he'd been taking all the heat, and he was going to bring me on board as an advisor so if we didn't find a killer, I'd have to take some of the blame," Berry said with a laugh.

Jerry Berry wasn't exactly Mr. Popularity with the detective division, but that wasn't who he was trying to be. If there was a chance they could all work together and get enough evidence to arrest someone for Ronda's murder, he would be more than content.

On February 3, 2010, Berry contacted Bing Spencer

in the Lewis County Jail. They met for the first time with a glass panel between them in an attorney-client visiting area.

Spencer quickly explained why he and the other guests at Jonathan's party had somewhat fuzzy memories. They had been smoking "dope"—marijuana.

However, Bing Spencer claimed to have had fairly good recall of the night of December 15–16. He said that Adam Skolnik was his best friend—and they were sharing a place near his parents' home in a small trailer. They had gone to the Reynolds house at about 8 P.M. Ron was there at the time, but he'd left because he had a meeting or a function that he had to attend. "I never saw him again that night."

"When did you see Ronda?"

"Around ten P.M. She stepped out of her bedroom and told us all to quiet down—that we were getting too loud."

Spencer admitted that he was the one who supplied marijuana to the Reynolds brothers.

"Do you know if there was someone there who drove an old pickup?" Berry asked.

"There was a piece-of-shit pickup truck there, but I don't know who it belonged to," Spencer answered. "Jonathan's older brother was there but I don't remember his name."

"Was everyone at the party doing drugs?"

"All but Adam. He only drank whiskey."

"What brand?"

"Black Velvet or Jack Daniels. I believe that he and I brought a bottle of Black Velvet to the party."

Berry tensed. Maybe the empty bottle of Black Velvet hadn't come from the Reynoldses' liquor cabinet at all.

"Sometime between midnight and two A.M., the

Reynolds brothers told us to leave and then come back in an hour or an hour and a half after things had quieted down."

And Bing Spencer believed that everyone had complied. He explained to Jerry Berry that his memory wasn't that clear—but that he'd kept a journal for ten years, often jotting down things about that night.

"You still have it?" Berry asked.

"My ex-wife does. I've got no way to get possession of it now. For all I know, she threw it away. I always felt like Jonathan and one of his brothers had something to do with Ronda's death, but I've been afraid to talk about it, and, besides, I didn't know who to talk to."

Jerry Berry kept his face calm, hiding the rush of hope that surged through him. As he walked to his car after the interview with Bing Spencer, some things fell into place in his mind. The heavy odor of incense the morning that Ronda's body was found could easily have been used to hide the smell of marijuana.

And when the Reynolds boys asked everyone to leave the house around midnight and come back in an hour or so, they would have had ample time to rape and/or kill Ronda.

The private detective had heard from many sources how much Jonathan hated Ronda. Maybe her complaining about the noise they were making had been the last straw for a mind muddled with marijuana.

Now, Berry revisited a man who had told him in 2009 that Katie Huttula said to him, "My son Jonathan killed his stepmother in Toledo."

The informant—Joey Martin*—also a doper, had been riding in a car with Katie and another man when she blurted that out.

"Do you recall the other guy's name?" Berry asked.

"Yeah . . . I stopped my car on the freeway, and we ran to his house," Joey said. "He'll remember what she said. Write down his name. It's Sam Berdelli*."

"Will you sign a statement about what you've just told me?" Berry asked.

"Yeah, sure."

For a detective looking for vital and solid evidence, drug addicts are not the most believable witnesses. They are vulnerable on the witness stand, and both opposing attorneys and jurors frown on them.

But to Jerry Berry, the jagged stories falling into place made an awful kind of sense.

Chapter Thirty-four

Lewis County detective Bruce Kimsey met Jerry Berry as he entered the Law and Justice Center. Kimsey told him he had just talked with Bing Spencer, and that he was trying to get him on a "contract," which probably meant that Spencer wanted to become a paid informant.

"He told me about the Reynolds thing," Kimsey said. "Probably the same thing he told you."

Berry wasn't quite ready to go to the sheriff's detectives with all the information he was gleaning from Spencer. He only nodded and wished Kimsey good luck.

Bing Spencer admitted to Berry that he had talked to Kimsey, and he had no idea why the sheriff's detective had asked him about the Reynolds case.

"I'm trying to get a contract to work with Kimsey and give up names and places with drug dealing."

Spencer was obviously not above playing both ends against the middle. He was looking out for himself, and for all Berry knew, he was being deceitful about the party on Twin Peaks Drive.

"Did you remember anything else about that?" Berry asked.

"I do—but I don't want to say at this time."

Berry waited a few minutes, but he wasn't going to play games with Bing Spencer.

"I'll keep in touch," Berry said as he picked up his files and walked out.

*   *   *

BERRY WAITED, but it wasn't until February 17 that he had a voice message from Sig Korsgaard. The jail chaplain had passed on a message from Bing: he wanted to talk with Berry again.

"I've got to go to Olympia," Berry said. "I'll contact him at the jail on my way through Chehalis."

Once more, they met in the awkward confines of a glass booth where they were visible to others.

"What do you want to tell me?" Berry asked, after they had exchanged greetings.

"I can tell you the whole story," Spencer said. "It wasn't the Reynolds boys who did it."

"Who pulled the trigger?"

Bing Spencer dropped his head and started to cry. He tilted his head toward a section of cells.

"Was it Adam?"

Bing nodded.

"How do you know?"

"Adam came home to change his clothes. He had some blood on the front of his shirt. It was a white Oregon State U tank top. When Adam took it off, I threw it in with my dirty clothes. I might still have it some-where."

Weeping again, Bing Spencer said that this secret had been on his chest and in his head for twelve years. He'd dreaded snitching about his best friend.

"And it's killing me."

As anxious as Berry was to hear everything Spencer had to say, he wanted to finish this version of the night of December 15–16 in a spot where there was a modicum of privacy.

"I need to talk to my attorney," Berry said, "to see how we should proceed—and I promise I'll find a better place to talk."

Back in his car, Berry called Karen and Sig Korsgaard. Did either of them remember finding a bloodied shirt twelve years before?

They did. Bing had told them he was in a fight and the blood came from that. They had believed him. He had also given Karen a pair of jeans to wash.

The next day, Jerry Berry visited Bing again. His informant was becoming more voluble and at ease with every interview.

Bing Spencer said that he had been sitting in the Reynolds' kitchen with Jonathan and Adam at about 8:30 in the evening of December 15 when first Ronda and then Ron had come in. Ron had opened a beer and offered one to Bing. Ron was dressed in a shirt, slacks, and sport coat, and shortly thereafter he left the house.

"Jack Walters* was there, too," Spencer said. "About a month before that, Jonathan had asked me to kill Ronda, and he offered me some ideas of how to do it. Later on this night as we were partying, Adam and Jonathan started talking about how they could kill Ronda.

"Jonathan said he wanted Ronda dead and he had for a long time. I could tell by the look in Adam's eyes that something bad was going to happen. First, they talked about making it look like a burglary that went bad.

"Later, they told us to leave the house for a while. I left and I think Jack Walters did, too, but Adam stayed there."

Bing said he'd gone to the trailer he shared with Adam, which wasn't far away. At about 2:30 to 3 A.M., Adam came home.

"He had blood on the right side of his face, and his shirt and jeans were very bloody. He told me, 'It's done.' We left the trailer around three A.M. and drove someplace on Michigan Hill. Adam pointed a snub-nosed automatic pistol at my head and he said, 'I'll kill you if you ever tell anyone what happened.' "

It sounded credible, but Berry knew he had to find some physical evidence all these years later to convince a prosecutor to file murder charges, and then persuade a jury that Ronda had died as Bing Spencer described.

He notified Barb Thompson of what he'd just heard, and asked her to call a forensic lab in Oregon to see if DNA from bodily fluids, including blood, might be analyzed successfully a dozen years after they were shed.

Barb learned it might be possible. But first they had to find the long-missing bloodied clothing. Karen Korsgaard remembered washing those clothes in 1998, and, even if they were found, they might not retain anything to test.

On February 26, Berry met with Sheriff Steve Mansfield and Chief Civil Deputy Stacy Brown at the Law and Justice Center in Chehalis. He gave them a copy of his ongoing investigation regarding the party alleged to have taken place on December 15–16. He also gave them a verbal summary of what he had learned. Now he asked Sheriff Mansfield what would be the best way to proceed. Steve Mansfield said he would read the report and get back to Jerry Berry in the next few days.

Jerry Berry was no longer a commissioned officer, but once he had given his report to the Lewis County detectives, he was essentially wearing that hat. Regretfully, he told Barb Thompson he could not share what he learned from this point on. It had to be kept secret—even from her. At least for the moment.

Bing Spencer was feeling cocky. He wanted special privileges. If he could only have his computer back and get out of jail, he was sure he could sit down and write out the whole story for Berry.

His parents, the Korsgaards, believed that Bing probably attended the party at the Reynolds house, but they couldn't accept that he might have actually done anything to harm Ronda. However, his mother said, "If you do the crime, you do the time."

Jerry Berry was having no luck finding the bloody clothes or the spiral notebook where Spencer said he had written down things he recalled about the night Ronda died. Now he sensed that the Korsgaards were becoming afraid that Bing might be in a lot of trouble—might even be charged in some way as an accessory to Ronda's murder.

He was correct. Karen and Sig wanted a signed document that would prevent that from happening. That was beyond Jerry Berry's power.

Nevertheless, Bing Spencer—still in jail for other drug-related crimes—continued to talk to Berry. He said he had walked to his travel trailer and retrieved some "dope," either marijuana or meth, and when he returned, there was no one outside, and no sign of Jonathan and Adam, who had been arguing.

"I believed they were fighting about how to kill Ronda. I walked into the house and started down the hallway just as Micah was coming out of their little brother's bedroom at the end of the hall. We looked at each other and we heard a gunshot go off—the sound coming from Ronda's room.

"I heard Jonathan say, 'Oh fuck!' and then Adam said, 'Help me!' A girl in the kitchen screamed and then ran outside. I turned around and ran back to my trailer and just sat on the couch not knowing what to do."

Again, he described Adam Skolnik coming in all bloody and with something that was possibly brain tissue on his clothes, too.

"It looked like the blood on his face had been 'sprayed or splattered.' "

This was apt description of high-velocity back spatter or "blowback" from a gunshot wound.

Anyone, including myself, would find this new story of a party without any parental supervision quite believable. Jerry Berry wanted very much to know for sure that he and Barb Thompson had tracked down the real killers at last.

Spencer kept summoning Jerry Berry back to the Lewis County Jail with "more information," most of it damning to his former best friend, Adam Skolnik.

"I was on my way home," Berry said, "when Bing told his stepfather that he'd forgotten to tell me something. So I turned around and went back to the jail.

"Bing told me that Adam and he had gone to Denny's restaurant on the morning Ronda died—and this was after Adam had held a gun to Bing's head and threatened to kill him if he ever told what happened," Berry recalled. "He said that Adam had leaned across the table and asked him, 'Do you want to know what it felt like?' "

Bing had asked his best friend, "What did what feel like?"

"What it felt like when I done her?"

"No, Adam," Bing had said. "What did it feel like?"

"You know what it feels like when you have a buck in your sights? It felt like that—only *after* I pulled the trigger."

*   *   *

BING SPENCER BELIEVED he was the fair-haired boy with detectives. He was looking forward to his "contract" to become a drug snitch, and he was also getting serious attention from Jerry Berry and the other detectives.

But he slipped up. And then the narration of Bing Spencer began to disintegrate, like safety glass hit by a bullet.

On March 5, 2010, Jerry Berry introduced Bing Spencer to Lewis County detectives Jamey McGinty and Kevin Engelbertson. Berry stayed in the interview room only about five minutes, asking Spencer to be truthful and tell the detectives everything he had told Berry.

"I told Bing that I trusted the detectives one hundred percent and I was asking him to do the same."

Four days later, Chief Stacy Brown led Berry into a room, and Detective Kimsey pointed to a chair where there was a clear view into the interview room. Bing Spencer was sitting at a table beyond the one-way glass with Engelbertson and McGinty. Someone handed Berry a headset so he could listen to what was being said in the interview. His eyes widened as he listened.

"Bing was telling the detectives things that were different from what he had told me. He told them that he did not believe Adam Skolnik would have killed Ronda and that he now thought Ronda had shot herself," Berry said. "He also stated that I had put words in his mouth and led him to believe that he would be allowed to go home!"

Jerry Berry went into the hall with Stacy Brown after some time, and asked to talk with Sergeant Dusty Breen. He explained that Bing Spencer was clearly playing to whoever was interviewing him.

So had Spencer made the party story up out of whole cloth?

After the interview was finished, there was a meeting in the sheriff's conference room, attended by Stacy Brown, Sergeant Breen, Detectives Kimsey, McGinty, and Engelbertson, and Berry. Kimsey felt that Bing Spencer had made up the whole thing, and McGinty and Engelbertson had found him too "wishy-washy" to be believable.

It was a serious loss for Jerry Berry, as Chief Brown and Sergeant Breen told him that the investigation would continue until more facts were known.

*   *   *

THERE WAS ANOTHER young man alleged to be at that curious "party": Jack Walters. None of the detectives had located him but, with Berry's help, Barb Thompson tracked him to Cascade County, Montana. He was living there, and the Cascade County Sheriff's Office was only too glad to arrest him when they learned Walters was a convicted sexual predator who had never reported his presence to their offices as required by law.

Jeff Ripley, the Montana deputy Barb talked to, said he would personally call Sergeant Dusty Breen at the Lewis County Sheriff's Office to offer assistance. After being briefed on Ronda's story by Berry, Ripley even offered to interview Walters himself if the Lewis County detectives would write out a list of questions.

He waited for a call from them.

And waited. They never contacted Cascade County.

CHAPTER THIRTY-FIVE

SOME LONG-AGO EVIDENCE turned up in the spring of 2010: Sheriff Mansfield reported that they had located female DNA samples from Ronda and male DNA from Ron Reynolds. It appeared that it *was* his semen that had been swabbed from Ronda's vaginal vault. There apparently had been no sign of other semen present. There was no way to know how carefully the sample was preserved back in 1998.

Scrapings from Ronda's torn fingernail were located, too. There was no male DNA caught in the nail. She hadn't broken the nail fighting for her life; it was probably the result of some mishap when she packed to move or drained the waterbed—if, indeed, she ever had.

Bing Spencer had woven a hideous story. Was that the way his mind worked—or had he really seen and heard what he said he had? He knew many of the facts: the Black Velvet bottle, the arguments his mother had also observed, the times that seemed to coordinate accurately with Ronda's time of death, and the condition of her body.

Over a dozen years, there had been several articles written about the mystery of Ronda's death. It was possible that Spencer had researched the details—like the whiskey bottle—but he hardly seemed the type to go to so much trouble.

Bing Spencer had recanted the story he told Jerry Berry. In late April, after demurring at first, he agreed to take a polygraph examination. He passed it, admitting that he had no knowledge of Ronda's shooting. He stated that he had made it all up so he could trade favors and get out of jail.

Adam Skolnik also took a polygraph—and passed it, denying that he had any involvement in Ronda's murder.

It was a major let-down, but Jerry Berry and Marty Hayes continue to believe that Bing Spencer *was* at a party at Ronda's house the night she died. He also believes Micah Reynolds was there, because Spencer's mother substantiated both facts. Berry considers her a very credible witness.

*   *   *

MICAH MIGHT WELL have been in his father's house that night in December and, if he was, he may know what happened. Still, no one has ever suggested he had any participation in Ronda's death. The consensus was that there would be no effort to locate or question him.

On April 27, 2010, Jerry Berry wrote his final report.

> *All information and leads were brought to the Lewis County Sheriff's Office by this investigator. The original witness, Tom "Bing" Spencer, provided false information which hampered the investigation . . .*

I am closing my private investigation into the death of Ronda Reynolds at this time. However, should reliable and verifiable information become available in the future, I will turn it over to the Lewis County Sheriff's Office for follow up.

> *Respectfully,*
> *West Coast Investigative Services*
> *Jerry C. Berry, Owner*
> *Private Detective*

PART SIX

Likely—and

Unlikely—Suspects

Chapter Thirty-six

WE CAME TO KNOW by the summer of 2010 that Ronda Reynolds did not commit suicide in 1998. Twelve jurors had quickly agreed that the four death certificates issued by the Lewis County Coroner's Office listing the manner of her death were wrong.

That in itself was a tremendous comfort to Barb Thompson.

But Judge Richard Hicks was hampered by statute from legally declaring Ronda a murder victim. As he denied Royce Ferguson's motion on the last day of the November 2009 hearing, one got the sense that Hicks *wished* he could accede to Ferguson's request.

I believe that Ronda Reynolds was a homicide victim. Her family has never wavered in their conviction that someone deliberately killed her. Private investigator Jerry Berry, former Lewis County deputy Bob Bishop, gun expert Marty Hayes, and Attorney Royce Ferguson all agree that she died at a murderer's hand (or at murderers' hands). Thousands of people who have followed Ronda's case since December 1998—many of them strangers—have sent their support to her mother.

It is easier to reach a conclusion that Ronda was murdered than it is to prove who killed her. Many individuals had motivations to want her gone from this earth; there may well be some we still don't know about. There are undoubtedly those who *know* what happened, but for their own reasons are afraid to come forward.

In a homicide case, particularly one that occurs in the home of a victim with a spouse, the first person law enforcement officers look at as a possible suspect is that spouse or romantic partner. After that, they expand the circle of suspicion a little more, concentrating on other people who were close to the fatally injured party.

Love can turn to hate. Infidelity and jealousy often poison a marriage. Emotions erupt, burning like a forest fire out of control.

There are even occasions where the motivation is coldly a matter of business. Humans kill each other for myriad reasons.

Ron Reynolds was, of course, the first suspect, and he remains one. From the beginning, his affect was peculiar: he hardly seemed like a grieving widower, and he was anxious to suggest the suicide theory.

Perhaps the hardest part of his story to accept was his denial that he heard the fatal gunshot—when he said he was only about ten feet away.

But why would Ron want his about-to-be ex-wife to die?

I suggest that his reasons would have been financial. Every one I talked to, many of whom had known Ron from his childhood to middle age, mentioned his greediness. As a child, he didn't share his toys or his room. His parents spoiled him, adding to his sense of entitlement. As an adult, he was attracted to women of means—whether it came from their families or their own efforts.

If they were attractive, all the better.

Although Ron denied it, Ronda *did* give him $15,000 to help buy the house on Twin Peaks Drive, and he knew she was due to receive about $7,000 from the sale of property she owned with her former husband, Mark Liburdi.

Ron was still stung by the almost $100,000 the divorce judge had ordered him to pay Katie Huttula. With their five sons, and the twenty-some years Katie had been married to him, it wasn't an inordinate amount, but for him it was a stab to his financial worth.

Couldn't Ron Reynolds simply divorce Ronda after their eleven-month marriage? Yes, she was disappointed that her second marriage had failed, but she was quite ready to start over with her life. She was making plans, deciding where she would live, and planning advances in her store-security career. She probably would have married David Bell—although not as rapidly as she had wed Ron after her first divorce.

But Katie had cost Ron $100,000, and he must have been apprehensive of what Ronda might ask for.

Ron believed that Ronda had $300,000 worth of life insurance. He knew he was her primary heir. That is the kind of motivation that shows up in fiction—and in fact.

Katie Huttula and Ron began an affair within three or four months of his marriage to Ronda. Both of them apparently had regrets about splitting up after so many years.

They seemed almost addicted to each other. Katie told a number of people that she wanted to reunite with Ron. Indeed, she had been vehement when she spoke about that with a woman who had been in the same graduating class at Elma High School.

"I want Ron back," she said. "And I'll get him. I don't care *what* I have to do to make that happen!"

On the night Ronda died, Katie and Ron were allegedly still having their affair. Katie wanted her family all together. She adored her sons even though her drug use had continued while she was pregnant with some of them. They *were* extremely intelligent and multitalented—but several of them were using drugs by the time they were in their mid-teens.

That wasn't surprising, given the fact that both their biological parents had problems with drugs, although Ron seemed to stop as he grew older. Katie's addictions clung to her like moss, blurring her intelligence and decision making.

And Katie sent that email to Barb in June 2004 that said she knew Ronda had been murdered. She denied knowing who the killer was—and referred to more than one murderer. That puzzled Barb at the time. It still does.

How much does Katie actually know about Ronda's death?

Even if the recent revelations by Tom "Bing" Spencer about a party at Ron and Ronda's house on December 15–16 turn out to be only partially true, it's quite possible neither Ron nor Katie was in the house for most of that night.

It seems more than likely that Ron didn't go home after the school Christmas pageant—but drove north instead to Katie's house.

Their three younger sons were whisked out of the house on Twin Peaks Drive when the first deputies arrived. They were not questioned by investigators before they left. Why hadn't any of the three youths heard the gunshot? Did anyone ask them?

And when Barb arrived some thirty hours later, she was stunned to see Katie walk out of what had been Ron and Ronda's bedroom. Katie had apparently slept in their waterbed the night Ronda died!

Was it possible that Ron's story about his arriving home at about 10 P.M. and spending the next seven hours trying to talk Ronda out of committing suicide had no basis in fact?

Quite possible. He might have left Ronda alone in the house, vulnerable to his sons and others who attended the alleged alcohol and drug party.

Here's one scenario to consider:

An early morning phone call from his panicked sons telling him that Ronda had died would certainly have brought Ron and Katie rushing from Olympia to help cover up a murder and make it look like suicide.

Perhaps the reason that Ron Reynolds did not hear the gunshot that killed Ronda was that he was twenty-five miles away—not ten or twelve feet away.

The fatal incident at the alleged party would have occurred about 2 A.M., a time that matched the amount of lividity and rigor mortis in Ronda's body. Ron and Katie probably didn't know about after-death changes. She would have left for Olympia about 5 A.M., *before* Ron called 911. Her sons had followed two hours later.

But that's only one scenario.

Mark Liburdi was Ronda's ex-husband, which put him in a small circle of those who were close to her—or had been. While their divorce hadn't been particularly friendly, they were on speaking terms. Both of them had remarried soon after their divorce. They were established in new lives when Ronda was shot.

Most convincing about Liburdi's innocence: he had been on patrol, talking with WSP radio often, at the time Ronda died.

"Jerry even checked out David [Bell]," Barb told me with a tinge of regret in her voice. "That had to be done, but David was right where he said he was in the early morning hours—on patrol in Des Moines."

Bell probably knew that Berry had checked on him. He was a trained and experienced cop and understood the process of winnowing out suspects.

An investigator who didn't know him could have wondered if Bell was angry and jealous that Ronda had decided to stay with her husband that fatal night. Bell wasn't her lover when she was killed—but he had been a decade earlier. That put him in the second tier of suspects.

What about Cheryl Gilbert? She was obsessed with Ronda, and frequently proclaimed that she was Ronda's "very best friend."

Was her attraction to Ronda romantic or sexual? No one knows. But she attached herself to Ronda. She could well have been upset when she found the keys to her house, which Ronda had tossed inside on the evening of December 15. Cheryl was thrilled by Ronda's decision to move into her extra bedroom when she left Ron. She'd even bought a bed for herself. Cheryl had counted on picking Ronda up to drive her to the airport in Portland, having breakfast on the way and a good conversation.

For some reason, Ronda changed her mind about the living arrangement, and she decided to have David Bell pick her up. Possibly she began to feel smothered by Cheryl's constant attention, which may have sometimes felt like stalking. Or maybe she just wanted a backup driver to be sure she got to the airport on time.

Cheryl certainly enjoyed being the center of the investigators' attention for some hours on the day Ronda died—and thereafter. She was talkative and animated when she met with detectives. Subsequently, she changed her story many times—and ended by agreeing a year or so later that Ronda probably had killed herself. Cheryl also lied numerous times.

Ronda never called Cheryl her "very best friend," because she wasn't. But Ronda often felt sorry for her, unaware that Cheryl had fashioned a bizarre imaginary relationship. Ronda had never been attracted to women. Was Cheryl? If Cheryl had gone to Ronda's house while Ron was at Katie's apartment all night, could Cheryl Gilbert have been so distraught—feeling betrayed—that she could have shot Ronda?

Or did Jonathan Reynolds kill Ronda? It is well documented that he hated her. Add to that, she was a beautiful woman, thirty-three years old, and he could well have felt some sexual attraction to her, even though she was his stepmother. That would have caused a love/hate schism in his mind.

Ronda believed that Jonathan or one of his brothers killed one of her dogs. She believed he had a cruel streak that made other creatures' pain attractive to him. One of his friends told Barb of an incident that happened when he was trying to get a trapped bird out of his fireplace chimney so he could light a fire.

Jonathan came by his house, saw the situation, and swiftly lit a match, holding it to the kindling in the fireplace.

"I saw his face when that poor bird burned alive," his friend recalled. "It excited him to see that."

Whether there was or wasn't a drug party going on at the house on Twin Peaks Drive the night Ronda was shot—and accepting that Ron Reynolds probably was not there—Ronda needed to get some sleep that night. There may have been raucous voices and loud music. She would have done what she always did when she needed some peace and quiet, or surcease from an argument: grab a pillow and a blanket and find some out-of-the-way spot to sleep.

High on drugs, Jonathan may have been extra angry to hear Ronda call out, telling whoever was there to quiet down. Ronda may even been a little frightened by the drugged teenagers, who were as large as men.

And Jonathan might have decided to kill her, and get rid of her once and for all. He knew where the gun was—he had probably watched David Bell empty it of bullets and put the gun in the drawer under his father's side of the waterbed. The bullets themselves would still have been where Bell had tossed them.

According to Bing Spencer—who admitted lying about a number of things—Jonathan had cried out right after the gunshot echoed through the house. And Adam Skolnik had run from the room, terrified.

Then there were the polygraphs. Polygraphs are not as reliable as many laypersons think. True sociopaths can often fool the lie detector; they are so confident in their own power that they can be fearless. They have no consciences and don't feel guilt, so they don't show physical reactions during polygraphs as most subjects do. Their heart rates stays steady, they don't sweat, their blood pressure doesn't go up.

And so much of what Bing Spencer said fits the known facts.

There is one person of interest who has never been

interviewed: Jack Walters, whom Bing counted among those who were at the house on Twin Peaks Drive the night Ronda was shot.

With Jerry Berry's help, Barb Thompson had tracked him to Montana after she checked on Walter's "rap sheet" to see if he'd ever been arrested. He had been.

In 2003, Jack Walters sexually attacked a fifteen-year-old girl, and he had other sexually related charges in the past—enough so he was deemed a "sexual predator." Carrying that official tag, he was legally bound to register with local police departments when he moved to a new location. He should have checked in when he moved to Montana.

But Walters never did.

Barb found his corrections officer, Scott Albert, who had a warrant for Jack Walters.

"He worked so hard to help me," Barb remembers. "Something on the warrant needed to be changed—so he rewrote the whole thing. Everyone in Cascade County, Montana, was kind to me—but Scott went several extra miles."

With Albert's help, she located the address where Walters was living, and Sheriff's deputy Jeff Ripley arrested him for failure to register as a sexual predator.

If Walters verified that there had, indeed, been a party that night, Barb and Jerry Berry felt, it would move the investigation ahead rapidly. They waited to hear what the Lewis County detectives had found out.

Weeks after the Washington investigators were given Walters's contact information, Barb and Jerry Berry were shocked to learn that no one had called Ripley to arrange an interview.

By that time, Jack Walters was no longer in the Cascade County Jail. Ripley said they had kept him locked up as long as they legally could, but it would be difficult to locate him now.

Barb Thompson was angry. "I practically gave Lewis County Walters on a silver platter," she said. "And they couldn't be bothered bringing him back to Washington, or flying to Montana to talk with him face-to-face."

Barb had offered to buy Jerry Berry a ticket to go to Montana to interview Jack Walters, but he thought it would be better to let Lewis County detectives go. When they learned that Lewis County hadn't followed up, Berry regretted his decision.

"If Jack Walters had been interviewed, and he said that there *had* been the party Bing Spencer described, we would have been much farther ahead—but Lewis County didn't seem to want to open that possibility."

Still, Jack Walters is a sexual predator who might have knowledge about how Ronda died. Even if interviewed, he might have shaded the truth to protect himself.

Walters joined the list of possible suspects.

Katie Huttula moved in with Ron right after Ronda was murdered. It's possible they joined forces to protect their sons. Perhaps they joined forces to keep an eye on each other, but living together didn't work.

There also remains a slight possibility that Ronda died in a home invasion.

She had made some enemies—both as a state trooper when she arrested angry felons, and as a store security officer. She might not have known if there was someone out there who harbored a paranoid grudge. She wouldn't be that hard to find. She lived in a small town where people knew each other's business.

Ronda was an extraordinarily beautiful woman, the kind of woman who could attract a stalker, a man—or woman—

who knew her routines, knew when she was alone in her house. If she was there by herself on the night she died, the Reynolds boys probably hadn't bothered to lock the front door.

As I have often written, there is indeed such a thing as the "perfect murder." That usually requires a stranger-to-stranger encounter. One could describe Ronda's world while she was living with Ron as rife with shady characters, druggies, juvenile delinquents, and at least one known sexual predator. She handled herself safely and efficiently as a trooper and a store detective, but whoever wanted her dead in December 1998 had been crafty as a fox.

She never saw danger coming.

*   *   *

BARB THOMPSON AND I have continued our detective work, a pair of slightly older Cagney and Laceys. In July 2010, we drove once again to Lewis County to interview people we had been unable to reach earlier, and to talk again with Jerry Berry and Marty Hayes.

We went first to the home of Karen and Sig Korsgaard. Sig had once been a Lewis County deputy himself, and both he and Karen had been frustrated when their initial attempts to give information to the sheriff's office were ignored. They had tried since 1998 to tell the detectives about the party at Ron and Ronda's home on December 15–16, but none of them had responded. And Jerry Berry had never been handed the message to call them. Finally, after the verdict in Terry Wilson's hearing had come down, they tried once more.

Two detectives came to the Korsgaard's home and said, "Sheriff Mansfield told us to come out and talk to you."

"It seemed like they weren't really interested," Karen Korsgaard said, "and they were only here because the sheriff sent them. Maybe we were feeling snubbed because Sheriff McCroskey had ignored us when he was in office, but we still felt slighted. It was our son who had come up with so much information, and we thought he *did* tell most of the truth. We know he isn't always truthful, but this time we believed him."

Both Karen and Sig remembered the bloodied clothes that Bing brought home on December 16, 1998. "He said he'd been in a fight—or maybe it was Adam who had been in a fight—and that was why the clothes were bloody. But that didn't seem right," Sig said. "Those jeans had way too much blood on them to have come from a fight. They were absolutely sodden with blood. The shirt had very little blood on it."

But Bing had stuck to his story, and Karen had washed the blood-soaked jeans in cold water.

As we talked, all four of us realized that the only way jeans could have been so drenched in someone's life fluid was if the person who owned them had *kneeled* in a pool of blood. Ronda's body was found lying in that much blood.

Whatever Bing Spencer's faults were, neither his mother nor his stepfather believed he was capable of killing anyone or, for that matter, any creature. They acknowledged his weakness for drugs and his tendency to exaggerate—and even outright lie.

Karen was temporarily angry with her son for being so stupid and sneaky—but she believed 90 percent of his recall of the night Ronda died.

The Korsgaards were slowly going through all the belongings of their four children that were stored out in their shed. They said they hoped to find the notebook that Bing had kept for years after Ronda's murder. Sig was a chronic diary keeper, and Bing had picked that up from him.

"I always taught him to write things down, keep good records—things like that," Sig said. "And as far as I know, he did."

The Korsgaards confided other information to Barb Thompson and myself—very important things that I am not at liberty at this point to reveal. And I realized that they probably held the key to the suspects who murdered Ronda Reynolds.

It felt strange—but good—for me to be actually working as a "detective" again after all these years. And I could see that Barb was a bulldozer, but a tactful one, who never gave up until she was exhausted.

We drove by the house with the blue trim, the house where Ronda had died a dozen years before. Of course Ron no longer lived there; an elderly couple had bought it, saying they didn't feel any darkness or danger there.

Barb pointed to a large patch of tall and thorny weeds. "I think the holster for Ron's father's gun might be somewhere out there," she said. "You know, they never found it. I'm going to look for it myself."

"Now?" I asked, reminding her that it was 95 degrees out.

She laughed. "Not now—but someday."

A day later, we tried our best to find Katie Huttula. This time wasn't any more successful than our first try back in November although we drove to several addresses. No one we talked to admitting knowing her. One of the apartment complexes was supposed to be her current address. There was little doubt that it was a drug house, and there were several residents in their early twenties having a barbecue in the parking lot. We smelled marijuana and saw that one woman was clearly high on pills, but they all said they had never heard of Katie Huttula.

We went back three times, positive that they *did* know Katie, but they were adamant that they didn't. They smirked at us and seemed to share a secret joke—but maybe that was the pot.

It was growing dark, and we finally gave up the search.

Some tipsters say that Katie is in California. We called the apartment manager there and got only a recorded message. We have been unable to locate Katie Huttula. She may be dead. She is more likely alive, perhaps living far from Lewis and Grays Harbor counties. She is one person I would sincerely like to talk to. I'm sure she knows something, but she is afraid to tell.

Many of the main characters in the sad saga of Ronda Reynolds continue to reside in Lewis County. Others have virtually vanished.

Ron Reynolds is still the principal at the same school. If the school district should fire him because of any suspicions about him, they would probably face a lawsuit, as nothing has been proven that involves him. He refuses all media interviews. If he or he and Katie Huttula *did* rush to his Toledo home from Katie's apartment in Olympia to help their sons set up a scene to make Ronda's death look like a suicide, neither faces any charges of being accessories after the fact. The statute of limitations on that charge has run out.

Ron and his fourth wife live on a beautiful piece of acreage.

David Bell lives in Des Moines, Washington, five miles from my home, and he is still a sergeant with the Des Moines Police Department. He is single.

Some of the Reynolds sons—including Micah—have gone to Alaska to work on the mammoth fishing trawlers.

Jonathan has a band that appears in taverns around Lewis and Gray's Harbor County. Micah's wife recently had a baby.

Mark Liburdi is close to retirement from the Washington State Patrol.

Tom "Bing" Spencer is in prison for the next few years. At this point, his mother does not correspond with him.

Cheryl Gibson hasn't contacted Barb Thompson for years. The last she heard, Cheryl was living in either Lewis or Gray's Harbor County.

Jerry Berry, Marty Hayes, and Royce Ferguson continue in their professions. Berry and Hayes have both run—unsuccessfully—for coroner of Lewis County. They are not registered for this term's election.

Berry's private detective agency—West Coast Investigative Services—is thriving. He is a remarkably thorough detective and I recommend him to correspondents often.

Marty Hayes continues to operate his Firearms Academy of Seattle and is very close to getting his law degree. A visit to his home, close to the gun range, takes a little getting used to. Every so often, the air is filled with the sound of what seems like a hundred guns as his students fire at targets in a field below his house.

Royce Ferguson has just filed his brief in response to Terry Wilson's appeal for a new trial.

No matter what they may say, the triumvirate will *never* stop working on Ronda Reynolds's case until her killer is in custody.

*   *   *

BARB THOMPSON CONTINUES to live on her ranch in Spokane. She still breeds and trains American quarter horses, and she and her dog, Trooper, were present at the birth of several colts this spring. I called her two weeks ago and she answered her cell phone while she was up on her barn roof repairing it! She lives by the slogan she and Ronda shared: "No fear."

She is one tough lady who manages to remain pretty and feminine.

The next time I talked with her, Barb was lame, because yet another horse kicked her in the shin. It took a lot of persuasion on my part to get her to go to her doctor. Her leg was infected—but it got better. She had healed up enough to go on a pack-mule trip with friends up into the mountains last weekend.

In a week or so, she will bring some horses over the Snoqualmie Pass to their new owners, and then I will join her for yet another trip to Lewis County. We have people to interview, witnesses with new information.

Like so many others before me, I have caught the fever of finding justice for Ronda. It is contagious.

We are so very close to the killer (or killers) now.

Acknowledgments

I NEEDED A GREAT DEAL of help as I researched the story of Ronda Reynolds, even though I had been following it in the background of my mind since December 1998. Fortunately, scores of people came forward and remembered the heartwarming, exciting, and sometimes tragic details of Ronda's too-short life. With their help, Ronda came alive for me, just as she had for the three men—Jerry Berry, Marty Hayes, Royce Ferguson—all forensic specialists in their own areas of expertise. Each of them worked virtually pro bono for years to remove the blindfold across Justice's eyes and unveil the truth.

This is Ronda's book, but it is also her mother Barb's book. To quote from *The Ladies' Home Journal*: "Never underestimate the Power of a Woman."

Some of the people listed below shared vital information with me, some taught me forensic science that I needed to know, and some had my back during the challenges I faced when I began to write about Ronda.

My sincere thanks to all of you:

Lois Duncan, a wonderful writer who maintains a web site for those who seek the truth about their loved one's fate: www.realcrimes.com, Dr. John Demakas, Dr. Michael Gruber, Rowdy Berry, Susan Berry, Richard and Donica Fletcher, Pete Erickson, Robert Bishop, and Dr. Jeffrey Reynolds,

"Smurf," Gila Hayes, Sarita McClellan, Jerry Johnston, Kathy Neu, Kurt Wetzold, Vernon Geberth, Raymond Pierce, Alan and Ella McDonnell, Robert Zielke, Sue Sampson, Juanita Vaughn, Tony and Belinda Rodriguez, Connie Riker, Darrell Prowze, Linda Eller, Larry and Judy Semanko, Julie Colbert, Claudia Self, and Danita Rakov.

Sharyn Decker, Ian Ith, Tracy Vedder, and Kiyomi Taguchi of KOMO-TV.

My gratitude goes to the Lewis County attentive jurors who made a unanimous decision in a difficult case: Angel, Debra, Pete, Denise, Nathan, Sandy, Opal, Elaine, Scott, Corina, Josie, and Don. Several shared their thoughts with me, following the judge's orders about what they could say *after* their verdict.

Lauren Sund, Pat Henning of Centralia, Kate Jewell, First Reader Gerry Hay, Rod Englert, David Bell, Freeman Thompson, Joanne Gonzales, Lee Shallat, Eric Roberts, Dan Pearson, Dave and Marion Nordquist, Donna Anders, Glade Austin, Gary Aschenbach, Rahma Starret, Abe Miller—Mr. Happy Computer, Betty May Settecase, the staff at Best Western in Chehalis, Kim Edmondson, Steve and Glenda Larson, Scott Albert, Dr. Michael Nevins, Dr. Nathan Green, and Dr. Diane Dozois of Group Health.

Special thanks to the International Association of

Women Police (IAWP), and, of course, to Barb Thompson, Jerry Berry, Marty Hayes, Royce Ferguson, and Blair Connery.

To my family: Matt, Andy, Lindsey, Mike, Marie and Holland Rae Rule, Bruce, Machell, Olivia, Tyra, and Logan Sherles. Family includes my Michigan and Ohio cousins: Chris and Linda, Jim and Mary, Sara Jane, Bruce and Diane, Jan and Eby, Sherman, David, Lucetta May, and Glenna.

To Ronda's family: Freeman Thompson, Virginia Ramsey, William Ramsey, Don Hennings, Beverly Branom, Bill Clark and the support of hundreds of their friends too numerous to list.

To the thousands of ARF's—Ann Rule Fans—who visit my web site at www.annrules.com—to ask questions, give me tips on cases, comments, and, bless you, praise. You always lift me up when I get discouraged and have temporary writers' block!

And thank you once again to my literary agents of thirty-five years: Joan and Joe Foley, who have never let me down, and to my theatrical agent Ron Bernstein of International Creative Management, who magically turns books into movies!

And, as always, I appreciate my long association with Free Press, Pocket Books, and Simon & Schuster. I've been with them for more than two decades, and the team that helps me write, print, and publish my books is one any author would envy. My publisher Martha Levin, who stands solidly behind me, my editor Mitchell Ivers, whose critiques are incisive but tactful, his assistant Jessica Webb, who works with me to create the photo sections and handles a thousand other details and is always cheerful, my keen-eyed copyeditor Thomas Pitoniak, and copyediting supervisor Carol de Onís, managing editor Isabel Tewes, my attorneys

Elisa Rivlin, Felice Javit, and Duane Bosworth, and my publicist Carisa Hays.

In the Still of the Night is probably one of the three most difficult books I have ever written. I could not possibly have done it without the help of so many people who cared.

—Ann Rule

REWARD • REWARD • REWARD

Through auctions, donations, and fund-raisers, we are now in a position to offer a reward for information leading to the arrest and conviction of one or more person or persons who carried out a plan to murder Ronda Reynolds. At this point, the reward is over $30,000.

To find out more about this—the guidelines and stipulations—please contact me at About13time@aol.com or P.O. Box 98846, Seattle, WA 98198—or Barbara Thompson at BarbsWash@aol.com or P.O. Box 607, Airway Heights, WA 99001

REWARD • REWARD • REWARD

ANN RULE is the author of thirty *New York Times* bestsellers, all of them still in print. A former Seattle police officer, she knows the crime scene firsthand. She is a certified instructor for police training seminars and lectures to law enforcement officers, prosecutors, and forensic science organizations, including the FBI. For more than three decades, she has been a powerful advocate for victims of violent crime. She has testified before U.S. Senate Judiciary subcommittees on serial murder and victims' rights, and was a civilian adviser to the VI-CAP (Violent Criminal Apprehension Program). A graduate of the University of Washington, she holds a Ph.D. in Humane Letters from Willamette University. She lives near Seattle and can be contacted through her web page at www.annrules.com.